# Cambridge Greek Testament for Schools and Colleges

---

THE GENERAL EPISTLE OF

# ST JAMES.

London: C. J. CLAY AND SONS,
CAMBRIDGE UNIVERSITY PRESS WAREHOUSE,
AVE MARIA LANE.
Glasgow: 263, ARGYLE STREET.

Leipzig: F. A. BROCKHAUS.
New York: THE MACMILLAN COMPANY
Bombay: E. SEYMOUR HALE.

# Cambridge Greek Testament for Schools and Colleges

GENERAL EDITOR :—J. ARMITAGE ROBINSON B.D.

NORRISIAN PROFESSOR OF DIVINITY

---

## THE GENERAL EPISTLE OF

# ST JAMES

*WITH NOTES AND INTRODUCTION*

BY THE

## REV. ARTHUR CARR M.A.

VICAR OF ADDINGTON SURREY

FORMERLY FELLOW OF ORIEL COLLEGE OXFORD

**STEREOTYPED EDITION.**

## CAMBRIDGE

AT THE UNIVERSITY PRESS.

1899

*First Edition* 1896.   *Reprinted* 1899.

# PREFACE

## BY THE GENERAL EDITOR.

THE Greek Text upon which the Commentaries in
this Series are based has been formed on the following
principles: Wherever the texts of Tischendorf and
Tregelles agree, their readings are followed: wherever
they differ from each other, but neither of them agrees
with the Received Text as printed by Scrivener, the
consensus of Lachmann with either is taken in preference to the Received Text: in all other cases the
Received Text as printed by Scrivener is followed. It
must be added, however, that in the Gospels those
alternative readings of Tregelles, which subsequently
proved to have the support of the Sinaitic Codex,
have been considered as of the same authority as
readings which Tregelles has adopted in his text.

In the Commentaries an endeavour has been made
to explain the uses of words and the methods of con-

struction, as well as to give substantial aid to the student in the interpretation and illustration of the text.

The General Editor does not hold himself responsible except in the most general sense for the statements made and the interpretations offered by the various contributors to this Series. He has not felt that it would be right for him to place any check upon the expression of individual opinion, unless at any point matter were introduced which seemed to be out of harmony with the character and scope of the Series.

J. ARMITAGE ROBINSON.

CHRIST'S COLLEGE,
*February,* 1893.

# CONTENTS.

# CONTENTS

# INTRODUCTION.

## CHAPTER I.

### THE AUTHORSHIP AND CANONICITY OF THE EPISTLE.
### ST JAMES THE LORD'S BROTHER.

#### *I. External Evidence of Authenticity.*

THE Epistle of St James has not been admitted into the Canon of the New Testament without dispute. The most important early testimony in regard to its authenticity is found in Eusebius, *H. E.* II. 23, where, after citing accounts of James the Lord's brother from various authorities, the historian adds that to him is attributed the first of the Epistles called Catholic, but that it is regarded by some as spurious, not many of the ancient writers having mentioned either this Epistle or that which is attributed to Jude, although they were both publicly read in the Churches. Further on, in another passage containing a list of the Scriptures which are acknowledged (ὁμολογούμενα) as well as of those whose authenticity is disputed (ἀντιλεγόμενα), the Epistle of St James is included in the latter group: τῶν δ' ἀντιλεγομένων, γνωρίμων δ' οὖν ὅμως τοῖς πολλοῖς, ἡ λεγομένη Ἰακώβου φέρεται καὶ ἡ Ἰούδα. Eus. *H. E.* III. 25.

On this testimony it may be remarked that the doubt as to the authenticity of the Epistle seems to have arisen not from any improbability of the alleged authorship, or from erroneous doctrine contained in it, but from the absence of citation by succeeding writers. But this is a fact quite capable of explanation in the case of an Epistle singularly free from controversial subjects and addressed to Jewish Christians, a community which shortly afterwards was either absorbed into the Churches of Gentile Christians, or became discredited by a lapse partly into Gnosticism, partly into a form of Christianity hardly distinguishable from Judaism.

In the catalogue of the Canonical books called the Muratorian Fragment, a document belonging to the end of the second century, the Epistle of St James is omitted. It is however found in the Syriac and Egyptian versions (with regard to which see below p. xlvii), and in the lists of Origen (†A.D. 254), Cyril of Jerusalem (A.D. 348), Gregory of Nazianzus (c. A.D. 381), Athanasius in his 39th Festal Letter (A.D. 367), in those of the Councils of Laodicea (A.D. 363) and Carthage (A.D. 397), and of the so-called Apostolic Canons. The authenticity of the Epistle is also recognised in the writings of St Jerome and St Augustine.

More important than the testimony cited above are the un-doubted traces of this Epistle to be found in Clement of Rome (*Ep. to Corinthians*, A.D. 95; see c. 23, c. 30, c. 33), in the *Didaché*, written probably early in the second century (see ii. 4, iv. 3, iv. 14 and other passages cited by Mayor, p. liii), and in Hermas, who wrote his allegorical work not much later. The presence of St James's influence in *Hermas* appears in a most interesting way, not so much by direct quotation as by a per-vading sense of his teaching which penetrates the whole book, together with a constant use of his most characteristic termino-logy. A significant instance of this is the frequent occurrence of δίψυχος, διψυχία, διψυχεῖν, words highly characteristic of St James but rare elsewhere. No one can read *The Shepherd* without feeling how great an impression the Epistle of St James had made on the writer's mind.

References to the Epistle are also discernible in the writings of Barnabas (c. A.D. 95), Ignatius (c. A.D. 115), and Polycarp (c. A.D. 155).

Such evidence enables us to trace the existence of this Epistle to the beginning of the post-Apostolic age. And if this be so it is hardly conceivable that at that early epoch any Christian writer would have ventured to put forth a forged epistle in the name and with the authority of St James. On the whole the external evidence leads us to infer that the Epistle, at first better known in the East than in the West, gradually won its way into full recognition by the Church, and in the fourth century was placed without question in all the authorised catalogues of the Canonical books.

## II. *Internal Evidence of Authenticity.*

But if there are points of weakness in the external testimony to the genuineness of the Epistle, the internal evidence is unusually strong and convincing in favour of the authorship of St James the Lord's brother, in accordance with the traditional view stated by Eusebius[1].

### (1) *The relationship of the 'Brethren of the Lord' to Jesus.*

The force of this evidence can be best appreciated by a survey of St James's life, of his relations to our Lord, of his position in the Church, and of the time and circumstances in which we may suppose the Epistle to have been written.

But two questions still remain: (*a*) whether James or Jacob the Lord's brother is to be identified with any one of those who bear the same name in the Gospel narrative, and (*b*) what relationship to the Lord is indicated by the term 'brother.'

The two questions are intimately connected and may be discussed together, for the identification of James the Lord's brother with James the son of Alphæus, and possibly also with James the son of Clopas, would probably never have been suggested except for the purpose of supporting one of the three theories respecting the relationship of the brethren of the Lord to Jesus, which may now be stated.

---

[1] The grounds on which the authorship has been ascribed to James the son of Zebedee hardly deserve serious consideration. Little has been advanced to support this contention except a supposed probability that an apostle of so leading a position must have left some record behind him, and secondly that the close verbal similarity to the words of the Sermon on the Mount points to the evidence of one who had listened to that discourse. Of these arguments, the first applies with at least equal force to the brother of the Lord, and the second, so far as it has any weight, must fall before considerations named below.

(2)  *Early opinions on the subject.*

Up to the fourth century after Christ two opposing views were held. By the great majority of Christian writers it was maintained that the Mother of the Lord remained ever Virgin, and that the Brethren of the Lord, whose names are given in the Synoptic Gospels (Matt. xiii. 55, Mark vi. 3), were sons of Joseph by a former marriage.

The other opinion was that the word ἀδελφοί was used in the ordinary sense of brothers, and that 'the brethren of the Lord' were sons of Joseph and Mary, and younger brothers of Jesus. The fact that this view, although apparently the more natural and obvious one, received but little support among the more ancient Christian writers creates a strong presumption against it.

(3)  *Another view put forward in the fourth century.*

Towards the close of the fourth century, however, a fresh suggestion was made. It was a time when the subject of celibacy was keenly disputed in the Church. And the assumed fact that sons and daughters were born to Joseph and Mary was urged strongly against the more rigorous defenders of a celibate life. This assumption therefore was opposed with great force by St Jerome, who himself put forth a third and new hypothesis as to the relationship of the Brethren of the Lord.

By this hypothesis 'the brethren' were first cousins of the Lord, being sons of Mary wife of Clopas, who was according to this theory, and by a possible inference from S. John xix. 25, a sister of the Virgin Mary. A further identification, etymologically possible, between Clopas and Alphæus (which was not however made by Jerome himself) would give the result that James the son of Alphæus, James 'the little' (ὁ μικρός, Mark xv. 40), and James the brother of the Lord were one and the same person.

The view was further strengthened by supposing the expression, Ἰούδας Ἰακώβου, which occurs in the lists of the Apostles, Luke vi. 16 and Acts i. 13, to mean Judas *brother* of James. For then James the son of Alphæus (or Clopas) is shewn to have brethren named Judas and Joses, the three names corresponding to those of the names of the 'Brethren of the Lord.'

(4) *Arguments against this view.*

Apart from the novelty of this view, in itself a considerable objection, the extreme improbability of two sisters bearing the same name seems to be fatal to it. The theory also involves a strain on the meaning of ἀδελφοί, for even if ἀδελφοί be used to signify 'cousins,' it is most improbable that St Paul would employ the word ἀδελφός with that signification in the singular number to indicate the relationship of St James to our Lord.

As to the identification of Alphæus with Clopas, and consequently that of James the son of Alphæus with James the son of Mary and Clopas, one argument adduced in support of it by the translation of Ἰούδας Ἰακώβου by 'Judas the *brother* of James' is, to say the least, extremely doubtful. But a more serious objection against this identification of James the son of Alphæus and James the Lord's brother lies in the statement of St John, (vii. 5) that 'even His brethren did not believe on Him,' which precludes the possibility of any of the Lord's brethren being among the number of the Twelve. This being so, the identification of Clopas with Alphæus, which, as stated above, was not recognised by Jerome himself, would weaken rather than strengthen his theory.

In addition to these arguments it may be said that the close and intimate relation in which 'the brethren' stand to the Mother of the Lord is wholly against the probability of St Jerome's hypothesis.

If, then, we reject the ingenious hypothesis of St Jerome, which would probably never have been advanced except for the purpose of controversy, the dispute must continue to lie between the antagonistic views which were opposed to each other before Jerome's argument was put forward.

(5) *Argument in favour of the view that the 'Brethren' were sons of Joseph and not of Mary.*

And although the dispute is one which admits of no certain solution, the theory that the brethren of the Lord were sons of

Joseph and not of Mary has the support of a very ancient and scarcely contradicted tradition in its favour. The very existence of such a tradition in spite of what seems to be the more obvious meaning of the Evangelist's words is in itself strong evidence for its truth. For it cannot be said that the tradition originated from a desire to exalt the virtue of celibacy, although it was undoubtedly used for that purpose in the fourth century.

It is a theory which gives a natural meaning to the term ἀδελφοί. Indeed those who were regarded as half-brothers of our Lord could be designated by no other term, as is shewn by the familiar instances of the twelve patriarchs, who are repeatedly called brethren, though sons of different mothers.

Again, the allusions to the brethren of the Lord in connexion with Jesus tend to the inference that they were older rather than younger 'brethren.' The phrase 'Thy mother and thy brethren seek thee' (Matt. xii. 47) seems to suggest authority in the brethren as well as in the mother. The more natural explanation of the references to the brethren in the Synoptic Gospels is that they were better known, and therefore older than Jesus: 'Is not this the carpenter's son? Is not his mother called Mary? and his brethren James, and Joses, and Simon, and Judas? And his sisters are they not all with us?' (Matt. xiii. 55, 56. Comp. Mark vi. 3.) And the unbelief of the brethren mentioned by St John (vii. 5) suits the natural disregard by the older sons of a younger brother's opinion or claims.

But perhaps the argument which weighs most against the nearer relationship of the brethren is that which is drawn from our Lord's words from the Cross, in which He committed His mother into the charge of John the son of Zebedee. It is improbable that Jesus would have withdrawn His mother from the natural protection of her own sons if that close tie had existed. But if we suppose that the sons of Zebedee were first cousins of our Lord, the relationship was closer with John than with 'the brethren,' who (according to this view) were not strictly speaking related.

The evidence of the Apocryphal gospels sustains the hypothesis that 'the brethren' were sons of Joseph born before his espousals

with Mary; and this evidence is so far valuable that it points to
the current opinion in the second and third centuries after
Christ[1].

If the opinion be adopted that Jesus was younger than 'the
brethren,' interest is added to the parallel between the position
of Jesus in the family at Nazareth and that of Joseph among
the sons of Jacob, and of David among the sons of Jesse. In
each case there are traces of wonder and jealousy in the choice
of the younger son.

(6) *The childhood of St James and the influence of the home
at Nazareth.*

But even if it be admitted that the brethren of the Lord
were not kinsmen according to the flesh, their relationship to
Joseph and their close association with Mary and her divine
Son which is apparent in the Gospel record, would bring them
under the same educational influences in which the child Jesus
grew up.

It is these influences which in their depth and subtilty
form a part of the link between the mind of Christ and the words
and thoughts of James. For the life and teaching of Christ were
the outcome of those silent years of education in which He in-

---

[1] See *St James*, in *Camb. Bible for Schools*, Introd. § vi.
The objection has been raised: How could our Lord through
Joseph have been the heir to David's throne (according to the
genealogies) if Joseph had elder sons? A sufficient answer is that
the succession among the Jews was not always carried on through the
elder son. There are conspicuous examples to the contrary in Bible
history—Jacob himself, David and Solomon are instances. The
principle is stated in the words of Jehu, 'Choose out the fittest
of your master's sons.' It has also been asked what became of the
six young motherless children when Joseph and the Virgin first went
to Bethlehem, then to Egypt; and why are the elder sons not mentioned on the occasion of the visit to the Temple? The answer to the
first question is that there were near relations in Galilee, and that the
absence of Joseph and the Virgin was unexpectedly prolonged; the
answer to the second is that there was no occasion to mention the
elder brethren if they had been in Jerusalem, but that the occasion
was a special one for Jesus, Who might therefore have come alone
with His mother and Joseph. See Edersheim, *Life of Jesus the
Messiah*, vol. I. p. 364.

creased in wisdom. And in those years the brethren of the Lord
must have known Him as no other men knew Him. And when
conversion revealed the full meaning of that close intercourse
to James and his brethren, words, looks, thoughts and acts must
have come back with all the vividness of early impressions.

It is this subtle infusion and penetration of Christ in St James's
character which gives an indefinable force to his teaching. It is
probably rather to these recollections of intercourse and inter-
change of thought in youth and early manhood than to express
quotations that the parallelism is due between St James's writings
and the Sermon on the Mount.

What these influences were we partly learn from the opening
chapters of St Luke's Gospel, which present to us, as closely
associated with the early life of Jesus, a group of pious Israelites
whose hearts had been divinely prepared for the revelation of the
Messiah. Simeon, with evident reference to Isaiah xl., was
waiting for the consolation (παράκλησιν) of Israel; Anna, a
prophetess, spake of the child Jesus to all them that were looking for the redemption of Jerusalem (ii. 38). The hymn of Mary
brings into prominence two leading Messianic thoughts—the exaltation of the meek and lowly and the unitedness of Israel—and
Zacharias connects the Messianic hope with the house of David
with the oath sworn to Abraham, and with the extension of the
gospel to the Gentiles (i. 79); and His last thought is emphasized
in the Song of Simeon. Two other characteristics are discernible
in this part of St Luke's Gospel as belonging to that circle which
immediately surrounded the infant Saviour, both of them
features of the religious life of Israel which were largely developed in the post-Exile period, one of these is 'righteousness,' the
other 'wisdom.'

Righteousness in the technical post-Exile sense (see Deut. vi.
25) consisted in an exact and scrupulous performance of the
requirements of the Law. It was the corner-stone on which the
whole system of Judaism was reared. It was in virtue of his
righteousness that James was called 'the Just' (ὁ δίκαιος); it is
expressly attributed to his father Joseph (δίκαιος ὤν, St Matt. i.
19), and to Zacharias and Elisabeth (δίκαιοι ἀμφότεροι ἐναντίον

τοῦ θεοῦ, πορευόμενοι ἐν πάσαις ταῖς ἐντολαῖς καὶ δικαιώμασιν τοῦ κυρίου ἄμεμπτοι, Luke i. 6); it appears in the offering at the circumcision of Jesus, and in the visit to Jerusalem for the Passover, and in the words of Jesus at His baptism: οὕτω γὰρ πρέπον ἐστὶν ἡμῖν πληρῶσαι πᾶσαν δικαιοσύνην, Matt. iii. 15.

Another religious and intellectual conception which filled a large space in the thought of the post-Exile period, and which indeed created a literature of its own, was the conception of wisdom, in its highest sense closely identified with the creative power of God, but extending over the whole field of human knowledge.

A further marked characteristic in the circumstances of the Nativity distinguishing the family and kinsfolk of Jesus, and those in closest sympathy with them, is the revival of the Hebrew poetical genius which produced the Benedictus, the Magnificat, and the Nunc dimittis, and which appears repeatedly in a form of supreme beauty in the words of Jesus. But all these thoughts of the kingdom, these hopes, aspirations, religious tendencies, and intellectual gifts which surrounded and inspired the childhood of Jesus must also have influenced the spiritual growth of St James. The effect is visible in the Epistle, when, apart from the close and special parallelism to the words of Jesus, the thoughts of this gospel of the childhood are also traceable: as e.g. the unity of Israel[1], implied in the greeting

---

[1] It is interesting to trace in the names of the 'brethren of the Lord' some indication of such Messianic thoughts as the reunion of the twelve tribes of Israel and the restoration of the kingdom. Jacob (James) and Joseph, Simon and Judas, are representative names. Jacob by his second divinely imparted name is the eponymous hero of Israel, Joseph the second founder of the race: to shew they signify the restored unity of Israel, comp. 'O thou Shepherd of Israel, thou that leadest Joseph like a sheep,' Ps. lxxx. 1. Simon and Judas are memorable Maccabean names; Judas, the warrior who organised victory for his people, B.C. 166, and Simon, the mighty high-priest and king in whose reign the sovereign right of coining money was secured for the Jews, B.C. 142. And that hopes of a Maccabean restoration, or of a kingdom restored on the lines of Maccabean sovereignty, were mingled with the hopes of a Davidic monarchy in the Messianic expectation appears among other proofs from the title

with which the Epistle opens; the excellence of wisdom ($\sigma o \phi \acute{\iota} a$), ch. i. 5, iii. 15; the reverence for the Law; the exaltation of the poor, the attribute of peace, St Luke i. 73, ii. 14 (comp. St James iii. 18); and above all the gift of poetical expression conspicuously present in this Epistle. See *infra* p. xli.

### (7) *The unbelief of the 'Brethren' during our Lord's Ministry.*

Soon after Jesus entered on His ministry Nazareth ceased to be His home. He left His mother and His brethren 'for the sake of the Gospel.' In John ii. 12, we read that after the miracle in Cana He 'went down to Capernaum, he and his mother and his brethren and his disciples: and there they abode not many days.' But when Jesus returned from Judæa (John ii. 43, 54), and revisited Nazareth, He was rejected by His fellow-townsmen (Luke iv. 16—30), after which He made Capernaum His home (Matt. iv. 13; Luke iv. 31).

The reason for this separation from His kinsfolk may be traced in His answer to one who told Him that His mother and His brethren desired to speak with Him: "Who is my mother? and who are my brethren? For whosoever shall do the will of my Father which is in heaven, the same is my brother, and sister, and mother" (Matt. xii. 47—50; Mark iii. 32—35; Luke viii. 20, 21). The tone of rebuke for unbelief discernible here is intensified even to indignation on the occasion of a second visit to Nazareth (Matt. xiii. 54—58; Mark vi. 1—6), when His own brethren having joined in the rejection of Jesus, He exclaimed, "A prophet is not without honour, but in his own country, and among his own kin, and in his own house": St Mark (vi. 4) adds: "He marvelled because of their unbelief." This prepares us for the explicit statement in St John vii. 2—10, "Even his

'King of the Jews,' which dates from Maccabean times, and is not found in the earlier history of Israel.

That this nomenclature cannot have been accidental appears from the fact that three out of those named appear in the group of friends and disciples who immediately surrounded Jesus, and in comparatively few instances beyond that group. Of the twelve Apostles, two are named Simon, two Judas, and two James or Jacob.

brethren did not believe on him" (οὐδὲ οἱ ἀδελφοὶ αὐτοῦ ἐπίστευον εἰς αὐτόν); the tense indicates the persistent unbelief.

The passage, however, shews continued intercourse between Jesus and His brethren, while indicating a profound difference in religious position, and inability on their part to recognise Christ or to understand His work: "The world cannot hate you; but me it hateth, because I testify of it, that its deeds are evil." The context marks the intention of Jesus to be independent of His brethren, in action—which like elder brethren they endeavoured to control. The answer to them is the same in effect as the answer to Mary at the marriage in Cana. Comp. John vii. 8, with John ii. 4.

(8) *The Conversion of St James.*

We now pass to the days which followed the Resurrection. When the Eleven Apostles were gathered together after the Ascension the brethren of the Lord were with them (Acts i. 14). A momentous change had taken place in their spiritual lives, of which very little is said in Holy Scripture. One expression, how-ever, of St Paul explains everything. Speaking of the risen Lord St Paul writes (1 Cor. xv. 7): "then he appeared unto James; then to all the apostles." The result of that appearance of the risen Lord was a changed life and a changed belief. James was re-ceived without hesitation among the number of believers; and shortly afterwards we find him occupying the highest position in the Church at Jerusalem. "He was," says Eusebius (*H. E.* II. 1), "the first to be entrusted with the See (θρόνον) of the Church in Jerusalem."

A strange tradition is preserved in *The Gospel according to the Hebrews* that the Lord went to James and appeared unto him, for James had sworn that he would not eat bread from that hour wherein he had drunk the cup of the Lord, until he saw Him rising again from the dead...bring a table and bread...and he took up the bread and blessed and broke and afterward gave to James the Just, and said to him, 'My brother, eat thy bread, for the Son of Man is risen from them that sleep.' (Nicholson, *The Gospel according to the Hebrews*, pp. 66—68.)

From the great difficulty of supposing the presence of James the brother of the Lord at the Last Supper, Bishop Lightfoot has suggested that the true reading is *Dominus* not *Domini,* the familiarity of the expression 'the cup of the Lord' having misled the scribe. In that case the words would be, "wherein the Lord had drunk the cup." (Lightfoot's *Galatians,* p. 266.)

The tradition may contain a substratum of truth. Substantially indeed it falls in with St Paul's record of the Lord's appearance to St James referred to above.

(9) *Position in the Church of Jerusalem.*

The circumstances of St James's election to the presidency or bishopric of the Church in Jerusalem are not narrated in the Bible. But it is not difficult to conjecture the motives which led to the choice. The brother of the Lord had now become a believer, he had been honoured by a special revelation from the risen Christ: he had already gained a reputation for sanctity of life both among the disciples and the Jews[1]. The rest would follow naturally. His near kinship to the Lord—possibly the nature of the communication when He appeared to His 'brother' —possibly a resemblance of voice and manner and looks such as is found in those who have been associated from childhood— would combine to give to St James an authority and position in the Church which would be tacitly and unhesitatingly admitted by all the brethren.

(10) *His great influence.*

The few direct references to St James in the Acts and Epistles point to his leading position in the Church. The news of St Peter's release from prison is sent expressly and at once to "James and the brethren" (Acts xii. 17). He presides and pronounces the decision at the Conference held at Jerusalem on the admission of Gentiles to the Church (Acts xv. 13—21); and again

---

[1] So high was this reputation with the Jews that his death was assigned as one of the causes which called down the wrath of God upon Jerusalem that ended in its destruction. St James held a position which was only once possible in the history of the Christian Church.

at a gathering of the brethren, to receive a report of St Paul's mission work, the preeminence of St James is indicated by the language of St Luke: "And on the day following Paul went in with us unto James; and all the elders were present" (Acts xxi. 18). In Galatians ii. 9, St James is named before Cephas and John as one of those "who were reputed to be pillars." In this passage the division of mission work is named, "that we (Paul and Barnabas) should go unto the Gentiles, and they unto the Circumcision." An injunction very characteristic of St James is added: "Only they would that we should remember the poor."

The passage shews complete agreement between the two great leaders, St James and St Paul, and is also quite in harmony with the decision of the Conference at Jerusalem (Acts xv. 18). The expression however in verse 12 of the same chapter of Galatians, τινὰς ἀπὸ Ἰακώβου, and the incident which follows, seem to point to a deepening difference between the Jewish and Gentile divisions of the Christian Church. The words, however, have been unduly pressed, and it is quite possible that the envoys or disciples of St James may have gone far beyond St James's own views in their language and acts.

### (11) *His ascetic life.*

Some further particulars of St James's life are recorded in a fragment of Hegesippus preserved in Eusebius (*H. E.* ii. 23), "He was holy from his mother's womb, he drank not wine nor strong drink (σίκερα, Heb. שֵׁכָר: comp. St Luke i. 15), nor did he eat flesh; no razor came to his head, nor did he anoint himself with oil, nor use the bath. To him alone was it permitted to enter the holy place, for his clothing was of linen, not of wool. Alone he used to go into the temple (ναόν) and would be found upon his knees praying for the remission of his people's sins, so that his knees became hard like those of a camel through continuously bending them in the worship of God. On account of his exceeding righteousness he used to be called δίκαιος καὶ ὠβλίας." The meaning of the second word is explained to be περιοχὴ τοῦ λαοῦ καὶ δικαιοσύνη.

(12) *His death.*

In the end the Scribes and Pharisees finding that the faith of Christ greatly increased through the preaching of St James, persuaded him to stand on the pinnacle of the Temple, in the hope that he would there dissuade the people, from following the Crucified One. St James, however, cried with a loud voice : "'Why ask ye me concerning Jesus the Son of Man ? He is seated in Heaven on the right hand of the mighty power, and He will come on the clouds of heaven.' Thereupon they flung down the Just One, and then stoned him, since he was not killed by the fall. Then he turned and knelt, saying, 'I beseech thee, Lord God, Father, forgive them, for they know not what they do.' Then one of the priests of the sons of Rechab cried saying, 'Cease, what are ye doing ? the Just One prayeth for us.' And then one of them, a fuller, took the club with which he beat the clothes and smote the Just One on the head. And in that manner did James suffer martyrdom." Hegesippus adds : "And they buried him in the place beside the Sanctuary (τῷ ναῷ)."

There is no reason to doubt the substantial accuracy of this account. The narrative is natural and unforced and describes a death in harmony with what is known of the life of St James.

(13) *Agreement of the Contents of the Epistle with the above facts.*

Tested by the features and incidents of that life which are known to us, the internal evidence for the authenticity of the Epistle is both strong and subtle. Strong in direct harmony with acknowledged circumstances of his life, and subtle in undesigned coincidence with position and antecedents.

Of the topics of the Epistle, some are precisely such points as might have been referred to the Bishop of the Church in Jerusalem, points on which direction from him might have been expected. Some of them irresistibly recall the spirit of religious thought which pervades the utterances of the group of pious Jews to which the holy family belonged. Among these are the praise of wisdom, the doom of the proud, the excellence of poverty, the indifference to external rank. Other expressions again suggest, without verbally repeating, the teaching of the Lord Jesus in such a way as to indicate the result of long familiar intercourse rather than the express reproduction of a scholar. Other features of the Epistle reflect the personal character of the author. The ascetic tone—the contempt of riches—the sense of freedom and of spiritual independence—the stern attitude towards the rich oppressor—the pious belief in the efficacy of prayer—the joy in conversions.

An argument against the authenticity of the Epistle has been drawn from the excellence and originality of the Greek style in which it is written. But such an argument implies a preconception of the possibilities of learning available for James, which does not rest on evidence. At the same time the perfection of the style has been exaggerated. Full of force and vigour it undoubtedly is—words and phrases are admirably suited to the exact expression of the ideas intended to be conveyed. But the form and idiom are for the most part Hebraic. There is an absence of the more delicate uses of Greek construction, and certainly an absence of that facility of expression and idiomatic usage which are characteristic of a writer using his native tongue.

The subject-matter and some features in the style of the Epistle may be explained by the position held by St James and the circumstances of the time.

We have seen that it was to St James that the news of St Peter's escape from prison was first conveyed, and that when St Paul went up to Jerusalem after his conversion he saw none of the Apostles except Cephas and James the brother of the Lord. Again, when St Paul revisited Jerusalem on his return from Greece and Macedonia St Luke tells us that, 'on the day following he went in with us unto James, and all the elders were present' (Acts xxi. 17). What was done by St Paul must have been done by thousands of Christians who came up to Jerusalem. Bishops and Elders from distant Churches would find that the greatest interest of a visit to Jerusalem centered in the person of the Lord's brother. Every question concerning the welfare of the Church, every dispute in doctrine, each instance of persecution or suffering would be referred to the Bishop of Jerusalem.

In these circumstances it would be natural to expect from St James an authoritative message to distant communities of Jewish Christians such as this Epistle contains. There is a certain abruptness of style, an absence of introduction and of constructive links between the topics treated of which would be naturally characteristic in a letter written, not as a treatise on Christian doctrine, but in answer to appeals made from a distance to a central living authority. The variety and range of subjects and the emphasis laid on special points may well be due to the same cause.

(14) *Recent objections to the authenticity of the Epistle noticed.*

From the fifth century downwards the claim of this Epistle to Apostolic authority was scarcely questioned, until in the 16th century the early doubts were revived on entirely different grounds. In his prolegomena to the New Testament (A.D. 1522) Luther terms the Epistle of St James, 'an Epistle of straw' (eine recht strohende Epistel), partly (1) because of its supposed antagonism to Pauline doctrine and its assertion of righteousness by works, partly (2) because of the absence of such important topics as the sufferings, the death, the resurrection and the ascension of Christ. It is shewn below (ch. v.) that the first of these objections rests on a misconception of St James's argument and its relation to St Paul's teaching. (2) The argument from omission is always precarious and in this case the circumstances in which the Epistle originated would fully account for the omissions noticed by Luther.

More recent criticism has laid stress on : (1) the difficulty of finding an occasion for the Epistle : why, it is asked, should St James have written to the Dispersion ? (2) the improbability that St James, the Lord's brother, should have written in opposition to St Paul ; (3) the supposed inconsistency between St James ii. 25 and Hebrews xi. 31 ; (4) the improbability that a Galilean peasant like St James should possess the power of writing in the Greek style of this Epistle.

The answer to these questions will, it is hoped, be found in the foregoing remarks. On (3) it may be added that there is no real opposition between righteousness by faith and righteousness by works that spring from faith.

On the whole the ancient tradition may be confidently re-affirmed. The weakness of the external evidence is more apparent than real, and the internal testimony is indisputably strong and cogent.


## CHAPTER II.

### THE DATE OF THE EPISTLE AND THE CIRCUMSTANCES IN WHICH IT WAS WRITTEN. *45 or 46*

If we admit the validity of the argument for the authenticity of this Epistle the question of date is confined to a narrow limit of time. Nevertheless it is important to determine, if possible, whether St James wrote before or after the Epistles of St Paul had become widely known in the Church, as this is a point which bears on the exegesis of the Epistle : and further whether he wrote before or after the great Conference held in Jerusalem A.D. 52, in regard to the admission of the Gentiles into the Christian Church.

There are two considerations which point to a very early date for the Epistle :—(1) the Judaic type of Christianity apparent in it ; (2) the absence of controversy on subjects which came into dispute about the time of the Conference in Jerusalem or soon afterwards.

1. It may be safely asserted that, for some years after the memorable Day of Pentecost and the birth of the Christian Church, there was no visible and external separation between the disciples of Christ and the Jewish community. The Christians still worshipped in the Temple and in the synagogues, and practised circumcision.

In this the first disciples followed the example of the Lord

Jesus Christ, who uniformly taught in the synagogues, or in the Temple, and with His fellow-countrymen observed the appointed feasts and ordinances of the Law.

St Paul himself, to whom the Apostleship to the Gentiles was divinely entrusted, was no exception to this rule. In every city which he visited in the course of his missionary journeys he resorted in the first instance to the synagogues of the Jews (Acts xiii. 14 ff., xv. 1 ff., xvi. 13, xvii. 1, 10, xviii. 4). Moreover when the larger infusion of Gentile converts had excited the wrathful jealousy of the Jewish Christians (Acts xxi. 20), St Paul by the advice of St James and the other Apostles took certain men who were under a vow, and "purifying himself with them went into the temple, declaring the fulfilment of the days of purification, until the offering was offered for every one of them" (Acts xxi. 26); thus purposely and conspicuously declaring his adherence to the ancient rites.

It is clear then that even after the Conference at Jerusalem A.D. 52, the Jewish converts as distinct from the Gentiles were expected to observe exact conformity with the Law. Before that Council, and at the period in which we are disposed to place the date of this Epistle, the Church in Jerusalem must have consisted almost entirely of converts from Judaism among whom the question of separation from their brethren had not yet been stirred.

Such was the condition of the Judæo-Christian Church over which St James presided and from which the Jewish communities of the Eastern Dispersion derived their Christianity. It may be noted that this phase of Christianity was not destined to last long. At the date when the Epistle to the Hebrews was written the Christian Church appears at any rate to have been dissociated from the Temple services, and the fall of Jerusalem finally broke the link between Judaism and the form of Christianity allied with it. What remained of Judæo-Christianity lapsed into Ebionism and various forms of heresy.

The very circumstance of the limited duration of Judæo-Christianity serves to fix the date of the Epistle to St James; if our contention be correct, that it was addressed to a Christian community whose relations with Judaism were still close, and at a time when Christianity had not been generally recognised as hostile to the synagogue and Temple worship.

One specially interesting indication of the early epoch in the history of Christianity at which the Epistle was written is the occurrence of the word 'synagogue' to denote the Christian place of assembly (ch. ii. 2). Nothing is more natural than that, in the circumstances which we have sketched, the new brotherhood should form synagogues of its own. This was no unusual thing. Hundreds of small communities in Judaism had separate synagogues. The Rabbinical writers counted 480 of these in Jerusalem alone : and, although the number may be exaggerated, the fact that small bodies of Jews like the Libertines and the Cyrenians had their own synagogues in Jerusalem confirms the substantial truth of the statement (see Acts vi. 9).

The Christian synagogue would answer precisely to the meeting place of one of these Jewish communities. In its main features the service would follow the pattern of the Jewish synagogue ritual. Indeed traces are discernible in the 2nd chapter of the Acts of the formation of such a Christian synagogue in which the disciples met for instruction and worship and the celebration of the Eucharist.

The Christian synagogues like those of the Jews would be open to all who chose to enter. And to the poor Christian Jews it would be a temptation, which can be understood, to welcome the appearance of a rich man—a possible convert—within the walls of their little synagogue.

It is easy to believe that a Church constituted on these principles and having its origin in Jerusalem would look for guidance and inspiration to the brother of the Lord. All questions of difficulty would be referred to him for decision, and by means of the frequent communications between the Jews in Jerusalem and their brethren in distant provinces, St James would be kept informed of the spiritual condition of the Churches of the Dispersion. Such an Epistle as this which we possess would be the natural outcome of questions and information of this kind : its informal character—the abruptness of its beginning—the variety and to a certain extent the simplicity of the topics treated of may be explained on this hypothesis.

The existence of persecution is supposed to point to a later date for this Epistle. But the persecutions alluded to are of a primitive type and such as that which arose after the death of St Stephen, a persecution which extended as far as to the distant settlement of Jews in Damascus. It was such a persecution as that in which St Paul himself engaged in his unconverted days; such as he too himself was exposed to when he taught that Jesus is the Christ in the cities and synagogues of Pisidia and Macedonia. It was persecution not by the Gentiles as yet, but by the Pharisaic party among the Jews, who resented that which appeared to be an attack upon the Law and the traditions. It was persecution of the poor by the unscrupulous and irresponsible rich, such as had appeared in every period of Jewish history, and which was specially denounced by the Hebrew prophets when it shewed itself among the ancestors of the Jews of the Dispersion.

That persecution under the form of judicial process (ch. ii. 6) was possible is shewn by recently discovered inscriptions, which prove the autonomy of Jewish communities in the cities of the Roman Empire previous to A.D. 70, but not after that date[1].

2. It is by referring the Epistle to this primitive stage in the history of the Christian Church, that we are able to account for the absence of much of the controversial matter which enters into other Epistles. There were no Judaizers to be attacked, because as yet Gentile Christianity had not taken a recognised position in the Church, and Judaism did not yet exist in that hostile form which it afterwards assumed. Nor as yet had such heresies crept in as were afterwards found at Colossæ—no false doctrine about the resurrection as at Corinth—no despondency as to the delay in the Advent of Christ, and therefore no need of such warnings and consolations as were addressed to the Thessalonians or to the Hebrews a few years later.

---

[1] See Professor Ramsay in *Expositor* for April, 1895, p. 273.

## CHAPTER III.

### THE FIRST READERS OF THE EPISTLE. THE TWELVE TRIBES IN DISPERSION.

THE dispersion of Israel originated in the deportation of the inhabitants of the Northern Kingdom to Assyria after the conquest of Samaria by Sargon (B.C. 722). The cities in which the captives were placed, Halah and Gozan, point to the districts known to Ptolemy as Chalcitis and Gauzanitis; and Habor, 'the river of Gozan' (2 Kings xvii. 6), is identified with the Khabour, an affluent of the Upper Euphrates. In a little more than a hundred years from the captivity of Israel, Judah shared the same fate, and, with the exception of a small remnant, was carried in captivity to Babylon and the adjoining regions.

The successive returns under Zerubbabel (B.C. 537) and Ezra (B.C. 458) left a large proportion, probably the vast majority of Israel and Judah, in Babylonia and the surrounding countries.

Hence the captivities of Israel and Judah, which were in the first instance penal, resulted in the permanent settlement of large and flourishing Hebrew colonies in the regions bordering on the Euphrates and the Tigris.

At the fall of Jerusalem the stream of Jewish migration began to flow into Egypt. And subsequently many thousands of Jewish families sought refuge in that country from the persecution of the Syrian kings. In Alexandria two of the five quarters of the city were chiefly inhabited by Jews. And in Egypt generally there were according to Philo hardly less than a million Jewish settlers, οὐκ ἀποδέουσι μυριάδων ἑκατὸν οἱ τὴν Ἀλεξάνδρειαν καὶ τὴν χώραν Ἰουδαῖοι κατοικοῦντες ἀπὸ τοῦ πρὸς Λιβύην καταβαθμοῦ μέχρι τῶν ὁρίων Αἰθιοπίας, Philo, *in Flaccum*, § 6. From Egypt numbers of Jews found their way to Cyrene. In 340 B.C. Artaxerxes Ochus carried Jewish captives from Egypt to the settlements of their kinsfolk in Babylon, and to Hyrcania and the shores of the Caspian Sea.

Subsequently Antiochus the Great (223—187), who shewed the utmost consideration to the Jews, removed 2000 of their families from Mesopotamia and Babylonia to Lydia and Phrygia with the view of infusing a loyal element in the disaffected population of those countries. The same system of deportation pushed the Dispersion still further west, for in the year 63 B.C. Pompey caused thousands of Jewish prisoners to be conveyed to Rome, where several gained their freedom and settled in the Trastevere (Philo, *De Leg. ad Caium*, p. 1014, § 23). But there was another cause which tended in the same direction. The Jew had now become a keen and experienced trader. With this object he passed from city to city and from province to province. Syria and Asia Minor, the Greek islands and Roman colonies were frequented by Hebrew merchants[1]. In this way the Jewish race gained a footing in every region of the civilised world, and not being confined as other nations within the limits of a single region in many places almost outnumbered the native populations.

The list in Acts ii. 9—11 indicates the extent of the Dispersion both in the East and West. But between these two branches there was a wide and well-marked difference which it is important to note. The Western Dispersion were Hellenists separated in language and in mode of thought and manner from the strict Hebrew-speaking Jews who constituted the Eastern Dispersion, and who in common with their Syrian and Palestinian brethren bore the honourable title of 'Hebrews,' or even in a special sense 'the Dispersion,' as distinguished from 'the Dispersion of the Greeks'—comp. St John vii. 35, μὴ εἰς τὴν διασποράν τῶν Ἑλλήνων μέλλει πορεύεσθαι, καὶ διδάσκειν τοὺς Ἕλληνας; see also Acts vi. 1[2].

---

[1] In Antioch and Damascus and other Syrian cities there was an enormous Jewish population (Joseph. *Bell. Jud.* II. 20. 2, VII. 8. 7), and in the provinces of Asia Minor they were almost if not quite as numerous. Comp. Joseph. *Antt.* XIV.7. 2; *Bell. Jud.* II. 16. 4, VII. 3. 3; also πᾶσα δὲ γαῖα σέθεν πλήρης καὶ πᾶσα θάλασσα, *Orac. Sybill.* III. 27; see Philo, *de Leg. ad Caium*, p. 1023 B.

[2] Edersheim's *Life and Times of Jesus the Messiah*, vol. I. pp. 7, 9, 14.

Rabbinical expressions are cited[1] shewing the equality of the Israelites dwelling in the Eastern Dispersion, and even their superiority over the Jews of Palestine. "Unlike the heathen countries, whose very dust defiled, the soil of Syria was declared clean like that of Palestine itself. So far as purity of descent was concerned, the Babylonians indeed considered themselves superior to their Palestinian brethren. They had it that when Ezra took with him those who went to Palestine, he had left the land behind him as 'pure as fine flour[2].'"

It is reasonable then to suppose that when St James writes to 'the twelve tribes which are of the Dispersion,' without any qualifying addition that he addresses himself to the Eastern as distinct from the Western or Hellenist Dispersion : in other words, to the Jews settled in Syria and Babylonia, who were in a preeminent sense 'the Dispersion.' How vast that population was in those regions may be gathered from the words of Josephus : Αἱ δὲ δέκα φυλαὶ πέραν εἰσὶν Εὐφράτου ἕως δεῦρο μυριάδες ἄπειροι καὶ ἀριθμῷ γνωσθῆναι μὴ δυνάμεναι, Joseph. *Antt.* xv. 2. 2.

It is apparent also that the Christians to whom St James wrote belonged to the poorer classes, the rich who are alluded to in the Epistle being unconverted Jews and not members of the Christian Church ; see notes on i. 10, ii. 1, iv. 13. This condition of things corresponds with what we read elsewhere of the early Church. The relief of the poor became the first act of Church organization, and notwithstanding the generosity of wealthier members the Church in Jerusalem relapsed into poverty and stood in need of pecuniary assistance (Acts vi. 1; Rom. xv. 26). Probably too St Paul's description of the Church of Corinth (1 Cor. i. 26—28) applied to many other Christian communities. During the first decades of its history then the Church was the Church of the poor. Moreover it was a persecuted Church. This appears both from the Epistle of St James and from the Acts of the Apostles.

Further than this internal evidence does not permit us to

---

[1] See Lightfoot, *Hor. Hebr.* Addenda to 1 Cor. xiv. ch. ii. §§ 1 and 2, p. 568.

[2] Edersheim's *Life and Times of Jesus the Messiah*, vol. i. p. 9.

specialise. We cannot say to what particular Church or Churches, Syrian or Babylonian, the Epistle was originally sent, or even whether it was strictly speaking encyclical, as the opening words suggest, or called forth by definite circumstances of a special community. A certain vividness and force of expression seems to indicate actual occurrences. The incident of the rich man entering the synagogue (ch. ii. 1—4) reads like the description of a scene from life, the wavering of some, the views of others concerning faith and temptation, the description of internal quarrels and particular acts of oppression—all these seem drawn from the actual experience of some one Christian community. At the same time what was specially applicable to one Church would be full of lessons to all where the general circumstances and characteristics would be similar.

It is, however, an interesting and important point that in addressing his Epistle to the twelve tribes St James expresses the belief in a still complete and united Israel, which appears as a settled conviction in post-Exilian thought.

Thus in the letter of Aristeas relating to the LXX. translation the high-priest Eleazar is represented as sending to Ptolemy Philadelphus seventy-two men, that is, six from each of the twelve tribes; and though four only of the priestly courses returned from exile (Ezr. ii. 36) the original representative number of twenty-four was restored. In the New Testament the same belief appears in the number of the twelve Apostles, and in the promise that they should sit on thrones judging the twelve tribes of Israel (Matt. xix. 28; Luke xxii. 30); in the twelve gates of the heavenly Jerusalem (Rev. xxi. 12); and in the sealing of the twelve tribes (Rev. vii. 4, foll.). St Paul speaks of 'the twelve tribes ($\tau\grave{o}$ $\delta\omega\delta\epsilon\kappa\acute{a}\phi\upsilon\lambda o\nu$) earnestly serving God day and night,' Acts xxvi. 7: and in Rom. xi. 25 the Israel alluded to includes all the children of Abraham.

Long after the Apostolic age the Talmudists made legal enactments in regard to intermarriage with the ten tribes, whose settlements they still recognised in the regions of the Euphrates, to which they had been first carried in captivity (Lightfoot, *Hor. Hebr.*, Addenda to 1 Cor. xiv. ch. III.).

This survival of Israel in its completeness is in accordance with such Old Testament predictions as that of Amos ix. 9, 'I will sift the house of Israel among all the nations, like as corn is sifted in a sieve, yet shall not the least grain fall upon the earth'; and that of Isaiah xi. 12, 'He shall assemble the outcasts of Israel and gather together the dispersed of Judah from the four corners of the earth....Ephraim shall not envy Judah, and Judah shall not vex Ephraim.' See also Hosea i. 11, 'The children of Judah and the children of Israel shall be gathered together, and they shall appoint themselves one head, and shall go up from the land.' Comp. also Hosea iii. 5, 'Afterward shall the children of Israel return, and seek the Lord their God, and David their king.'

## CHAPTER IV.

### THE CONTENTS OF THE EPISTLE.

The informal character of the Epistle renders a logical analysis difficult. It is not a formal treatise, but an authoritative reply to questions which had arisen, a bishop's ruling on incidents and questions of Church life and discipline which had been reported to him.

It may be regarded as a discourse on two practical rules of the Christian life : (a) Resistance to temptation, or ὑπομονή : temptation being a necessary condition of the Christian life. (b) Activity in the Christian graces, of which πίστις and ἔλεος are leading examples.

The various topics of the Epistle may be exhibited more in detail as follows :

Introduction. i. ver. 1.

1. Temptation. (a) From without, i. 2—4. (1) Wisdom, prayer, stedfastness, the Divine helps in temptation, 5—8. (2) Temptation, implying oppression, introduces the connected subject of the rich and poor, and the Old Testament problem of the prosperity of the wicked (as a cause of

The ethical and practical character of the Epistle is a note of the earlier stage of the Christian Church, when the first and most necessary step was to secure pure and honest and noble lives in those who were members of the brotherhood.

That the great Christian teachers of the first generation should have felt it especially needful to guard the moral side of the Christian life, can surprise no one who has even an elementary knowledge of the society out of which the Christian convert had emerged. On all sides there were in Greek, Roman and Oriental civilization moral evils of the gravest kind. In every city to which the Jewish Christian trader went he would find some fresh form of vice, some new kind of 'temptation' for protection against which the Apostolic warnings were hourly needed. See Döllinger, *Gentile and Jew*, I. 356 n.

But the preponderance of this ethical teaching certainly points to a period in which controversy had not yet become acute. Hence the absence in this Epistle of that developed Christology which is found in the later N. T. writers. In this Epistle there is no mention of the Incarnation, or of the sufferings and Crucifixion, or of the blood of Christ or of the Atonement or the High-priesthood of Christ, or of prophecy or of Baptism or the Eucharist. And in other regions of thought there are no less striking silences: there is no mention of the Christian attitude to slavery, or to magistrates and rulers: no discussion of questions of marriage, or of the Christian ministry. Such omissions are, however, all explicable in view of the special circumstances which seem to have called forth the Epistle, and are indeed if properly considered evidences both of its genuineness and of its early date.


## CHAPTER V.

### ST JAMES AND ST PAUL—FAITH AND WORKS.

THE supposition of an antagonism between St James and St Paul on the subject of faith and works rests on a very slender foundation, and would probably have had very inconsiderable influence on Christian thought had it not been for the great influence of Luther.

If indeed the words of St James (ch. ii. 14, foll.) are an attack upon St Paul, the immense significance of them can hardly be overrated. For to oppose St Paul on this point, and to assert the saving efficacy of the works of the law, would be to advocate Judaism in the Christian Church. It would mean that this Epistle contains a protest against the position authoritatively maintained by St Paul and sanctioned by the conscience of Christendom throughout the Christian centuries—a wholly untenable proposition. And yet those who see in these words an argument against the Pauline view of Christianity can take no middle course. St James is either the advocate of that form of Jewish Christianity which St Paul condemns, or he is not.

But if it is to be supposed that these words contain a deliberate argument against St Paul's position, what an inadequate treatment this would be of that great crucial question! Again, is it conceivable that the Church would have sanctioned and left in the Canonical Scriptures two contradictory views of this essential matter?

Happily it is only a very superficial view of the passage that demands an hypothesis of this kind. No 'reconciliation' is needed; for the arguments of the two great Apostles are not on the same plane. The errors attacked are fundamentally different.

St Paul's argument is in opposition to those who claimed to be justified by an exact performance of an external ritual, and who desired to carry into Christianity the whole Jewish ceremonial law. St James, on the other hand, is opposing the conception that faith without works is possible or that in any sense it can be the saving and central principle of the Christian life. The teaching of St James is that of the Epistle to the Hebrews, where the activity of a living faith is shewn to have been the inspiring principle of Hebrew history from Abraham to the time of the Maccabees. It is also the teaching of St Paul, comp. Titus iii. 1, 8, 14: the Christians must be: πρὸς πᾶν ἔργον ἀγαθὸν ἑτοίμους....Titus is to exhort ἵνα φροντίζωσιν καλῶν ἔργων

προΐστασθαι οἱ πεπιστευκότες θεῷ, and see as strictly in accordance with St James's teaching, Rom. ii. 13, οὐ γὰρ οἱ ἀκροαταὶ τοῦ
νόμου δίκαιοι παρὰ τῷ θεῷ, ἀλλ᾽ οἱ ποιηταὶ νόμου δικαιωθήσονται.

Up to this time indeed the observance of the Law was un-
questioned by Jewish Christians. The controversy in which
St Paul was engaged originated when the growth of the Gentile
element in the Church and the rise of the Judaizing faction
created the necessity of a further development of Christianity,
and of a clearly defined relationship to Judaism, which had then
assumed an attitude of hostility to the preaching of St Paul.

The danger against which St James directs his argument is,
that an unfruitful theoretical belief should take the place of
activity in good works. The danger corresponded, indeed, to
Pharisaism in the Jewish Church. With the Pharisees 'dead
works,' the mechanical carrying out of defined rules uninspired
by a living faith, ruined true religion. The corresponding danger
against which St James contends was, that a dead or dormant
faith without works should destroy the vital energy of the
Christian life.

The two Apostles have indeed the same moral standpoint,
and whenever a close similarity of expression occurs it is probable that the original teaching is to be referred to St James
rather than to St Paul. St James was a follower of Christ
before St Paul. And when St Paul visited Jerusalem after his
conversion, the exposition of Christianity by St James with the
authority of the Lord's Brother may well have contributed to
the moulding of his faith.

## CHAPTER VI.

SOME LEADING THOUGHTS IN THE EPISTLE : σοφία—πίστις—
πειρασμός—ὑπομονή.

IF this Epistle is the earliest of Christian documents which
has descended to us, it becomes of special interest and importance to examine the leading words and expressions which occur

in it, and to consider more fully than is possible in the notes the thoughts and associations which are attached to them.

1.   Twice in the Epistle St James speaks of σοφία or wisdom; in ch. i. 5, where with a kind of abruptness, as though σοφία would be acknowledged as the first object of desire, it is mentioned as a subject of prayer, and in ch. iii. 13—18, where there is a contrast between σοφία ἄνωθεν κατερχομένη and ἐπίγειος σοφία.

The inquiry to be made then is, what was St James's conception of σοφία, and what is meant by the distinction between the two wisdoms (iii. 13—18)?

The term σοφία conveyed a very definite series of meanings to the Greek mind before it came in contact with Hebrew thought.   It meant first of all skill in any art or handicraft in its most excellent and subtle form: οὐδὲν ἄλλο σημαίνοντες τὴν σοφίαν ἢ ὅτι ἀρετὴ τέχνης ἐστίν, *Eth. Nic.* VI. vii. 2.   In a higher sense it is the most exact of sciences, ἀκριβεστάτη τῶν ἐπιστημῶν: lastly it is a science of that which is most prized, the highest of existences, that is, the Divine existence of pure immutable being.

In some of these senses the use of σοφία and σοφός in the LXX. is synonymous with their use in Greek philosophical literature.   Oholiab and Bezalel are σοφοί, just as Phidias and Polycletus are σοφοί.   And the highest conception of σοφία in Greek thought approaches very nearly to the 'wisdom from above' described by St James.   But the Hebrew idea of σοφία has a meaning and history of its own.   The Hellenic σοφία is indeed deliberately set aside by St Paul as alien to the Christian system, 1 Cor. i. 18—28; and in Phil. iv. 8 the leading philosophic terms ἀρετή and ἔπαινος are named with evident disparagement.   When St James therefore speaks of σοφία in this Epistle it is the σοφία of Hebrew thought and literature.   It was a conception of great beauty, which grew up in the later part of the post-Exile period.   When, side by side with the zeal of Judaism for a minute and careful observance of the Law, a passion had arisen for the pursuit of wisdom, σοφία, the most comprehensive word of Greek thought, had been chosen to represent this purely Hebrew conception, which is embodied and illustrated in the sapiential books of the Bible and the Apocrypha. But the Hebrew *chokmah* or wisdom has a far wider signification than the Greek σοφία. According to the author of the Wisdom of Solomon it is the most perfect principle of guidance in human action : πρὸς ὑμᾶς οὖν, οἱ τύραννοι, οἱ λόγοι μου, ἵνα μάθητε σοφίαν καὶ μὴ παραπέσητε...λαμπρὰ καὶ ἀμάραντός ἐστιν ἡ σοφία, vi. 9, 12. Step by step σοφία leads to union with God : προσοχὴ δὲ νόμων (observance of the laws) βεβαίωσις ἀφθαρσίας· ἀφθαρσία δὲ ἐγγὺς εἶναι ποιεῖ θεοῦ, 18—20...τιμήσατε σοφίαν ἵνα εἰς τὸν αἰῶνα βασιλεύσητε, 21. It is a direct emanation from God : πᾶσα σοφία παρὰ Κυρίου καὶ μετ' αὐτοῦ ἐστιν εἰς τὸν αἰῶνα, Ecclus. i. 1 ; and the breath of His power and the reflexion of His brightness : ἀτμὶς γάρ ἐστιν τῆς τοῦ θεοῦ δυνάμεως...ἀπαύγασμα γάρ ἐστι φωτὸς ἀιδίου καὶ ἔσοπτρον ἀκηλίδωτον τῆς τοῦ θεοῦ ἐνεργείας καὶ εἰκὼν τῆς ἀγαθότητος αὐτοῦ, Wisdom of Solomon, vii. 25, 26.

This exalted view of σοφία gives a depth of meaning to the description of the Lord's growth : καὶ Ἰησοῦς προέκοπτεν τῇ σοφίᾳ κ.τ.λ., Luke ii. 52, and τὸ δὲ παιδίον ηὔξανεν, καὶ ἐκραταιοῦτο, πληρούμενον σοφίᾳ, ii. 40.

This then, we cannot doubt, was the glowing picture present to St James's mind when he spoke of σοφία as the most exalted subject of prayer, and as that which cometh from above. This latter expression sounds like an echo of the phrase in the Book of Wisdom where σοφία is described as 'an influence flowing from the glory of the Almighty' (ἀπόρροια τῆς τοῦ παντοκράτορος δόξης εἰλικρινής), vii. 25.

It is less easy to determine what the Apostle means us to understand by that opposing 'wisdom' which he describes as earthly, sensual, devilish, ἐπίγειος, ψυχική, δαιμονιώδης.

While it is true that the notes of the psychic wisdom as given by St James are, from a Christian standpoint, a justifiable criticism of the prevailing philosophic systems, the question arises whether such a warning against the dangers of Greek philosophy would be specially needed in those Hebrew communities to which the Epistle was addressed, and whether St James's argument is not rather directed against dangers to be found in the distinctively Jewish tendency to a spirit of zeal

and fanaticism. At this early stage of Christian history the
evils which threatened Judaism equally threatened the Judæo-
Christian body. 'Zeal for the Lord' was an historic word with
the Jew and had inspired great actions, and the Maccabean
victories were still a practical argument of success. But this
noble enthusiasm of former days had now degenerated into a
blind hatred of foreign domination, and was rapidly tending to
the fierce spirit which broke out in wild excesses at the siege
of Jerusalem.

Therefore, though a more general interpretation need not be
excluded, it is probable that by the false wisdom of which
St James speaks, and which is clearly associated with zeal and
contention and rivalry (ἐρίθεια), is primarily meant that other
system of life which found many supporters at this period and
which Josephus expressly calls a φιλοσοφία, *Antt.* XVIII. i. 1,
τῇ δὲ τετάρτῃ τῶν φιλοσοφιῶν ὁ Γαλιλαῖος Ἰούδας ἡγεμὼν κατέστη
κ.τ.λ. This φιλοσοφία represented the mundane and material
side of the Maccabean revival. It fostered the expectation of an
earthly kingdom, and of a Messiah who should overcome the
armies of the aliens and free Israel from Roman domination;
it was ἐπίγειος. It looked to a time of material prosperity and
to the satisfaction of desires: it was ψυχική and not πνευματική.
Again, the moving energetic element in this system, that spirit
of enthusiasm and desperate resistance to foreign power or to
any infringement of the national religion in its extreme phase,
exhibited characteristics which closely approached the phenomena of demoniacal possession: it was δαιμονιώδης.

2. Another leading thought in this Epistle is embodied
in the word πίστις. So far from this conception being absent, or
unimportant, in St James's scheme of the Christian life its preeminent position is implied from the first, ch. i. 2. The object
of St James's teaching is not to eliminate faith as a leading
principle, but to secure the sacredness and efficiency of it, and to
guard against the danger of esteeming faith to be merely an
intellectual assent to a creed, or a belief in a fact which a man
might hold without receiving vital inspiration from it.

Faith as conceived by St James then is an active principle—

the energy of the soul in its relation to God. It implies work
achieved under an invisible and eternal influence which it instinc-
tively apprehends and appropriates. It is the same inspiring
quality of great and holy men which the writer of the Epistle to
the Hebrews enlarges upon as the key to the Divine history of
Israel. Accordingly works that spring from faith justify in virtue
of the inseparable union with a living faith.

3. And if faith is thus the essence and determining quality
of the Christian life, so that οἱ πιστεύοντες—the believers—the
possessors of πίστις, form the Christian community, it follows
that conditions must exist by which πίστις should be continuously exercised and tested. If the Christians as a body are οἱ
πιστεύοντες, they are also οἱ πειραζόμενοι. Through πειρασμός
faith becomes an ἐνέργεια, instead of being simply a δύναμις.
That this was the condition of the Master's life is shewn by the
expression : ὑμεῖς δέ ἐστε οἱ διαμεμενηκότες μετ' ἐμοῦ ἐν τοῖς πειρασμοῖς μου, Luke xxii. 28. It also agrees with St Paul's important
rule : ὅτι διὰ πολλῶν θλίψεων δεῖ ἡμᾶς εἰσελθεῖν εἰς τὴν βασιλείαν
τοῦ θεοῦ, Acts xiv. 22, and with many other passages of Holy
Scripture.

4. But from this exercise of faith, in which it is being con-
tinually tested by different forms of trial (πειρασμοῖς ποικίλοις),
there results another quality highly and specially characteristic of
the Christian life, namely, ὑπομονή, patience or resistance. πίστις
represents the active principle, ὑπομονή the passive principle,
though in ὑπομονή there is also an element of action. ὑπομονή
engages itself in resisting evil, πίστις in producing good—in
activities which result from the divinely illuminated attitude of
the soul.


## CHAPTER VII.

### THE POETICAL ELEMENT IN THE EPISTLE.

POETICAL form is so marked a characteristic of this Epistle
and bears so close a relation to the interpretation of it in parts,
that some explanation of the principles and laws of Hebrew

poetry seems to be required in an Introduction. Certain poetical elements, such as beautiful and exact expression of observed facts in life and nature, suggestiveness, imagination, taste, delicate choice of words, find a place in the poetry of all nations and of all times. But in regard to form there is great diversity. For instance, metre, the chief characteristic of Greek and Latin verse, does not in its strict sense of measured syllables regularly disposed enter into the art of the Hebrew poet, and rhyme, which gives a special charm to much of modern European poetry, is also absent from Hebrew poetical composition. At the same time the examples quoted below exhibit lines of corresponding length, and there are many instances where a play on the sound of words produces an effect similar to rhyme.

One characteristic device of Hebrew poetry is a system of acrostics exhibited in several of the Psalms, of which the 119th is a specially complex and ingenious example. Other instances are Prov. xxxi. 10—31, and Lamentations i. ii. iii. iv.

But by far the most distinctive feature of Hebrew poetry is parallelism; by which is meant a correspondence by way of likeness or dissimilarity of words, thoughts and clauses, a response of line to line and word to word. (1) The commonest form of parallelism is where the thought of the first line is repeated in the second and emphasized (*a*) by intensified expression; as,

> The wicked watcheth the righteous,
> And seeketh occasion to slay him.
> I have seen the wicked in great power,
> And spreading himself like a green tree in his own soil.
>                                   Ps. xxxvii. 32, 35.

(*b*) Or by contrast as:

> The full soul loatheth an honeycomb:
> But to the hungry soul every bitter thing is sweet.
>                                   Prov. xxvii. 7.

(2) Sometimes the parallelism consists of identity of structure without either contrast or necessary similarity in sense, as:

> Fire and hail, snow and vapour;
> Stormy wind, fulfilling his word:

> Mountains and all hills;
> Fruitful trees and all cedars.  Ps. cxlviii. 8, 9.

These are examples of parallelism in its simplest form.  But the scheme is capable of great variety and extension.  Sometimes from four to eight lines are required to complete the system, sometimes the parallelism is shewn in triplets or in stanzas of five lines, as :

> Let that day be darkness;
> Let not God regard it from above,
> Neither let the light shine upon it.   Job iii. 4.

Sometimes the first line answers to the third and the second to the fourth, as :

> As the heavens are high above the earth,
> So high is his goodness over them that fear him:
> As remote as the east is from the west,
> So far hath he removed from us our transgressions.
>                                     Ps. ciii. 11, 12.

A still more complex structure, called by Bishop Jebb 'introverted parallelism,' is when the corresponding lines in a stanza are the first and fourth, and the second and third, as :

> My son, if thine heart be wise,
> My heart shall be glad, even mine:
> Yea, my reins shall rejoice,
> When thy lips speak right things.  Prov. xxiii. 15, 16.

Other instances of this complex character are Psalm lxxxiv. 5—7, where the stanza consists of six lines : "Blessed is the man...appeareth before God in Zion" : and Psalm cxxxv. 15—18, an instance where eight lines are required to complete the parallelism : "The idols of the nations...every one that trusteth in them."

Many other examples might be given of the various modes in which the parallelism of Hebrew poetry is exhibited.  It was a system which required the same constructive skill as the classical system, and created a pleasure in expectancy of response at least equal to that of the rhymed couplet of English poetry.

It may also be observed that Hebrew poetry loses less by

translation than the poetry of any other nation. It is quite possible to retain in a foreign language many of its chief characteristics—length of lines, position of words, the response (or contrast) of thought to thought, and even the rhythm which gives it its special charm and grace. It is indeed chiefly this underlying poetical form and diction of the original to which the English Bible owes its strength and beauty of style.

The strain of poetical inspiration in the Old Testament revived in the New. Evidence of this continued gift meets us at the opening of the Gospel. In the hymn of Zacharias and Simeon and in the Psalm of the Blessed Virgin Mary, the beauty of artistic form and expression and the peculiar charm of Hebrew parallelism reappear in perfection. And it is with the deepest and most solemn interest that we trace the same vein of poetry in the discourses of our Lord. This is especially observable in the most momentous utterances of the Gospel. As instances of these may be cited: Matt. x. 34—39, xi. 28—30, xx. 25—28, and even in the hour of the Passion, Luke xxiii. 28—31. But nowhere is this characteristic more completely and beautifully exhibited than in the Sermon on the Mount, which is indeed from first to last thrown into the form of a varied and impressive poem, the artistic structure of which can be shewn by analysis[1]. It is significant and deeply suggestive that in this poetic structure, next to our Lord's own discourses, this Epistle of St James, the brother of the Lord, ranks highest.

The whole argument is more like the argument of a poem than of a regularly constructed treatise. The gradual evolution of ideas, one springing from another by which it is suggested, the linked digressions and the repeated return to the original and pervading thought, bear the same character of a noble and artistic poem.

Among other examples of genuine poetical excellence are the vigorous passages on the evils of the tongue (iii. 3—13), the scene in the Christian synagogue on the entrance of the wealthy Jew (ii. 2—4), the vivid description of trade activity (iv. 13—v. 6), and of the cruel and miserly landlord, with the picturesque personifi-

---

[1] Bishop Jebb's *Sacred Literature*, Sect. ix.

cation of the rust or tarnish on the hoarded gold, or the hire of the labourers unjustly withheld, itself crying out in accusation. And throughout this work there is the poet's grasp of what is real and eternal, in contrast with the false and fleeting character of human opinion.

Some further remarks on the poetical passages of the Epistle will be made in the notes, but two points of special interest may be indicated here. (*a*) The revival of a poetical gift in a marked and striking way in the family of the poet king David is a memorable fact. We have seen that it was a characteristic charm of our Lord's discourses, that it is noticeable in those hymns and psalms which celebrated the events and significance of His birth, and that it is found again richly developed in the Epistle of the Lord's brother. All this implies in that family or group of families the study not only of the words but of the form of ancient prophecy, and a proficiency in the same Divine art which must have been cultivated in the ancient schools of the prophets. (*b*) It is a fair inference from this ordered beauty of form and artistic diction that such an Epistle as this is not a hasty or desultory composition, but the finished result of natural powers carefully trained and divinely illuminated. And we may further believe that it was purposely moulded in a poetical form with a view to the deeper impression and more lasting memory which such a form would ensure.

## CHAPTER VIII.

### THE GREEK TEXT OF ST JAMES.

THE text of this Epistle, like other portions of the N.T., rests on the evidence of the ancient MSS., Versions, and quotations in the works of early writers and liturgies.

Of the MSS. the following important Uncials are referred to in the notes.

ℵ. *Codex Sinaiticus,* assigned to the middle of the ivth century. Of the correctors ℵ[a] was probably a contemporary, ℵ[b] belongs to the vith century, ℵ[c] to the beginning of the viith century. This valuable Codex was recovered by Tischendorf in an interesting way from the convent of St Catharine on Mt Sinai in the year 1859. It is now at St Petersburg.

A. *Codex Alexandrinus,* vth century.

This MS. was presented to Charles I. in 1628 by Cyril Lucar, Patriarch of Constantinople, formerly Patriarch of Alexandria. It passed with the royal collection to the British Museum in the year 1753.

B. *Codex Vaticanus,* ivth century.

This is the oldest vellum MS. of the New Testament in existence, and of great value and authority in determining the text. As the name implies, it is in the Vatican Library, where it has been so jealously guarded that for a long time no complete collation was possible. Recently however an excellent facsimile of the whole has been published.

C. *Codex Ephraemi,* a palimpsest of the vth century, of great critical value, now in Paris.

The following ixth century MSS. are also cited in these notes. K. *Codex Mosquensis,* in the Library of the Holy Synod at Moscow. L. *Codex Angelicus Romanus,* in the Angelican Library of the Augustinian Monks in Rome. P. *Codex Porphyrianus* (a palimpsest), so called from Bishop Porphyry of St Petersburg, to whom it belonged.

*The Versions* cannot be used except rarely for the verification of Greek words, but they give evidence of the presence or omission of words or clauses, and in some cases are so literal that their testimony is available for the order of words. The following are of the greatest value :

I. *Latin.* There is very little evidence for a Latin version of the Epistle of St James earlier than the 4th cent. It is not quoted by any early Latin writer, and it is absent from the Cheltenham Stichometry, which probably dates from about

400 A.D. It has however a place in the Claromontane Stichometry, and it is quoted, though rarely, by Latin Fathers of the
4th cent.

Of 'Old Latin' texts we have

*ff* = *Cod. Corbiensis*, saec. ix, formerly at Corbie in Picardy,
now at St Petersburg. This MS. now contains the Epistle
complete, preceded by Ps. Tertullian on Jewish Meats and the
Epistle of Barnabas. It is not therefore a Biblical MS. It
ascribes the Epistle to James the son of Zebedee.

*m* = quotations in the 'Speculum Augustini,' a collection of
Biblical extracts arranged under headings.

The text of *ff* agrees with the quotations of Chromatius of
Aquileia, a friend of St Jerome. The text of *m* in this Epistle
is almost identical with that of the quotations of Priscillian, a
Spanish heretic of the 5th century. Both our non-Vulgate
authorities may therefore claim the title of Old Latin, though it
is obvious what a different meaning and authority the term Old
Latin has here compared with the case of the Gospels where the
forms of the 'Old Latin' can be traced back to the second
century.

We have also in the Vulgate an already existing text slightly
revised by St Jerome. The best MSS. of the Vulgate are, as in the
other books, *am* (= *Cod. Amiatinus*, circ. 700 A.D.) and *fuld*
(= *Cod. Fuldensis*, 546 A.D.).

There are exhaustive essays on the Latin texts of the Epistle
by Bishop John Wordsworth and Dr Sanday in *Studia Biblica*,
I. (1885).

II. *Syriac.* "There are three stages in the history of the
Syriac Canon. The first ignored the Catholic Epistles [including
therefore our Epistle] altogether. This is represented by the
*Doctrine of Addai* and by the Homilies of Aphraates, which are
definitely dated between the years 336—345. The second stage
is marked by the Peshitto Version, which has been called the
Syriac Vulgate. As far back as that version can be traced it
included three of the Catholic Epistles, St James, St Peter,
1 St John. How far this stage overlapped the first it will need

closer investigations than have yet been made to determine. The great body of the Syrian Church accepted the three Epistles which are found in the Bibles alike of the Nestorians and of the Jacobites who broke away from orthodox standards in the fifth and sixth centuries" (Dr Sanday, _Studia Biblica,_ III. pp. 245, 246). The third stage was the reception of all seven Catholic Epistles.

It will be seen from this that our Epistle, though not at first received by the Syrian Church, gained for itself a place in that fourth century revision of the Old Syriac N.T. which is commonly called the Peshitto. Whether any translation of the Epistle existed before the 4th cent. must therefore remain doubtful. The Epistle is of course included in the Harklean revision of A.D. 616.

III. _Egyptian._ The two most important Egyptian Versions of the N.T. are the Bohairic and the Sahidic. The Bohairic (formerly called Memphitic) was spoken in Northern Egypt, the Sahidic (formerly called Thebaic) in Southern Egypt. The date at which the N.T. began to be translated into these dialects is uncertain. As far as the Gospels are concerned some scholars place it as early as the end of the second century. The two Versions represent distinct types of text, the Northern Version being the purest, the Southern having some remarkable interpolations. The Sahidic Version of St James is known to us only in fragments[1].

[1] For the notes on the Latin and Syriac Versions the Editor is indebted to Mr F. C. Burkitt; for that on the Egyptian Version to Mr Forbes Robinson.

# ΙΑΚΩΒΟΥ ΕΠΙΣΤΟΛΗ

**1** ¹Ἰάκωβος θεοῦ καὶ κυρίου Ἰησοῦ Χριστοῦ δοῦλος ταῖς δώδεκα φυλαῖς ταῖς ἐν τῇ διασπορᾷ χαίρειν.

²Πᾶσαν χαρὰν ἡγήσασθε, ἀδελφοί μου, ὅταν πειρασμοῖς περιπέσητε ποικίλοις, ³γινώσκοντες ὅτι τὸ δοκίμιον
ὑμῶν τῆς πίστεως κατεργάζεται ὑπομονήν. ⁴ἡ δὲ ὑπο-
μονὴ ἔργον τέλειον ἐχέτω, ἵνα ἦτε τέλειοι καὶ ὁλόκληροι,
ἐν μηδενὶ λειπόμενοι. ⁵εἰ δέ τις ὑμῶν λείπεται σοφίας,
αἰτείτω παρὰ τοῦ διδόντος θεοῦ πᾶσιν ἁπλῶς καὶ μὴ
ὀνειδίζοντος, καὶ δοθήσεται αὐτῷ. ⁶αἰτείτω δὲ ἐν
πίστει, μηδὲν διακρινόμενος· ὁ γὰρ διακρινόμενος ἔοικεν
κλύδωνι θαλάσσης ἀνεμιζομένῳ καὶ ῥιπιζομένῳ. ⁷μὴ
γὰρ οἰέσθω ὁ ἄνθρωπος ἐκεῖνος ὅτι λήμψεταί τι παρὰ
τοῦ κυρίου, ⁸ἀνὴρ δίψυχος, ἀκατάστατος ἐν πάσαις
ταῖς ὁδοῖς αὐτοῦ. ⁹Καυχάσθω δὲ ὁ ἀδελφὸς ὁ ταπεινὸς
ἐν τῷ ὕψει αὐτοῦ, ¹⁰ὁ δὲ πλούσιος ἐν τῇ ταπεινώσει
αὐτοῦ, ὅτι ὡς ἄνθος χόρτου παρελεύσεται. ¹¹ἀνέτειλεν
γὰρ ὁ ἥλιος σὺν τῷ καύσωνι καὶ ἐξήρανεν τὸν χόρτον,
καὶ τὸ ἄνθος αὐτοῦ ἐξέπεσεν καὶ ἡ εὐπρέπεια τοῦ προσ-
ώπου αὐτοῦ ἀπώλετο· οὕτως καὶ ὁ πλούσιος ἐν ταῖς
πορείαις αὐτοῦ μαρανθήσεται. ¹²Μακάριος ἀνὴρ ὃς
ὑπομένει πειρασμόν, ὅτι δόκιμος γενόμενος λήμψεται

τὸν στέφανον τῆς ζωῆς, ὃν ἐπηγγείλατο τοῖς ἀγαπῶσιν
αὐτόν.

¹³ Μηδεὶς πειραζόμενος λεγέτω ὅτι ἀπὸ θεοῦ πειράζομαι. ὁ γὰρ θεὸς ἀπείραστός ἐστιν κακῶν, πειράζει
δὲ αὐτὸς οὐδένα. ¹⁴ ἕκαστος δὲ πειράζεται ὑπὸ τῆς ἰδίας
ἐπιθυμίας ἐξελκόμενος καὶ δελεαζόμενος· ¹⁵ εἶτα ἡ ἐπιθυμία συλλαβοῦσα τίκτει ἁμαρτίαν, ἡ δὲ ἁμαρτία
ἀποτελεσθεῖσα ἀποκύει θάνατον.

¹⁶ Μὴ πλανᾶσθε, ἀδελφοί μου ἀγαπητοί. ¹⁷ πᾶσα
δόσις ἀγαθὴ καὶ πᾶν δώρημα τέλειον ἄνωθέν ἐστιν
καταβαῖνον ἀπὸ τοῦ πατρὸς τῶν φώτων, παρ' ᾧ οὐκ
ἔνι παραλλαγὴ ἢ τροπῆς ἀποσκίασμα. ¹⁸ βουληθεὶς
ἀπεκύησεν ἡμᾶς λόγῳ ἀληθείας, εἰς τὸ εἶναι ἡμᾶς
ἀπαρχήν τινα τῶν αὐτοῦ κτισμάτων.

¹⁹ Ἴστε, ἀδελφοί μου ἀγαπητοί· ἔστω δὲ πᾶς ἄνθρωπος ταχὺς εἰς τὸ ἀκοῦσαι, βραδὺς εἰς τὸ λαλῆσαι,
βραδὺς εἰς ὀργήν· ²⁰ ὀργὴ γὰρ ἀνδρὸς δικαιοσύνην θεοῦ
οὐκ ἐργάζεται. ²¹ διὸ ἀποθέμενοι πᾶσαν ῥυπαρίαν καὶ
περισσείαν κακίας ἐν πραΰτητι δέξασθε τὸν ἔμφυτον
λόγον τὸν δυνάμενον σῶσαι τὰς ψυχὰς ὑμῶν. ²² γίνεσθε
δὲ ποιηταὶ λόγου, καὶ μὴ ἀκροαταὶ μόνον παραλογιζόμενοι ἑαυτούς. ²³ ὅτι εἴ τις ἀκροατὴς λόγου ἐστὶν καὶ οὐ
ποιητής, οὗτος ἔοικεν ἀνδρὶ κατανοοῦντι τὸ πρόσωπον
τῆς γενέσεως αὐτοῦ ἐν ἐσόπτρῳ· ²⁴ κατενόησεν γὰρ
ἑαυτὸν καὶ ἀπελήλυθεν, καὶ εὐθέως ἐπελάθετο ὁποῖος ἦν.
²⁵ ὁ δὲ παρακύψας εἰς νόμον τέλειον τὸν τῆς ἐλευθερίας
καὶ παραμείνας, οὐκ ἀκροατὴς ἐπιλησμονῆς γενόμενος
ἀλλὰ ποιητὴς ἔργου, οὗτος μακάριος ἐν τῇ ποιήσει
αὐτοῦ ἔσται. ²⁶ εἴ τις δοκεῖ θρησκὸς εἶναι, μὴ χαλιναγωγῶν γλῶσσαν αὐτοῦ ἀλλὰ ἀπατῶν καρδίαν αὐτοῦ,
τούτου μάταιος ἡ θρησκεία. ²⁷ θρησκεία καθαρὰ καὶ

ἀμίαντος παρὰ τῷ θεῷ καὶ πατρὶ αὕτη ἐστίν, ἐπισκέπτεσθαι ὀρφανοὺς καὶ χήρας ἐν τῇ θλίψει αὐτῶν, ἄσπιλον ἑαυτὸν τηρεῖν ἀπὸ τοῦ κόσμου.

2 ¹Ἀδελφοί μου, μὴ ἐν προσωπολημψίαις ἔχετε τὴν πίστιν τοῦ κυρίου ἡμῶν Ἰησοῦ Χριστοῦ τῆς δόξης. ²ἐὰν γὰρ εἰσέλθῃ εἰς συναγωγὴν ὑμῶν ἀνὴρ χρυσοδακτύλιος ἐν ἐσθῆτι λαμπρᾷ, εἰσέλθῃ δὲ καὶ πτωχὸς ἐν ῥυπαρᾷ ἐσθῆτι, ³καὶ ἐπιβλέψητε ἐπὶ τὸν φοροῦντα τὴν ἐσθῆτα τὴν λαμπρὰν καὶ εἴπητε· Σὺ κάθου ὧδε καλῶς, καὶ τῷ πτωχῷ εἴπητε· Σὺ στῆθι ἐκεῖ ἢ κάθου ὑπὸ τὸ ὑποπόδιόν μου, ⁴οὐ διεκρίθητε ἐν ἑαυτοῖς καὶ ἐγένεσθε κριταὶ διαλογισμῶν πονηρῶν;

⁵Ἀκούσατε, ἀδελφοί μου ἀγαπητοί. οὐχ ὁ θεὸς ἐξελέξατο τοὺς πτωχοὺς τῷ κόσμῳ πλουσίους ἐν πίστει καὶ κληρονόμους τῆς βασιλείας ἧς ἐπηγγείλατο τοῖς ἀγαπῶσιν αὐτόν; ⁶ὑμεῖς δὲ ἠτιμάσατε τὸν πτωχόν. οὐχ οἱ πλούσιοι καταδυναστεύουσιν ὑμῶν, καὶ αὐτοὶ ἕλκουσιν ὑμᾶς εἰς κριτήρια; ⁷οὐκ αὐτοὶ βλασφημοῦσιν τὸ καλὸν ὄνομα τὸ ἐπικληθὲν ἐφ' ὑμᾶς; ⁸εἰ μέντοι νόμον τελεῖτε βασιλικὸν κατὰ τὴν γραφήν· Ἀγαπήσεις τὸν πλησίον σου ὡς σεαυτόν, καλῶς ποιεῖτε· ⁹εἰ δὲ προσωπολημπτεῖτε, ἁμαρτίαν ἐργάζεσθε, ἐλεγχόμενοι ὑπὸ τοῦ νόμου ὡς παραβάται. ¹⁰ὅστις γὰρ ὅλον τὸν νόμον τηρήσῃ, πταίσῃ δὲ ἐν ἑνί, γέγονεν πάντων ἔνοχος. ¹¹ὁ γὰρ εἰπών· Μὴ μοιχεύσῃς, εἶπεν καί· Μὴ φονεύσῃς· εἰ δὲ οὐ μοιχεύεις, φονεύεις δέ, γέγονας παραβάτης νόμου. ¹²οὕτως λαλεῖτε καὶ οὕτως ποιεῖτε ὡς διὰ νόμου ἐλευθερίας μέλλοντες κρίνεσθαι. ¹³ἡ γὰρ κρίσις ἀνέλεος τῷ μὴ ποιήσαντι ἔλεος· κατακαυχᾶται ἔλεος κρίσεως.

¹⁴Τί τὸ ὄφελος, ἀδελφοί μου, ἐὰν πίστιν λέγῃ τις ἔχειν, ἔργα δὲ μὴ ἔχῃ; μὴ δύναται ἡ πίστις σῶσαι

αὐτόν; [15] ἐὰν ἀδελφὸς ἢ ἀδελφὴ γυμνοὶ ὑπάρχωσιν καὶ
λειπόμενοι τῆς ἐφημέρου τροφῆς, [16] εἴπῃ δέ τις αὐτοῖς ἐξ
ὑμῶν· Ὑπάγετε ἐν εἰρήνῃ, θερμαίνεσθε καὶ χορτάζεσθε,
μὴ δῶτε δὲ αὐτοῖς τὰ ἐπιτήδεια τοῦ σώματος, τί τὸ
ὄφελος; [17] οὕτως καὶ ἡ πίστις, ἐὰν μὴ ἔχῃ ἔργα, νεκρά
ἐστιν καθ᾽ ἑαυτήν. [18] ἀλλ᾽ ἐρεῖ τις· Σὺ πίστιν ἔχεις,
κἀγὼ ἔργα ἔχω· δεῖξόν μοι τὴν πίστιν σου χωρὶς τῶν
ἔργων, κἀγώ σοι δείξω ἐκ τῶν ἔργων μου τὴν πίστιν.
[19] σὺ πιστεύεις ὅτι εἷς ἐστιν ὁ θεός; καλῶς ποιεῖς· καὶ
τὰ δαιμόνια πιστεύουσιν καὶ φρίσσουσιν. [20] θέλεις δὲ
γνῶναι, ὦ ἄνθρωπε κενέ, ὅτι ἡ πίστις χωρὶς τῶν ἔργων
ἀργή ἐστιν; [21] Ἀβραὰμ ὁ πατὴρ ἡμῶν οὐκ ἐξ ἔργων
ἐδικαιώθη, ἀνενέγκας Ἰσαὰκ τὸν υἱὸν αὐτοῦ ἐπὶ τὸ
θυσιαστήριον; [22] βλέπεις ὅτι ἡ πίστις συνήργει τοῖς
ἔργοις αὐτοῦ, καὶ ἐκ τῶν ἔργων ἡ πίστις ἐτελειώθη, [23] καὶ
ἐπληρώθη ἡ γραφὴ ἡ λέγουσα· Ἐπίστευσεν δὲ Ἀβραὰμ
τῷ θεῷ, καὶ ἐλογίσθη αὐτῷ εἰς δικαιοσύνην, καὶ φίλος
θεοῦ ἐκλήθη. [24] ὁρᾶτε ὅτι ἐξ ἔργων δικαιοῦται ἄνθρωπος
καὶ οὐκ ἐκ πίστεως μόνον. [25] ὁμοίως δὲ καὶ Ῥαὰβ ἡ
πόρνη οὐκ ἐξ ἔργων ἐδικαιώθη, ὑποδεξαμένη τοὺς ἀγγέ-
λους καὶ ἑτέρᾳ ὁδῷ ἐκβαλοῦσα; [26] ὥσπερ γὰρ τὸ σῶμα
χωρὶς πνεύματος νεκρόν ἐστιν, οὕτως καὶ ἡ πίστις χωρὶς
ἔργων νεκρά ἐστιν.

**3** [1] Μὴ πολλοὶ διδάσκαλοι γίνεσθε, ἀδελφοί μου,
εἰδότες ὅτι μεῖζον κρίμα λημψόμεθα. [2] πολλὰ γὰρ
πταίομεν ἅπαντες· εἴ τις ἐν λόγῳ οὐ πταίει, οὗτος
τέλειος ἀνήρ, δυνατὸς χαλιναγωγῆσαι καὶ ὅλον τὸ
σῶμα. [3] εἰ δὲ τῶν ἵππων τοὺς χαλινοὺς εἰς τὰ στόματα
βάλλομεν εἰς τὸ πείθεσθαι αὐτοὺς ἡμῖν, καὶ ὅλον τὸ
σῶμα αὐτῶν μετάγομεν· [4] ἰδοὺ καὶ τὰ πλοῖα, τηλικαῦτα
ὄντα καὶ ὑπὸ ἀνέμων σκληρῶν ἐλαυνόμενα, μετάγεται

ὑπὸ ἐλαχίστου πηδαλίου ὅπου ἡ ὁρμὴ τοῦ εὐθύνοντος
βούλεται· [5]οὕτως καὶ ἡ γλῶσσα μικρὸν μέλος ἐστὶν καὶ
μεγάλα αὐχεῖ. ἰδοὺ ἡλίκον πῦρ ἡλίκην ὕλην ἀνάπτει·
[6]καὶ ἡ γλῶσσα πῦρ, ὁ κόσμος τῆς ἀδικίας, ἡ γλῶσσα
καθίσταται ἐν τοῖς μέλεσιν ἡμῶν, ἡ σπιλοῦσα ὅλον τὸ
σῶμα καὶ φλογίζουσα τὸν τροχὸν τῆς γενέσεως καὶ
φλογιζομένη ὑπὸ τῆς γεέννης. [7]πᾶσα γὰρ φύσις θηρίων
τε καὶ πετεινῶν ἑρπετῶν τε καὶ ἐναλίων δαμάζεται καὶ
δεδάμασται τῇ φύσει τῇ ἀνθρωπίνῃ, [8]τὴν δὲ γλῶσσαν
οὐδεὶς δύναται ἀνθρώπων δαμάσαι· ἀκατάστατον κακόν,
μεστὴ ἰοῦ θανατηφόρου. [9]ἐν αὐτῇ εὐλογοῦμεν τὸν
κύριον καὶ πατέρα, καὶ ἐν αὐτῇ καταρώμεθα τοὺς ἀνθρώπους τοὺς καθ᾽ ὁμοίωσιν θεοῦ γεγονότας· [10]ἐκ τοῦ αὐτοῦ
στόματος ἐξέρχεται εὐλογία καὶ κατάρα. οὐ χρή, ἀδελφοί μου, ταῦτα οὕτως γίνεσθαι. [11]μήτι ἡ πηγὴ ἐκ τῆς
αὐτῆς ὀπῆς βρύει τὸ γλυκὺ καὶ τὸ πικρόν; [12]μὴ δύναται,
ἀδελφοί μου, συκῆ ἐλαίας ποιῆσαι ἢ ἄμπελος σῦκα;
οὔτε ἁλυκὸν γλυκὺ ποιῆσαι ὕδωρ.

[13]Τίς σοφὸς καὶ ἐπιστήμων ἐν ὑμῖν; δειξάτω ἐκ τῆς
καλῆς ἀναστροφῆς τὰ ἔργα αὐτοῦ ἐν πραΰτητι σοφίας.
[14]εἰ δὲ ζῆλον πικρὸν ἔχετε καὶ ἐριθείαν ἐν τῇ καρδίᾳ
ὑμῶν, μὴ κατακαυχᾶσθε καὶ ψεύδεσθε κατὰ τῆς ἀληθείας. [15]οὐκ ἔστιν αὕτη ἡ σοφία ἄνωθεν κατερχομένη,
ἀλλὰ ἐπίγειος, ψυχική, δαιμονιώδης. [16]ὅπου γὰρ ζῆλος
καὶ ἐριθεία, ἐκεῖ ἀκαταστασία καὶ πᾶν φαῦλον πρᾶγμα.
[17]ἡ δὲ ἄνωθεν σοφία πρῶτον μὲν ἁγνή ἐστιν, ἔπειτα
εἰρηνική, ἐπιεικής, εὐπειθής, μεστὴ ἐλέους καὶ καρπῶν
ἀγαθῶν, ἀδιάκριτος, ἀνυπόκριτος. [18]καρπὸς δὲ δικαιοσύνης ἐν εἰρήνῃ σπείρεται τοῖς ποιοῦσιν εἰρήνην.

**4** [1]Πόθεν πόλεμοι καὶ πόθεν μάχαι ἐν ὑμῖν; οὐκ
ἐντεῦθεν, ἐκ τῶν ἡδονῶν ὑμῶν τῶν στρατευομένων ἐν

τοῖς μέλεσιν ὑμῶν; ²ἐπιθυμεῖτε, καὶ οὐκ ἔχετε· φονεύετε
καὶ ζηλοῦτε, καὶ οὐ δύνασθε ἐπιτυχεῖν· μάχεσθε καὶ
πολεμεῖτε· οὐκ ἔχετε διὰ τὸ μὴ αἰτεῖσθαι ὑμᾶς· ³αἰτεῖτε
καὶ οὐ λαμβάνετε, διότι κακῶς αἰτεῖσθε, ἵνα ἐν ταῖς
ἡδοναῖς ὑμῶν δαπανήσητε. ⁴μοιχαλίδες, οὐκ οἴδατε ὅτι
ἡ φιλία τοῦ κόσμου ἔχθρα τοῦ θεοῦ ἐστίν; ὃς ἐὰν οὖν
βουληθῇ φίλος εἶναι τοῦ κόσμου, ἐχθρὸς τοῦ θεοῦ
καθίσταται. ⁵ἢ δοκεῖτε ὅτι κενῶς ἡ γραφὴ λέγει;
Πρὸς φθόνον ἐπιποθεῖ τὸ πνεῦμα ὃ κατῴκισεν ἐν ἡμῖν;
⁶μείζονα δὲ δίδωσιν χάριν. διὸ λέγει· Ὁ θεὸς ὑπερη-
φάνοις ἀντιτάσσεται, ταπεινοῖς δὲ δίδωσιν χάριν. ⁷ὑπο-
τάγητε οὖν τῷ θεῷ· ἀντίστητε δὲ τῷ διαβόλῳ, καὶ
φεύξεται ἀφ᾽ ὑμῶν· ⁸ἐγγίσατε τῷ θεῷ, καὶ ἐγγιεῖ ὑμῖν.
καθαρίσατε χεῖρας, ἁμαρτωλοί, καὶ ἁγνίσατε καρδίας,
δίψυχοι. ⁹ταλαιπωρήσατε καὶ πενθήσατε καὶ κλαύσατε·
ὁ γέλως ὑμῶν εἰς πένθος μεταστραφήτω καὶ ἡ χαρὰ εἰς
κατήφειαν. ¹⁰ταπεινώθητε ἐνώπιον Κυρίου, καὶ ὑψώσει
ὑμᾶς.

¹¹Μὴ καταλαλεῖτε ἀλλήλων, ἀδελφοί. ὁ καταλαλῶν
ἀδελφοῦ ἢ κρίνων τὸν ἀδελφὸν αὐτοῦ καταλαλεῖ νόμου
καὶ κρίνει νόμον· εἰ δὲ νόμον κρίνεις, οὐκ εἶ ποιητὴς
νόμου ἀλλὰ κριτής. ¹²εἷς ἐστιν ὁ νομοθέτης καὶ κριτής,
ὁ δυνάμενος σῶσαι καὶ ἀπολέσαι· σὺ δὲ τίς εἶ, ὁ κρίνων
τὸν πλησίον;

¹³Ἄγε νῦν οἱ λέγοντες· Σήμερον ἢ αὔριον πορευσό-
μεθα εἰς τήνδε τὴν πόλιν καὶ ποιήσομεν ἐκεῖ ἐνιαυτὸν
καὶ ἐμπορευσόμεθα καὶ κερδήσομεν, ¹⁴οἵτινες οὐκ ἐπίστασθε τὸ τῆς αὔριον· ποία γὰρ ἡ ζωὴ ὑμῶν; ἀτμὶς γάρ
ἐστε ἡ πρὸς ὀλίγον φαινομένη, ἔπειτα καὶ ἀφανιζομένη·
¹⁵ἀντὶ τοῦ λέγειν ὑμᾶς· Ἐὰν ὁ κύριος θελήσῃ καὶ ζήσο-
μεν, καὶ ποιήσομεν τοῦτο ἢ ἐκεῖνο. ¹⁶νῦν δὲ καυχᾶσθε

ἐν ταῖς ἀλαζονείαις ὑμῶν· πᾶσα καύχησις τοιαύτη
πονηρά ἐστιν. ¹⁷εἰδότι οὖν καλὸν ποιεῖν καὶ μὴ ποι-
οῦντι, ἁμαρτία αὐτῷ ἐστίν.

5 ¹ᵛἌγε νῦν οἱ πλούσιοι, κλαύσατε ὀλολύζοντες ἐπὶ
ταῖς ταλαιπωρίαις ὑμῶν ταῖς ἐπερχομέναις. ²ὁ πλοῦτος
ὑμῶν σέσηπεν, καὶ τὰ ἱμάτια ὑμῶν σητόβρωτα γέγονεν,
³ὁ χρυσὸς ὑμῶν καὶ ὁ ἄργυρος κατίωται, καὶ ὁ ἰὸς αὐτῶν
εἰς μαρτύριον ὑμῖν ἔσται καὶ φάγεται τὰς σάρκας ὑμῶν
ὡς πῦρ. ἐθησαυρίσατε ἐν ἐσχάταις ἡμέραις. ⁴ἰδοὺ ὁ
μισθὸς τῶν ἐργατῶν τῶν ἀμησάντων τὰς χώρας ὑμῶν
ὁ ἀφυστερημένος ἀφ' ὑμῶν κράζει, καὶ αἱ βοαὶ τῶν θερι-
σάντων εἰς τὰ ὦτα Κυρίου Σαβαὼθ εἰσελήλυθαν.
⁵ἐτρυφήσατε ἐπὶ τῆς γῆς καὶ ἐσπαταλήσατε, ἐθρέψατε
τὰς καρδίας ὑμῶν ἐν ἡμέρᾳ σφαγῆς. ⁶κατεδικάσατε,
ἐφονεύσατε τὸν δίκαιον· οὐκ ἀντιτάσσεται ὑμῖν.

⁷Μακροθυμήσατε οὖν, ἀδελφοί, ἕως τῆς παρουσίας
τοῦ κυρίου. ἰδοὺ ὁ γεωργὸς ἐκδέχεται τὸν τίμιον
καρπὸν τῆς γῆς, μακροθυμῶν ἐπ' αὐτῷ ἕως λάβῃ πρόϊμον καὶ ὄψιμον· ⁸μακροθυμήσατε καὶ ὑμεῖς, στηρίξατε
τὰς καρδίας ὑμῶν, ὅτι ἡ παρουσία τοῦ κυρίου ἤγγικεν.
⁹μὴ στενάζετε κατ' ἀλλήλων, ἀδελφοί, ἵνα μὴ κριθῆτε·
ἰδοὺ κριτὴς πρὸ τῶν θυρῶν ἔστηκεν. ¹⁰ὑπόδειγμα λά-
βετε, ἀδελφοί, τῆς κακοπαθείας καὶ τῆς μακροθυμίας
τοὺς προφήτας, οἳ ἐλάλησαν ἐν τῷ ὀνόματι Κυρίου.
¹¹ἰδοὺ μακαρίζομεν τοὺς ὑπομείναντας· τὴν ὑπομονὴν
Ἰὼβ ἠκούσατε καὶ τὸ τέλος Κυρίου εἴδετε, ὅτι πολύ-
σπλαγχνός ἐστιν ὁ κύριος καὶ οἰκτίρμων.

¹²Πρὸ πάντων δέ, ἀδελφοί μου, μὴ ὀμνύετε, μήτε τὸν
οὐρανὸν μήτε τὴν γῆν μήτε ἄλλον τινὰ ὅρκον· ἤτω δὲ
ὑμῶν τὸ Ναὶ ναί, καὶ τὸ Οὒ οὔ, ἵνα μὴ ὑπὸ κρίσιν
πέσητε.

¹³Κακοπαθεῖ τις ἐν ὑμῖν; προσευχέσθω· εὐθυμεῖ τις;
ψαλλέτω. ¹⁴ἀσθενεῖ τις ἐν ὑμῖν; προσκαλεσάσθω
τοὺς πρεσβυτέρους τῆς ἐκκλησίας, καὶ προσευξάσθωσαν
ἐπ᾽ αὐτόν, ἀλείψαντες αὐτὸν ἐλαίῳ ἐν τῷ ὀνόματι τοῦ
κυρίου. ¹⁵καὶ ἡ εὐχὴ τῆς πίστεως σώσει τὸν κάμνοντα,
καὶ ἐγερεῖ αὐτὸν ὁ κύριος· κἂν ἁμαρτίας ᾖ πεποιηκώς,
ἀφεθήσεται αὐτῷ. ¹⁶ἐξομολογεῖσθε οὖν ἀλλήλοις τὰς
ἁμαρτίας, καὶ εὔχεσθε ὑπὲρ ἀλλήλων, ὅπως ἰαθῆτε·
πολὺ ἰσχύει δέησις δικαίου ἐνεργουμένη. ¹⁷Ἡλίας ἄνθρωπος ἦν ὁμοιοπαθὴς ἡμῖν, καὶ προσευχῇ προσηύξατο
τοῦ μὴ βρέξαι, καὶ οὐκ ἔβρεξεν ἐπὶ τῆς γῆς ἐνιαυτοὺς
τρεῖς καὶ μῆνας ἕξ· ¹⁸καὶ πάλιν προσηύξατο, καὶ ὁ
οὐρανὸς ἔδωκεν ὑετὸν καὶ ἡ γῆ ἐβλάστησεν τὸν καρπὸν
αὐτῆς.

¹⁹Ἀδελφοί μου, ἐάν τις ἐν ὑμῖν πλανηθῇ ἀπὸ τῆς
ἀληθείας καὶ ἐπιστρέψῃ τις αὐτόν, ²⁰γινωσκέτω ὅτι ὁ
ἐπιστρέψας ἁμαρτωλὸν ἐκ πλάνης ὁδοῦ αὐτοῦ σώσει
ψυχὴν αὐτοῦ ἐκ θανάτου καὶ καλύψει πλῆθος ἁμαρτιῶν.

# NOTES.

## CHAPTER I.

*Title.* Ἰακώβου Ἐπιστολή, as in BK and in the subscription of ℵ, which has no title, and of A where the title is lost. In C both title and subscription are lost.

**12.** The T.R. inserts ὁ κύριος with KLP (C has κύριος) as subject to ἐπηγγείλατο against the leading uncials ℵAB. This reading is clearly a gloss, as is partly evidenced by the variant ὁ θεός, which appears in some cursives, the Vulgate and other versions.

**17.** ℵ*B have the curious error τροπῆς ἀποσκιάσματος.

**19.** ἴστε. So ℵcABC and old Latin (*scitote*) and Vulgate (*scitis*). KLP have ὥστε. The change from ἴστε to ὥστε was probably the correction of an expert who inferred some error from the occurrence of the Attic syncopated form ἴστε (from ἴσημι), a form not elsewhere found in the N.T.

**20.** οὐκ ἐργάζεται with ℵABC³ and many cursives, against C*KLP and others, which have οὐ κατεργάζεται. There is a tendency in language towards the use of strengthened forms.

---

### Ch. I. 1. Introductory Address.

**1.** θεοῦ καὶ κυρίου Ἰησοῦ Χριστοῦ. καὶ is here disjunctive. James (or Jacob) is the δοῦλος of God and also of the Lord Jesus Christ. Grammatically it would be possible to regard θεοῦ καὶ κυρίου as a joint qualification of Ἰησοῦ Χριστοῦ, but the usage of the N.T. is against this: comp. Ἰησοῦ Χριστοῦ καὶ θεοῦ πατρὸς κ.τ.λ. (Gal. i. 1). See, however, St John xx. 28 ὁ κύριός μου καὶ ὁ θεός μου, where both terms are applied to Christ.

κύριος, frequent in LXX. as the Hellenistic equivalent for Jehovah, as well as in lower senses, is applied in N.T. as a title of reverence to Christ, 'the Master,' and is so used almost as a proper name, 'the Lord'; hence the absence of the article as here and frequently, especially when κύριος is governed by a preposition, or when it is in the genitive

case, or when it precedes Ἰησ. Χριστός. Winer, III. xix. 1, p. 154. Here
it is correlative to δοῦλος. Therefore, although the use of κύριος here
may not distinctly prove the truth of the Godhead of Christ, yet the
associations of the word certainly tend to connect the Lord Christ of
the N.T. with the Lord God of the O.T.

δοῦλος: (a) in reference to a king, a subject, all subjects of an
Oriental monarch being slaves: καὶ ἰδοὺ οἱ δοῦλοί μου μετὰ τῶν δούλων
σου, 1 Kings v. 6: Ἱεροβοὰμ δοῦλος Σολομῶντος, 1 Kings xi. 26, and
frequently. So in N.T. ὡμοιώθη ἡ βασιλεία τῶν οὐρανῶν ἀνθρώπῳ
βασιλεῖ ὃς ἠθέλησεν συνᾶραι λόγον μετὰ τῶν δούλων αὐτοῦ, St Matt. xviii.
23; where the δοῦλοι are satraps, or provincial governors. In Demosthenes the subjects of Philip are δοῦλοι, in contrast to the free
Athenians: κἂν αὐτὸς μὴ παρῇ τοὺς δούλους ἀγωνοθετήσοντας πέμπει,
Phil. III. 32: (b) in reference to a master, a slave; and in a special
sense (c) a slave consecrated to a god, ἱερόδουλος, a term applied to the
Nethinim, Joseph. Ant. xi. 5. 6: comp. εἴθ' οὕτως ἀεὶ Φοίβῳ | λατρεύων
μὴ παυσαίμην, ἢ | παυσαίμην ἀγαθᾷ μοίρᾳ Eur. Ion 151—153. All
three are Christian thoughts: (a) connects δοῦλος with the conception
of the βασιλεία τοῦ θεοῦ, (b) with the thought of personal service to a
Master, (c) who is divine.

St Peter calls himself δοῦλος καὶ ἀπόστολος Ἰησ. Χριστοῦ, 2 Pet. i. 1.
So St Paul, δοῦλος Ἰησ. Χριστοῦ, κλητὸς ἀπόστολος, Rom. i. 1; and in
conjunction with Timothy, Παῦλος καὶ Τιμόθεος δοῦλοι Χριστοῦ Ἰησοῦ,
Phil. i. 1.

The simplicity of this self-designation and the absence of any authoritative title tend to prove the authenticity of the Epistle.

ταῖς δώδεκα φυλαῖς. This conception of the solidarity of Israel is a
point in the enthusiasm of the Maccabean revival. Our Lord recognises it in the number of the Apostles and in their destination as
judges of the twelve tribes of Israel. See Introduction, p. xxxii.

ἐν τῇ διασπορᾷ. Though the expression would include the vast
area over which the Jews were scattered, when used without any
qualifying words it had the special meaning of the Eastern dispersion
in Syria, Mesopotamia, Media and Elam, and other districts in the
region of the Tigris and Euphrates. See Edersheim, Life and Times
of Jesus the Messiah, Vol. I. p. 6 ff., and Introduction, pp. xxix., xxx.

διασπορά, lit. a scattering of seed, is not classical but is frequent
in LXX. in the sense of (a) scattering or dispersion, Deut. xxviii. 25;
Jer. xxxiv. 17: (b) collectively, the Israelites dispersed in different
parts of the world, 'the Dispersion.' τὰς διασπορὰς τοῦ Ἰσραὴλ ἐπι-
συνάξει, Ps. cxlvi. 2.   τὴν διασπορὰν τοῦ Ἰσραὴλ ἐπιστρέψαι, Is. xlix. 6.
μὴ εἰς τὴν διασπορὰν τῶν Ἑλλήνων μέλλει πορεύεσθαι; John vii. 35. See
also 1 Pet. i. 1.

There is no single fixed term in Hebrew for 'the dispersion.'
Therefore in using the recognised expression ἡ διασπορά for a variety
of Hebrew words the LXX. translators defined and specialised the
meaning of the prophetic passage.

χαίρειν. Infinitive for imperative, where possibly λέγει or some similar word is to be supplied. Κλαύδιος Λυσίας τῷ κρατίστῳ ἡγεμόνι Φήλικι χαίρειν, Acts xxiii. 26. Sometimes χαίρειν λέγει is to be supplied, Παῦλος πᾶσιν τοῖς ἁγίοις...τοῖς οὖσιν ἐν Φιλίπποις, Phil. i. 1. Winer, III. lxiv. 6, p. 735. Comp. also ὑμεῖς ἄλλοθεν ἄλλος ἐρητύειν ἐπέεσσι, *Il.* II. 75. Such uses however may be connected with the original use and derivation of the infinitive as a dative of purpose. See Monro, *Hom. Gram.* § 242.

The same simple salutation is used in the encyclical letter addressed to the Gentile brethren by St James and the Church in Jerusalem, Acts xv. 23. St Paul's salutation is usually χάρις καὶ εἰρήνη, Rom. i. 7; 1 Cor. i. 3 and frequently.

2—18. (a) TEMPTATION FROM WITHOUT, 2—4; (1) WISDOM, PRAYER, STEDFASTNESS, THE DIVINE HELPS IN TEMPTATION, 5—8; (2) A SPECIAL FORM OF TEMPTATION—OPPRESSION BY THE RICH—THE OLD TESTAMENT PROBLEM OF THE PROSPERITY OF THE WICKED, 9—12; (3) VICTORY OVER TEMPTATION, 13.

(b) TEMPTATION FROM WITHIN—MORAL AND RELIGIOUS ERROR, 14—18.

2. πᾶσαν χαράν, **all joy**, nothing but joy, all that constitutes joy—*merum gaudium.* Comp. ἐν πάσῃ ὑπομονῇ, 2 Cor. xii. 12. μετὰ πάσης προθυμίας, Acts xvii. 11. πᾶν κέρδος ἡγοῦ ζημιουμένη φυγῇ, Eur. *Med.* 454, 'pure gain.' For the use of πᾶσαν compare also χάριν σοι ἔχω πᾶσαν, Arrian *Epict.* III. 5, 'I am entirely grateful.' Winer, P. III. § 18. 4. For the thought comp. 1 Pet. iv. 13 καθὸ κοινωνεῖτε τοῖς τοῦ Χριστοῦ παθήμασιν χαίρετε, ἵνα καὶ ἐν τῇ ἀποκαλύψει τῆς δόξης αὐτοῦ χαρῆτε ἀγαλλιώμενοι.

ἀδελφοί. The special word for the Christian community, ὑμεῖς ἀδελφοί ἐστε, St Matt. xxiii. 8: ἐξῆλθεν οὖν ὁ λόγος εἰς τοὺς ἀδελφοὺς κ.τ.λ., St John xxi. 23; ἀπαγγείλατε Ἰακώβῳ καὶ τοῖς ἀδελφοῖς, Acts xii. 17; just as it denoted the brotherhood of the Jewish Church: ἐξῆλθεν πρὸς τοὺς ἀδελφοὺς αὐτοῦ, Ex. ii. 11. καὶ ἄξουσιν τοὺς ἀδελφοὺς ὑμῶν ἐκ πάντων τῶν ἐθνῶν, Is. lxvi. 20.

ὅταν περιπέσητε. The aorist points to the several occasions of temptation in each single instance, as often as,—a single act—ye fall, &c., consider it all joy.

περιπίπτειν, **to fall around** or **upon**, generally, perhaps always, in connection with things evil: τοιούτῳ μὲν πάθει...περιπεσόντες, Thuc. II. 54. νοσήματι περιπίπτωμεν, Xen. *Cyr.* VI. 2. 27. ἑαυτῷ περιπίπτειν, 'to fall into one's own snare,' Hdt. I. 108. λῃσταῖς περιέπεσεν, St Luke x. 30. 'The word brings out the externality of the temptation,' Mayor.

πειρασμός. Not classical, a proof, putting to the test, trial, temptation, not primarily in the sense of enticement or allurement, though this thought is not excluded, enticement to pleasure being a 'trial' as well as pain or persecution. πειρασμός in LXX. is used to translate Hebr. *Massah*, Ex. xvii. 7 καὶ ἐπωνόμασεν πειρασμὸς καὶ λοιδόρησις. In the N.T. it is used in an important passage speaking of our Lord's

πειρασμοί: ὑμεῖς δέ ἐστε οἱ διαμεμενηκότες μετ' ἐμοῦ ἐν τοῖς πειρασμοῖς μου,
Luke xxii. 28.   Comp. δακρύων καὶ πειρασμῶν, Acts xx. 19.   Satan is
called ὁ πειράζων Matt. iv. 3 and 1 Thess. iii. 5, where the reference
is especially to a test of faith, as here.

**ποικίλοις.**  So also 1 Pet. i. 6 ἐν ποικίλοις πειρασμοῖς.  Here greater
prominence is given to the variety of trials by the position of ποικίλοις at
the end of the clause and by its separation from its substantive.  The
πειρασμοί of the Christian are varied; spiritual, intellectual, sensual.
The whole Epistle may be regarded as a treatise on πειρασμοί, and this
first clause is in brief the apostle's answer to the suffering Churches of
the dispersion.  πειρασμός is necessary to the active exercise of πίστις,
and without it ὑπομονή is impossible.  The emphatic position of πᾶσαν
χαράν shews the importance of the thought.

3.  **γινώσκοντες.**  The part. has a causal force giving the reason
for πᾶσαν χαρὰν ἡγήσασθε, 'inasmuch as ye recognise' &c.  The tense
implies a constantly recurring recognition.

**ὅτι τὸ δοκίμιον,** κ.τ.λ.  Πίστις, here assured belief in Jesus Christ,
is the supreme energizing principle of the Christian life.  Christian
life therefore consists in activity of faith, but this activity or exercise
of faith is rendered possible by πειρασμοί, or trials which are the test
or touchstone (τὸ δοκίμιον) of faith: the complete and perfect result
(the compound κατεργάζεται gives the force of completion) of an active
faith is ὑπομονή, patience, or endurance, or capacity of resistance
to evil.

For τὸ δοκίμιον see 1 Pet. i. 7, where the same expression occurs.

**ὑπομονή** is the principle of firmness in resistance to evil which
fences in and gives security to the spiritual life.  The word is rare in
the classical period, but comp. ὑπομ. λύπης, Plato Deff. 412 c: τὴν τῆς
μαχαίρας ὑπ. τῶν πληγῶν, Polyb. xv. 15. 8, where we have an important shade of meaning—there is a sense of activity in resistance as
well as of capacity of resistance.  It is not a mere passive quality,
comp. the use of ὑπομένειν, Xen. Mem. ΙΙ. 8. 6 τῶν πραγμάτων ὅσα
μὲν δύνασαι ποιεῖν [χρή] ὑπομένειν: Ign. Polycarp 6 ἡ ὑπομονή ὡς
πανοπλία.  In N.T. the word both in its verbal and substantival forms
receives an accession of meaning from its use by our Lord Himself:
ὁ ὑπομείνας εἰς τέλος σωθήσεται, Matt. xxiv. 13; or, as the saying is
reported in Luke xxi. 19, ἐν τῇ ὑπ. ὑμῶν κτήσεσθε τὰς ψυχὰς ὑμῶν,
and in Luke's version of the parable of the Sower καρποφοροῦσιν ἐν
ὑπομονῇ, viii. 15.  The word does not occur in the other synoptics or
St John's Gospel, but is frequent in the Pauline Epistles; see especially Rom. v. 3 εἰδότες ὅτι ἡ θλῖψις κ.τ.λ., a passage strictly parallel to
this, ἡ θλῖψις corresponding with the τὸ δοκίμιον τῆς πίστεως of St James.
And, as in Aristotle's system, the repeated act produces the habit, from
which in turn corresponding action springs.

So completely had ὑπομονή become identified with Christian character that it gave point to the Emperor Julian's sneer, when the
Christians complained of their treatment by pagan governors: "Bear
it patiently," he said, "as your God commands you," Socr. H. E.
III. 14.

**4.   ἔργον τέλειον, a perfect result**, that result which is the τέλος of ὑπομονή, its final cause; *opus consummatum* O.L., *o. perfectum* V. The character that repels and quenches evil results in perfectness and completeness.   Each act of resistance strengthens character and developes new force, so completeness of resistance results in completeness of character.

**τέλειοι** are those who attain the aim or purpose for which they were intended and for which they were created, **ὁλόκληροι** (here and 1 Thess. v. 23 only in N.T.), those who retain all that was allotted to them from the first; comp. Acts iii. 16 ἡ πίστις ἡ δι᾽ αὐτοῦ ἔδωκεν αὐτῷ τὴν ὁλοκληρίαν ταύτην, all this (physical) completeness.   ὁλόκληρος is used (Ezek. xv. 5 LXX.) of a vine branch that is unimpaired: οὐδὲ ἔτι αὐτοῦ ὄντος ὁλοκλήρου οὐκ ἔσται εἰς ἐργασίαν, and very beautifully of perfect righteousness: τὸ γὰρ ἐπίστασθαί σε ὁλόκληρος δικαιοσύνη, Wisdom xv. 3.

The germ of this thought is in our Lord's words, Matt. v. 48 ἔσεσθε οὖν ὑμεῖς τέλειοι ὡς ὁ πατὴρ ὑμῶν ὁ οὐράνιος τέλειός ἐστιν.   Comp. 2 Sam. xxii. 26 (Ps. xviii. 25).   It is noticeable and suggestive that in the parallel passage, St Luke vi. 36, οἰκτίρμονες and οἰκτίρμων take the place of τέλειοι and τέλειος.   See also for τέλειοι Eph. iv. 13 μέχρι καταντήσωμεν...εἰς ἄνδρα τέλειον.   Col. i. 28 ἄνθρωπον τέλειον ἐν Χριστῷ.

**ἐν μηδενὶ λειπόμενοι** explains ὁλόκληροι.

**5.**   The clauses are connected, λειπόμενοι...λείπεται.

**σοφίας**, a term far wider in signification than the Greek conception of σοφία.   A whole cycle of Hebrew literature is devoted to the praise and definition of Wisdom.   According to the author of the Wisdom of Solomon σοφία is the most perfect principle of guidance in human action: λαμπρὰ γὰρ καὶ ἀμάραντός ἐστιν ἡ σοφία (vi. 12); it is won by those who seek it: εὐχερῶς θεωρεῖται ὑπὸ τῶν ἀγαπώντων αὐτήν, καὶ εὑρίσκεται ὑπὸ τῶν ζητούντων αὐτήν—an expression closely bearing on this passage.   Step by step σοφία leads to union with God: προσοχὴ δὲ νόμων (giving heed to her laws) βεβαίωσις ἀφθαρσίας, ἀφθαρσία δὲ ἐγγὺς εἶναι ποιεῖ θεοῦ· ἐπιθυμία ἄρα σοφίας ἀνάγει ἐπὶ βασιλείαν, vi. 19, 20; ...τιμήσατε σοφίαν ἵνα εἰς τὸν αἰῶνα βασιλεύσητε.   Again ch. vii. 25 ἀτμὶς γάρ ἐστιν τῆς τοῦ θεοῦ δυνάμεως...ἀπαύγασμα γάρ ἐστιν φωτὸς ἀϊδίου, καὶ ἔσοπτρον ἀκηλίδωτον τῆς τοῦ θεοῦ ἐνεργείας. Human wisdom is conceived of as an emanation from the divine wisdom which was with God at the creation of the world, πᾶσα σοφία παρὰ κυρίου καὶ μετ᾽ αὐτοῦ εἰς τὸν αἰῶνα, Ecclus. i. 1.

This exalted view of σοφία gives force to the description of the Lord's growth: καὶ Ἰησοῦς προέκοπτεν τῇ σοφίᾳ, Luke ii. 52: τὸ δὲ παιδίον ηὔξανεν καὶ ἐκραταιοῦτο πληρούμενον σοφίᾳ, Luke ii. 40.

**αἰτείτω.**   In the Wisdom of Solomon prayer is indicated as the effectual means of attaining σοφία.   διὰ τοῦτο ηὐξάμην καὶ φρόνησις ἐδόθη μοι, ἐπεκαλεσάμην καὶ ἦλθέν μοι πνεῦμα σοφίας, Wisdom vii. 7. Comp. also Ecclus. li. 13 ἐζήτησα σοφίαν προφανῶς ἐν προσευχῇ μου. In St Matt. xi. 19 (Luke vii. 35), ἐδικαιώθη ἡ σοφία ἀπὸ τῶν ἔργων αὐτῆς, the meaning of σοφία seems to be the plan of divine wisdom which rules and governs all things. For the construction comp. γνώμας λειπομένα σοφᾶς, Soph. *El.* 474.

In the prominence which St James gives to σοφία we trace the surpassing influence of the Wisdom literature in this age. In a question of completeness or perfection of religious equipment it would be natural to treat of σοφία as the highest religious excellence, without which perfection was inconceivable.

So also St Paul places σοφία at the head of spiritual gifts. 1 Cor. xii. 8 ᾧ μὲν γὰρ διὰ τοῦ πνεύματος δίδοται λόγος σοφίας, ἄλλῳ δὲ λόγος γνώσεως κ.τ.λ.

**αἰτείτω.** *αἰτεῖν*, Lat. *peto*, generally, though not always (see Luke i. 63; John iv. 9), used of requests made by an inferior to a superior. See Matt. vii. 9 τίς ἐστιν ἐξ ὑμῶν ἄνθρωπος ὃν αἰτήσει ὁ υἱὸς αὐτοῦ ἄρτον κ.τ.λ.; Acts iii. 2 ὃν ἐτίθουν...τοῦ αἰτεῖν ἐλεημοσύνην; Acts xii. 20 ᾐτοῦντο εἰρήνην. Hence our Lord never uses *αἰτεῖν* of His own requests to the Father, but ἐδεήθην (Luke xxii. 32) and ἐρωτήσω (John xvi. 26). See Trench, *N.T. Syn. sub voc.* on the important passage Joh. xvi. 23 ἐμὲ οὐκ ἐρωτήσετε οὐδέν...ἄν τι αἰτήσητε τὸν πατέρα δώσει ὑμῖν ἐν τῷ ὀνόματί μου.

**ἁπλῶς, with simplicity,** without secondary motive, *simpliciter*, O.L., rather than *affluenter*, V. Comp. ὁ μεταδιδοὺς ἐν ἁπλότητι, Rom. xii. 8; δοξάζοντες τὸν θεὸν ἐπὶ τῇ ὑποταγῇ...καὶ ἁπλότητι τῆς κοινωνίας εἰς αὐτοὺς καὶ εἰς πάντας, 2 Cor. ix. 13. In the classics ἁπλοῦς is opposed to what is deceitful, ἁπλᾶ τῆς ἀληθείας ἔπη—ἁπλοῦς ὁ μῦθος, Aesch. *Cho.* 554; ἁπλοῖ τρόποι opp. to δόλος, Ar. *Plut.* 1158.

**καὶ μὴ ὀνειδίζοντος, not reproaching,** for ingratitude. The two elements to be avoided in giving are: (1) secondary motives on the *do ut des* principle; (2) complaint on account of favours unreturned, τοῖς εὖ παθοῦσιν ὀνειδίσαι τὴν χάριν, Libernus, D. xxxii. (quoted by Wetstein): *Odiosum sane genus hominum beneficia reprobantium, quae meminisse debet is in quem collata sunt, non commemorare qui contulit,* Cic. *Lael.* 20.

From these two human defects divine gifts are absolutely exempt. (1) Interested motive is impossible with God; and (2) man's ingratitude is no barrier to divine love: ὅτι αὐτὸς χρηστός ἐστιν ἐπὶ τοὺς ἀχαρίστους καὶ πονηρούς, Luke vi. 35.

**6. ἐν πίστει.** πίστις here, reliance on a promise, trust in the character of God, the faith which was the necessary condition of a miracle.

**διακρινόμενος.** In middle voice διακρίνεσθαι = to get a thing decided, to decide for oneself, to set two issues before oneself; so **to doubt,** to be in a critical state of mind. The thought is of judicial hesitation which ceases when the verdict is given; hence, to dispute. See Acts xi. 2 διεκρίνοντο πρὸς αὐτόν. Jude 9 τῷ διαβόλῳ διακρινόμενος. The tense implies a continuance of hesitation which is not a Christian attitude. Comp. Matt. xxi. 21 ἐὰν ἔχητε πίστιν καὶ μὴ διακριθῆτε, οὐ μόνον τὸ τῆς συκῆς ποιήσετε κ.τ.λ., a passage reflected here. πορεύου σὺν αὐτοῖς μηδὲν διακρινόμενος, Acts x. 20. See Page on Acts *loc. cit.* and St Matthew in this series *loc. cit.*

**κλύδων.** Only here and Luke viii. 24 in N.T., but frequent in classics.

**θαλάσσης.** The absence of the article with this word is very rare. See Winer, P. III. § 19, and comp. ἠχοῦς θαλ. καὶ σάλου, Luke xxi. 25. κινδύνοις ἐν θαλάσσῃ, 2 Cor. xi. 26.  κύματα ἄγρια θαλάσσης, Jude 13.

**ἀνεμιζομένῳ καὶ ῥιπιζομένῳ.** qui a vento fertur et circumfertur, V. Neither of these words is found in LXX. or elsewhere in N.T. ἀνεμίζεσθαι is ἅπαξ λεγ., but comp. for the thought κάλαμον ὑπὸ ἀνέμου σαλευόμενον, Matt. xi. 7. ῥιπίζειν is used in Aristoph. in the sense of fanning a flame: τεμάχη ῥιπίζεται, Eccl. 842. ῥιπή expresses any rapid movement of wave, wind, fire, stars, ῥιπαὶ ἀστέρων, Soph. El. 106: the verb here possibly of the tide. Comp. ῥιπαὶ κυμάτων ἀνέμων τε, Pind. P. IV. 346. Comp. the proper name Εὔριπος, where the tide ebbed and flowed with unusual violence; hence the word is applied as here to an unstable man: τῶν τοιούτων γὰρ μένει τὰ βουλήματα καὶ οὐ μεταρρεῖ ὥσπερ Εὔριπος, Eth. Nic. IX. 6. 3.  See also Eph. iv. 14, where κλυδωνιζόμενοι (ἅπ. λεγ.) καὶ περιφερόμενοι παντὶ ἀνέμῳ expresses the same idea and is possibly modelled on these words or similar words in St James' teaching.

**7. γάρ.** See Winer, LIII. 3.  The ἄρα in γάρ draws the inference, the γε corroborates it.  'Let not then that man,' &c.

**8. δίψυχος.** Not classical, and here only in N.T.; it does not occur in LXX.; possibly a word coined by St James himself.  (In Ps. cxix. 113 the Hebr. for 'them that are of a double mind' is vaguely rendered παρανόμους in the LXX.)  ψυχή is regarded as the seat of desires, volition; hence δίψυχος, one who is torn by conflicting desires.  The word, elsewhere rare, is very frequent in Hermas' *Pastor*, so much so that the treatise reads like an amplification of St James' teaching. As one instance out of many bearing the impress of this passage, comp. ἆρον ἀπό σου τὴν διψυχίαν καὶ μηδὲν ὅλως διψυχήσῃς αἰτήσασθαι παρὰ τοῦ θεοῦ, Herm. *Past.* M. 9.  It is difficult to decide whether ἀνὴρ δίψυχος is to be taken as a subject with ἀκατάστατος as a predicate, or whether both are in apposition to ὁ ἄνθρωπος ἐκεῖνος.  On the whole the latter view seems preferable.

**ἀκατάστατος.** Here only in N.T.  The noun ἀκαταστασία and the adjective are classical in the sense of political instability and confusion; in Polybius ἀκατάστατος is used of youthful fickleness: διά τε καὶ φύσει μὲν καὶ ἀκατάστατον ὑπάρχειν [τὸ μειράκιον] ἔτι δὲ μᾶλλον ὑπ' ἐκείνων τότε μετεωρισθέν, VIII. 4. 6.  In this sense also Luke xxi. 9. See also 1 Cor. xiv. 33.

The separation between ὁ ἄνθρωπος ἐκεῖνος and ἀνὴρ δίψυχος gives emphasis to the words in apposition: comp. τὸ πάσχα ἡμῶν ἐτύθη Χριστός, 1 Cor. v. 7; Rom. viii. 28; 2 Cor. vii. 6.

**ἐν πάσαις ταῖς ὁδοῖς αὐτοῦ.** Comp. *infr.* v. 11 ἐν ταῖς πορείαις αὐτοῦ. The figure is so frequent in the O.T. as hardly to need illustration: διδάξει πραεῖς ὁδοὺς αὐτοῦ, Ps. xxv. 9.  νομοθέτησόν με, κύριε, ἐν τῇ ὁδῷ σου, Ps. xxvii. 11.  οἱ ὀφθαλμοί μου ἐπὶ πάσας τὰς ὁδοὺς αὐτῶν, Jer. xvi. 17.  Hence Christianity or the Church is preeminently ἡ ὁδός,

Acts xix. 9 κακολογοῦντες τὴν ὁδόν, and 23 τάραχος οὐκ ὀλίγος περὶ τῆς ὁδοῦ.

**9. καυχάσθω δὲ ὁ ἀδελφὸς ὁ ταπεινὸς** κ.τ.λ. The transition to the contrast between rich and poor is quite natural here. For the problem of the prosperity of the wicked and the suffering of the righteous is one with which the Wisdom literature occupied itself more anxiously than with any other. It is, for instance, the theme of the Book of Job.

The rejoicing in ταπείνωσις is parallel in spirit to the rejoicing ἐν πειρασμοῖς. The ταπείνωσις of the rich (his becoming *poor*) will save him from the fate of the rich. Comp. 1 Sam. ii. 10, LXX. (a passage not found in the Hebrew), μὴ καυχάσθω ὁ φρόνιμος ἐν τῇ φρονήσει αὐτοῦ, καὶ μὴ καυχάσθω ὁ δυνατὸς ἐν τῇ δυνάμει αὐτοῦ, καὶ μὴ καυχάσθω ὁ πλούσιος ἐν τῷ πλούτῳ αὐτοῦ.

**10. ὡς ἄνθος χόρτου.** Comp. πᾶσα σὰρξ χόρτος, καὶ πᾶσα δόξα ἀνθρώπου ὡς ἄνθος χόρτου· ἐξηράνθη ὁ χόρτος καὶ τὸ ἄνθος ἐξέπεσεν, Is. xl. 7, 8. ὥσπερ ἄνθος ἀνθῆσαν ἐξέπεσεν, Job xiv. 2. ἄνθρωπος ὡσεὶ χόρτος αἱ ἡμέραι αὐτοῦ, ὡσεὶ ἄνθος τοῦ ἀγροῦ οὕτως ἐξανθήσει, Ps. ciii. 14. See also Ps. xxxvii. 2. The whole Psalm is parallel in thought to this passage.

**χόρτος.** See note on St Matt. vi. 30 in this series. The first meaning of the word is (1) an enclosed place, especially for feeding cattle: αὐλῆς ἐν χόρτῳ, Hom. *Il.* xi. 774. Hence (2) provender, hay, θηρῶν ὀρείων χόρτον οὐχ ἵππων λέγεις, Eur. *Alc.* 495. Then (3) vegetation generally, flowers and grass, and even brushwood, which when dried are used for fuel in the East. Matt. vi. 31. In this sense χόρτος is not classical. The derivation is from a root meaning 'to seize,' hence 'to enclose'; it is cognate with χορός, 'an enclosed place for dancing'; *hortus*, 'garden,' 'yard,' &c. Curtius, *Gk Etym.* § 200. Skeat, *Etym. Dict.*, under 'Yard.'

**11. ἀνέτειλεν…ἐξήρανεν…ἐξέπεσεν…ἀπώλετο.** The use of the aorist here is to express the instantaneous effect produced by the καύσων. In English the present tense would be used to express this point of time; but the greater exactness of Greek thought and language places the events in the past. They are past in the very moment of describing them. See Winer P. iii. § xl. 1, p. 346, and notes on St Matt. in this series, and compare 1 Pet. i. 24 ἐξηράνθη ὁ χόρτος καὶ τὸ ἄνθος ἐξέπεσεν. By some grammarians these are cited as instances of the gnomic aorist. See Mayor *ad loc.* and Burton, *N. T. Moods and Tenses*, p. 21. Winer however does not recognise this use of the aorist in N.T.

**σὺν τῷ καύσωνι.** The καύσων is the hot wind or sirocco blowing at sunrise from the Eastern desert. ἐπάξει καύσωνα ἄνεμον (*urentem ventum*, V.; Hebr. קָדִים רוּחַ, *east wind*) ἐκ τῆς ἐρήμου, Hos. xiii. 15. ἀναλήμψεται γὰρ αὐτὸν καύσων, Job xxvii. 21. καὶ ἐγένετο ἅμα τῷ ἀνατεῖλαι τὸν ἥλιον καὶ προσέταξεν ὁ θεὸς πνεύματι καύσωνι συγκαίοντι, Jon. iv. 8. It was this wind that made the early morning hours so burdensome to the labourers, τοῖς βαστάσασι τὸ βάρος τῆς ἡμέρας καὶ τὸν καύσωνα, Matt. xx. 12, where see notes.

ἐξέπεσεν. A beautifully exact word to describe the dropping of the petals or corona out of the calyx, as an effect of drought, which would be more strikingly sudden under the hot eastern sun than in a temperate climate like ours.

εὐπρέπεια, here only in N.T.  Comp. ἐκ Σιὼν ἡ εὐπρέπεια τῆς ὡραιότητος αὐτοῦ, Ps. l. 2.  For the general sense of this passage comp. πᾶς ὁ ὑψῶν ἑαυτὸν ταπεινωθήσεται, ὁ δὲ ταπεινῶν ἑαυτὸν ὑψωθήσεται, Luke xiv. 11.  One of the notes of the Kingdom was the exaltation of the poor: 1 Sam. ii. 8; Pss. ix. 12, 18, lxxii. 2, 4, 12, 13, cvii. 41, cxiii. 7, 8.  In Is. xxv. 3 the LXX. version, εὐλογήσει σε ὁ λαὸς ὁ πτωχός, where the Hebr. is 'the strong people shall glorify thee,' is suggestive.  See also Luke i. 52, vi. 20.  The Gospel is especially a message to the poor, Matt. xi. 5.  The rich are regarded as synonymous with the wicked, the poor with the righteous.  See Is. liii. 9; Ecclus. xiii. 3; Luke xvi. 19—31.  Comp. Pss. x. and xi.

This aspect of the rich and poor respectively is a vein of thought which runs through all the prophetic writings.  It is a social result which has ensued in many epochs, when the wealthier class unrestrained by any unselfish principle gave themselves over to every indulgence of pride and passion.  It is a view which finds support in some of the words of Christ: εἰ θέλεις τέλειος εἶναι ὕπαγε πώλησόν σου τὰ ὑπάρχοντα καὶ δὸς τοῖς πτωχοῖς καὶ ἕξεις θησαυρὸν ἐν οὐρανοῖς, Matt. xix. 21.  See also vv. 23, 24.  It took effect in the earliest organisation of the Church. Acts ii. 44, iii. 6.  It was part of the religious thought of the day, as shewn in Essenism and Ebionism, the latter name being derived from a Hebr. word meaning 'poor.'  One of the great lessons of Christianity has been to teach the responsibility of wealth and its place in the service of Christ, whether by noble use or self-sacrificing abandonment.

ἐν ταῖς πορείαις αὐτοῦ, in his ways, possibly in a literal sense (1) in his journeys for traffic or business, (2) but more probably in the ordinary figurative sense of way or path in the O. T.  Comp. κατάρτισαι τὰ διαβήματά μου ἐν ταῖς τρίβοις σου ἵνα μὴ σαλευθῇ τὰ διαβήματά μου, Ps. xvii. 5.

12.  This verse closes the paragraph which begins with *v.* 2, referring back to the original thought of temptation and endurance.

τὸν στέφανον τῆς ζωῆς, the crown of life.  τῆς ζωῆς, gen. of apposition denoting that in which the crown consists.  The life, i.e. eternal life, is the promised crown.  στέφανον, not the imperial or royal crown (διάδημα), but the garland of victory and civic worth, or military valour, woven of oak, ivy, parsley, pine or olive; see however Rev. iv. 4, ix. 7, xiv. 14, στεφάνους χρυσοῦς.  στέφανος is used of the kingly crown, Matt. xxvii. 29 and parallels.  But there the word shewed the material of which the crown was composed.  See Trench, *N.T. Syn.* sub voc., and Bp Lightfoot on Phil. iv. 1.  Comp. κομιεῖσθε τὸν ἀμαράντινον τῆς δόξης στέφανον, 1 Pet. v. 4; πᾶς δὲ ὁ ἀγωνιζόμενος πάντα ἐγκρατεύεται, ἐκεῖνοι μὲν οὖν ἵνα φθαρτὸν στέφανον λάβωσιν, ἡμεῖς δὲ ἄφθαρτον, 1 Cor. ix. 25; ὁ τῆς δικαιοσύνης στέφανος, 2 Tim. iv. 8,

where see the context which is parallel to this passage. Still more
closely parallel is Rev. ii. 10 γίνου πιστὸς ἄχρι θανάτου καὶ δώσω σοι
τὸν στέφανον τῆς ζωῆς. Comp. also Wisdom v. 16.

The thought is finely illustrated by a noble statue of James, the
brother of the Lord, on the porch of Amiens Cathedral. Above the
head of the apostle, not on his head, but at a distance from it, is
represented a crown, to shew that the crown is not yet attained;
it is the inspiring hope of life to be struggled and fought for through
temptation and trial. This last thought is signified by a shield which
the apostle holds in his hand, on which is inscribed a banner or flag
such as used to be carried in the very forefront of battle. Such is
the teaching of St James here. See Ruskin, *The Bible of Amiens.*

ὃν ἐπηγγείλατο. The suppressed subject of ἐπηγγείλατο can only
be ὁ κύριος or ὁ χριστός. And the question arises: Is this promise
a saying of our Lord's not recorded in the Gospels? Or is it another
form of Matt. x. 22, ὁ δὲ ὑπομείνας εἰς τέλος οὗτος σωθήσεται or Luke
xxi. 19, ἐν τῇ ὑπομονῇ ὑμῶν κτήσεσθε τὰς ψυχὰς ὑμῶν? The connexion
between ὑπομονή and ζωή is the same in both expressions, and the form
of the expression here may be due to St James' love of poetical imagery.
On the other hand it is perhaps most natural to regard it as a direct
citation of words of our Lord remembered by St James, which distinctly conveyed a promise. For though the word of promise is only
explicitly stated here, it is clearly indicated in the form of each of the
above cited passages. See Resch, *Agrapha*, logion 52, p. 130.

τοῖς ἀγαπῶσιν αὐτόν. Comp. τοῖς ἠγαπηκόσι τὴν ἐπιφάνειαν αὐτοῦ,
2 Tim. iv. 8.

13. πειραζόμενος, while tempted, in the course of temptation.
Such a primitive form of error may have arisen from a perverted
inference from the petition in the Lord's Prayer: μὴ εἰσενέγκῃς ἡμᾶς
εἰς πειρασμόν, Matt. vi. 13. St James' words reveal the secret of
temptation. However external the inducements to it may appear, its
root is within. Comp. Ecclus. xv. 11 ff.

ἀπὸ θεοῦ. ἀπὸ denotes origin simply, not agency. Winer, P. III.
§ xlvii. *b* note 2.

ἀπείραστος, for classical ἀπείρατος. κακῶν, genitive of source,
'untempted by evil.' Comp. ἄκλαυτος φίλων, Soph. *Ant.* 847; κακῶν
ἀτρύμονες, Aesch. *Theb.* 875; Winer, P. III. § xxx. 4. Others render
as R.V. *marg.* 'untried in evil.' But ἀπείραστος is clearly in connexion with the attendant verbs πειράζομαι, πειράζει, and must have
the same signification which they bear. There is no real theological
difficulty. Absolute freedom from the power of temptation precludes
the possibility of tempting others.

14. A parable of sin and death. ὑπό implies direct personal agency.
Man is regarded as tempted by his own lust or desire, here personified.
The offspring of this union is sin; sin when mature becomes the mother
of death. Comp. for the thought generally: τὰ γὰρ ὀψώνια τῆς ἁμαρτίας
θάνατος, τὸ δὲ χάρισμα τοῦ θεοῦ ζωὴ αἰώνιος ἐν Χριστῷ Ἰησοῦ τῷ κυρίῳ
ἡμῶν, Rom. vi. 23; τὸ γὰρ φρόνημα τῆς σαρκὸς θάνατος, Rom. viii. 6.

ἐξελκόμενος καὶ δελεαζόμενος. Either (1) with Bede, cited by Mayor: *abstractus a recto itinere et illectus in malum;* two processes in temptation are indicated: persuasion through some strong motive to leave the right path, allurement to sin: comp. ἐγκράτειαν οὕτω μάλιστ᾽ ἂν ᾤετο ἀσκεῖσθαι, εἰ αὐτὸς ἐπιδεικνύοι ἑαυτὸν μὴ ὑπὸ τῶν παραυτίκα ἡδονῶν ἑλκόμενον ἀπὸ τῶν ἀγαθῶν, Xen. *Cyr.* VIII. 1. 32; or (2) the figure is drawn from the capture of fishes. The words are here in the order of thought; in act δελεαζ. would precede. Comp. *Moriamur et in media arma ruamus,* Verg. *Aen.* II. 353; *Castigatque auditque dolos,* ib., VI. 567; ἐξελκ. here only in N. T. δελεαζ., comp. δελεάζοντες ψυχάς, 2 Pet. ii. 14; δελεάζουσιν ἐν ἐπιθυμίαις, 2 Pet. ii. 18; γαστρὶ δελεαζόμενα, Xen. *Mem.* II. 1. 4; ἡδονὴ κακοῦ δέλεαρ, Plat. *Tim.* 69 D.

**15.** ἀποτελεσθεῖσα, perfected, of full age, mature. Comp. *jam matura viro, jam plenis nubilis annis,* Verg. *Aen.* VII. 53.

ἀποκύει, brings forth, R.V.

**17.** πᾶσα δόσις, κ.τ.λ. Note the hexameter rhythm here, πᾶσα... τέλειον; for similar instances see Heb. xii. 13; John iv. 35.

δόσις, strictly an act of giving. Comp. Phil. iv. 15 οὐδεμία μοι ἐκκλησία ἐκοινώνησεν εἰς λόγον δόσεως καὶ λήψεως, where, as Bp Light-foot notes, δόσεως καὶ λήψεως are used in the technical sense of 'credit and debit.' In the classics δόσις appears to signify the thing given, a gift, according to the lexicons, but in many of the examples quoted the active sense is still apparent, e.g. Hom. *Od.* VI. 208, δόσις δ᾽ ὀλίγη τε, φίλη τε, δόσις may well signify a giving rather than a gift, and this original and proper signification gives a real distinction between δόσις and δώρημα, which is lost if δόσις is rendered 'a gift' and becomes synonymous with δώρημα. δόσις is the act or mode of giving, which may be right or wrong, and δώρημα is the gift itself.

The position of ἀγαθή and τέλειον gives the force of an adverbial clause; if it be good or perfect it is a divine gift.

ἄνωθέν ἐστιν. This is rightly regarded as the predicate rather than ἄνωθεν ἐστιν καταβαῖνον. See however Winer, III. xlv. 5, where the second view is supported. ἄνωθεν from above, from heaven. See ch. iii. 15, 17 and John iii. 31, xix. 11, and comp. Col. iii. 1 τὰ ἄνω ζητεῖτε. Philo *de Profug.* T. I. p. 571. 2 speaks of σοφίαν ἄνωθεν ὀμβρηθεῖσαν ἀπ᾽ οὐρανοῦ.

τοῦ πατρὸς τῶν φώτων, the Father of lights. Primarily perhaps the Creator of the heavenly bodies, but also in a wider sense Father and Creator of light in all its manifestations; Giver of all gifts, spiritual, intellectual and moral, beauty of nature and excellence of art. For this use of the plural denoting the parts of which a whole is made up, comp. προφυλάττεσθαι ψύχη ἢ θάλπῃ, attacks of cold and heat, Xen. *Mem.* I. 4. 13. So in Latin: *artes,* Art in its various forms, works of art; *regna* the various elements in the *regnum* &c.

Although the expression τοῦ πατρὸς τῶν φώτων cannot be precisely paralleled, the association of light with the idea of God may be abundantly illustrated: the first creative word of God is "Let there be light," Gen. i. 3; comp. Is. xlv. 6, 7 "I am Jehovah, there is none else,

that form light and create darkness": ἐγὼ ὁ κατασκευάσας φῶς καὶ
ποιήσας σκότος. So in the manifestation of Jehovah the light of the
moon shall be as the light of the sun, and the light of the sun shall
be sevenfold as the light of seven days, Is. xxx. 26. Comp. also ἐν
τῷ φωτί σου ὀψόμεθα φῶς, Ps. xxxv. 9; σὺ κατηρτίσω ἥλιον καὶ σελήνην,
Ps. lxxiii. 16; καὶ ἀνατελεῖ ὑμῖν ἥλιος δικαιοσύνης, Mal. iv. 2. In
1 John i. 5 God is absolutely φῶς, and in Heb. i. 3 Christ is regarded
as the effulgence (ἀπαύγασμα) from the Father. So in Wisdom vii. 26
σοφία is described as being ἀπαύγασμα φωτὸς ἀϊδίου.

παρ᾽ ᾧ οὐκ ἔνι π., **with whom there is no possibility of change.** Lit.
'there is no room for.' See Lightfoot on Gal. iii. 28, who agrees with
Winer (P. II. § xiv. p. 96) that ἔνι is not a contraction for ἔνεστι, but a
form of ἐν or ἐνί with the accent thrown back as ἔπι, πάρα, &c. See
also Col. iii. 11.

παραλλαγή, transmission from one condition to another, change, as
π. κάλλους πρὸς αἶσχος, Arr. *Epict.* II. 23. 32. So here perhaps simply
change from light to darkness, in which case the predominant thought
both in this and the following expression would be absolute brightness,
the negation of darkness—rather than absolute immutability, the negation of change. The context of the passage however suggests that
παραλλαγή may be here used in a scientific sense, or at any rate in
a way suggestive of the scientific term *parallax*. It is true that
no instance is cited of such a use of παραλλαγή before the date of
this Epistle, but neither is there an instance cited of παράλλαξις used
in this sense earlier than Proclus, who, c. A.D. 440, wrote a paraphrase
on a work of the astronomer Ptolemy (fl. A.D. 139), and the Modern
Greek term for *parallax* appears to be παραλλαγή, not παράλλαξις. See
Sophocles, Modern Greek Lexicon *sub voc.* This may represent a very
ancient usage.

Parallax "may be defined in the most general way as the difference between the directions of a body as seen from two different
points," or, "apparent change in position produced by movement of
the earth." Newcomb's *Popular Astronomy*, pp. 165 and 206. "The
parallax of the sun was calculated, though erroneously, by Aristarchus
c. 250 B.C. and Hipparchus 162—127 B.C., a calculation adopted by
Ptolemy and adhered to for twelve centuries." Young's *Text-Book
of General Astronomy*, § 666. The thought therefore would be familiar in St James' time. Moreover he was writing to men living in
regions where astronomy had flourished from a remote antiquity.
That astronomical phrases were known to the Greek-speaking Jew in
the post-exile period appears from various passages in the LXX.
αὐτὸς γάρ μοι ἔδωκεν τῶν ὄντων γνῶσιν ἀψευδῆ εἰδέναι σύστασιν κόσμου
καὶ ἐνέργειαν στοιχείων, ἀρχὴν καὶ τέλος καὶ μεσότητα χρόνων, τροπῶν
ἀλλαγὰς καὶ μεταβολὰς καιρῶν, ἐνιαυτῶν κύκλους καὶ ἀστέρων θέσεις,
Wisdom of Solomon, vii. 17; καὶ καθ᾽ ὥραν γεννημάτων ἡλίου τροπῶν
καὶ ἀπὸ συνόδων μηνῶν, Deut. xxxiii. 14; ἐπίστασαι δὲ τροπὰς οὐρανοῦ, ἢ
τὰ ὑπ᾽ οὐρανὸν ὁμοθυμαδὸν γινόμενα; Job xxxviii. 33.

In the Book of Enoch, ch. lxxi., there is an elaborate treatise on the
laws and movements of the heavenly bodies, and the expression 'Father

of the lights' finds a parallel in such phrases as: 'The seasons, the years, and the days, Uriel shewed me; the angel whom the Lord of glory appointed over all the luminaries of heaven in heaven, and in the world,' &c. ch. lxxiv.

If this view of the meaning of παραλλαγή be accepted, the expression would indicate the immutability of the Eternal Father, and the thought would be intensified by the results of modern science, according to which the apparent displacement of the great majority of the fixed stars, due to parallax, is so minute as to elude our investigation. The παραλλαγή of the stars indeed is incalculable; with the Father of the lights παραλλαγή is inconceivable.

It is difficult to decide with certainty between these two possible senses of παραλλαγή. It is in favour of the first that the same thought of light and darkness would be retained in both expressions —παραλλαγή and τροπῆς ἀποσκίασμα. The second introduces the further thought of unchangeableness.

**τροπή**, turning or revolution, or perhaps the setting of a heavenly body. The genitive τροπῆς denotes occasion or cause.

**ἀποσκίασμα** is the shadow projected *from* one body on to another, or in any way caused by the movements of a body.

Hence τροπῆς ἀποσκίασμα is either (1) the shadow of night caused by the rotation of the earth, or, in popular phrase, by the setting of the sun (comp. οὔθ' ὁπότ' ἂν στείχῃσι πρὸς οὐρανὸν ἀστερόεντα | οὔθ' ὅτ' ἂν ἂψ ἐπὶ γαῖαν ἀπ' οὐρανόθεν προτράπηται· | ἀλλ' ἐπὶ νὺξ ὀλοὴ τέταται δειλοῖσι βροτοῖσιν, *Od.* xi. 17—19; τροπαὶ ἠελίοιο, ib. xv. 404, which Eustathius interprets of the west, τὰ δυτικὰ μέρη, the region of sunset): or (2) the shadow of eclipse caused by the revolution of a planet or its moons: a far more frequent occurrence in some parts of the celestial system than in the experience of our own planet: e.g. four of Jupiter's satellites are eclipsed at every revolution, i.e. at intervals varying from 12 hours to 7 days for the different satellites. The created luminaries suffer eclipse by projected shadow or darkness by turning from the source of light: with the Father of lights there is absolutely undimmed and continuous splendour: "the shadows vanish in the light of light." Tennyson.

Schleusner, following some of the Greek interpreters, takes ἀποσκίασμα as equivalent to ἴχνος, and renders it *ne levissimum quidem mutationis vestigium*, 'not a trace or vestige of change.' There is however no authority for this use of the word ἀποσκίασμα, and by this rendering the important conception of darkness or overshadowing, as a defect in the mundane luminaries, is lost. So also O. L. renders *modicum obumbrationis, vicissitudinis obumbratio*.

**18.  βουληθείς**, of His own wish, denoting absolute freedom from necessity or external cause of any kind. βούλομαι and βούλησις are strictly used of the end, not of the means to the end: εἰ δή τι τέλος ἔστι τῶν πρακτῶν δ δι' αὐτὸ βουλόμεθα, Arist. *Eth. N.* i. 2.1; ἡ μὲν βούλησις τοῦ τέλους ἐστὶ μᾶλλον, ἡ δὲ προαίρεσις τῶν πρὸς τὸ τέλος, *Eth. N.* iii. 2.9. See Stewart's *Eth. N. ad loc. cit.*

ἀπεκύησεν.  The recurrence of this rare word (see above, v. 15)
throws into forcible contrast the generation of sin, and the new birth
from the Father of lights.  This is the more striking as ἀποκύειν is a
word strictly used of the mother, not as here of the Father, 'begat.'
The word generally used in this sense is γεννᾶν.  Comp. the use of
τίκτειν, Il. II. 742; Aesch. Eum. 630.

The aorist points to the single act of regeneration, as in 1 Cor.
vi. 11 ἀλλὰ ἀπελούσασθε, ἀλλὰ ἡγιάσθητε, ἀλλὰ ἐδικαιώθητε ἐν τῷ ὀνόματι
τοῦ κυρίου, κ.τ.λ.

λόγῳ ἀληθείας, by the word of truth, the instrument by which the
work is effected.

λόγος ἀληθείας is the word or message which conveys the truth, the
revelation of the truth.  Comp. ὁ λόγος τῆς σωτηρίας ταύτης, Acts xiii. 26;
ὁ λόγος τῆς ἀληθείας τοῦ εὐαγγελίου, Col. i. 5; ὁ λόγος τῆς ἀληθείας,
2 Tim. ii. 15; ὃ ἦν ἀπ' ἀρχῆς ὃ ἀκηκόαμεν...περὶ τοῦ λόγου τῆς ζωῆς,
κ.τ.λ., 1 John i. 1.  Comp. also the frequent ἀμὴν λέγω of our Lord
(note the variant ἀληθῶς λέγω, Luke xii. 44); in St John always
the repeated ἀμὴν ἀμὴν λέγω.  See especially, as bearing on this passage,
St John iii. 3, 5 ἀμὴν ἀμὴν λέγω σοι, ἐὰν μή τις γεννηθῇ ἐξ ὕδατος καὶ
πνεύματος οὐ δύναται εἰσελθεῖν εἰς τὴν βασιλείαν τοῦ θεοῦ.

In the passages quoted above ὁ λόγος τῆς ἀληθ. or τῆς σωτηρίας is the
Gospel, that divine revelation by which God regenerated the world in
Christ,—a sense which it bears here; but there is a nearer approach to
the personal λόγος of John i. 1 here than in the other passages.  The
message of truth in Christ is proved to be the regeneration (ἡ παλιν-
γενεσία) first of Israel, then of the world.  The repeated ἡμᾶς points
to the privilege of Israel.

εἰς τὸ εἶναι.  A final clause denoting the end or object of the spiritual
creation.

ἀπαρχήν τινα, a kind of firstfruits.  τινα qualifies the boldness of the
expression, Winer III. 2 a.  In the Hebrew ritual ἀπαρχή meant the firstfruits of men and cattle and harvest, consecrated and offered to God:
οἴσετε τὸ δράγμα ἀπαρχὴν τοῦ θερισμοῦ ὑμῶν πρὸς τὸν ἱερέα, Lev. xxiii.
10.  See also Deut. xxvi. 2; Ex. xxiii. 19: ἀπαρχὴ therefore besides
the primary meaning of 'firstfruits' as the promise of harvest and
dedication of the coming harvest carried into the New Covenant the
thought of consecration to God.  Comp. οἴδατε τὴν οἰκίαν Στεφανᾶ, ὅτι
ἐστὶν ἀπαρχὴ τῆς Ἀχαίας, 1 Cor. xvi. 15; οὗτοι ἠγοράσθησαν ἀπὸ τῶν ἀνθρώπων ἀπαρχὴ τῷ θεῷ καὶ τῷ ἀ, νίῳ, Rev. xiv. 4.

τῶν αὐτοῦ κτισμάτων, His creatures.  The gift of the Incarnation
is literally and truly a new life, and the result is a new creature: ὥστε
εἴ τις ἐν Χριστῷ καινὴ κτίσις, 2 Cor. v. 17.  See Gal. vi. 15.  Thus
Christ is πνεῦμα ζωοποιοῦν, 1 Cor. xv. 45, because it is by the spiritual
communication of His own life that the new creature is effected.  With
this conception of the new birth as a gift of the Father of lights comp.
the use of φωτίζειν, φώτισμα, φωτισμός, as baptismal expressions: οἱ
φωτιζόμενοι ἑπτὰ ἡμέρας λαμπροφοροῦσιν, Suicer, sub voc. φωτίζειν.

### 19—27. The Christian Life, Character and Worship.

This theme incidentally arises from the thought of temptation, as moral or religious error, and is immediately connected with the expression ἀπαρχήν τινα τῶν αὐτοῦ κτισμάτων, v. 18.

It is a description of the life in union with Christ on the practical side. In view of prevailing pagan immorality and even of the ethics of philosophic paganism, the importance of moral teaching in the early Christian Church can hardly be over-estimated. The contrast between the Christian ideal and the pagan Society from which it was separated accounts for the repeated warnings even against gross forms of sin.

**19.** ἴστε. For the reading see above. The classical form ἴστε for the Hellenistic οἴδατε is found here only in N.T. 'Ye know it' refers to what precedes, emphasizing that, and leading on to its consequence—a new life.

ταχὺς εἰς τὸ ἀκοῦσαι. εἰς signifies aim or tendency; ταχὺς is constructed also with the infinitive alone: ὡς θέλοντα μέν μ' ἔχεις | σοὶ συμπονῆσαι καὶ ταχὺν προσαρκέσαι | βραδὺν δ' Ἀχαιοῖς εἰ διαβληθήσομαι, Eur. *Hec.* 861—3 : ταχὺς ἐν τῇ ἀκροάσει σου, Ecclus. v. 11. One of the sayings attributed by Mahommedan writers to Christ is, 'Asked by some how to win Paradise, He said, "Speak not at all." They said, "We cannot do this." He said then, "Only say what is good"' (Margoliouth, *Expository Times*, Dec. 1893). Comp. γλῶσσα ἀνθρώπου πτῶσις αὐτῷ, Ecclus. v. 13.

**20.** ὀργὴ γὰρ ἀνδρὸς κ.τ.λ. There is a suggestion of irony in this expression. ὀργή, primarily 'passionate impulse,' is as far as possible removed from justice in any case. How much greater the contrast between human ὀργή and divine δικαιοσύνη! On the other hand ὀργὴ θεοῦ is used of divine justice in its manifestation towards sinners, Rom. i. 18.

**21.** ἀποθέμενοι, of putting off a garment, τὰ ἱμάτια, Acts vii. 58; a burden, ὄγκον, Heb. xii. 1. More frequently figuratively, Rom. xiii. 12 τὰ ἔργα τοῦ σκότους. Eph. iv. 22, 25 τὸν παλαιὸν ἄνθρωπον...τὸ ψεῦδος. Col. iii. 8 τὰ πάντα, ὀργήν, θυμόν, κ.τ.λ. 1 Pet. ii. 1 πᾶσαν κακίαν. The tense implies a single, decisive effort.

πᾶσαν ῥυπαρίαν. πᾶσαν, **in its whole extent.** ῥυπαρίαν, ἅπ. λεγ. in N.T., uncleanness, comp. σαρκὸς ἀπόθεσις ῥύπου, 1 Pet. iii. 21; ὁ ῥυπαρὸς ῥυπανθήτω ἔτι, Rev. xxii. 11.

περισσείαν κακίας, **excess of wickedness.** περισσείαν not classical: ἅπ. λεγ. in N.T.

ἐν πραΰτητι, **with meekness.** πραΰτης is a note of the Kingdom. Pss. xxv. 9, xxxiv. 2, xxxvii. 11, lxxvi. 9, cxlvii. 6, cxlix. 4.
Christ calls Himself πραΰς Matt. xi. 29, and places the πραεῖς in the forefront of those who are 'blessed,' Matt. v. 4 (or 5). πραότης as an ethical term is concerned with anger, it means absence from resentment, meekness in suffering; it is mentioned with very faint praise by Aristotle, who says, ἐπὶ τὸν μέσον τὴν πραότητα φέρομεν πρὸς τὴν ἔλλειψιν ἀποκλίνουσαν, and again εἴπερ δὴ ἡ πραότης ἐπαινεῖται. It is

therefore one of those distinctively Christian terms which, like ὑπομονή, μακροθυμία, ταπεινοφροσύνη, point the divergence from pagan ethics. Closely associated with πραότης in N.T. are, ἐπιείκεια, 2 Cor. x. 1; ἐγκράτεια, Gal. v. 23; ταπεινοφροσύνη and μακροθυμία, Eph. iv. 2; Col. iii. 12; ὑπομονή, 2 Thess. iii. 5.    Comp. also 1 Cor. iv. 21; Gal. vi. 1; Titus iii. 2.   With the exception of this passage and 1 Pet. iii. 15 πραΰτης (πραΰτης) is a Pauline word.

δέξασθε τὸν ἔμφυτον λόγον.    Comp. μετὰ χαρᾶς δέχονται τὸν λόγον, Luke viii. 13.    ἐδέξασθε οὐ λόγον ἀνθρώπων ἀλλὰ καθὼς ἀληθῶς ἐστὶν λόγον θεοῦ, 1 Thess. ii. 13.

τὸν ἔμφυτον λόγον, the implanted word.   The word that becomes a part of the φύσις or character, that is worked into the nature just as the elements which go to form the plant are absorbed in it, and tend to its growth.   ἔμφυτον is formally proleptic here; it is implanted after its reception.   But in fact it expresses a constant quality of the λόγος and forms with it a single compound noun.

τὸν δυνάμενον σῶσαι κ.τ.λ.   Comp. infra iv. 12 ὁ δυνάμενος σῶσαι. The power there attributed to God is here attributed to the implanted Word, and in fact the implanted Word is scarcely distinguishable from the indwelling Christ.

22.   ποιηταὶ λόγου.   ποιητής is a characteristic word of St James, occurring four times in this Epistle, elsewhere in N.T. once in Romans ii. 13 ποιηταὶ νόμου, and in Acts xvii. 28, where it bears the classical sense of 'poet,' τινες τῶν καθ᾽ ὑμᾶς ποιητῶν.   In Tit. i. 12 St Paul uses the word προφήτης of a poet: εἰπέν τις ἐξ αὐτῶν ἴδιος αὐτῶν προφήτης.

παραλογιζόμενοι ἑαυτούς, deceiving yourselves, 'making a false or erroneous estimate': for this sense of παρά comp. παράσημος of a coin imperfectly stamped: δύναμις παράσημος αἴνῳ, Aesch. Agam. 780, power falsely stamped with praise; παραπείθειν, to persuade with fraud; παρακούειν, to misunderstand; παράγειν, to lead astray; σοφία δὲ κλέπτει παράγοισα μύθοις, Pind. Nem. VII. 34.

23.   ἀκροατὴς λόγου, 'he who only hears the word,' is compared to a man who by looking into a mirror observes (κατανοεῖ) the face of his γένεσις—his true individuality—the real meaning of himself (κατενόησεν γὰρ ἑαυτόν), but who instantly departing forgets what manner of man he was.    That is, if a man listens for a time only to divine teaching and is made to understand himself, to see himself in God's word, and then abandons it, the impression made by reading or instruction is momentary.  He is like the seed that fell in stony places or among thorns.  On the other hand the ποιητὴς λόγου, he who does the word, looks into the perfect law, the law of liberty, i.e. the word of God, and there sees reflected as in a mirror his own personality as it was created in the likeness of God (comp. ch. iii. 9); he abides in it, continues that earnest gaze, never losing sight of his ideal, of that which he was intended to be according to the purpose of his γένεσις or creation. "Is it not remarkable that St James dwells not on what the man learns about God in the Scripture, but on what he sees of God's

design, or delineation of what *he*, the beholder, was meant and made
to be?"  Archbp Benson, *Communings of a Day*, p. 8.

κατανοοῦντι, **closely observing**, attentively considering.  Comp.
Matt. vii. 3 δοκὸν οὐ κατανοεῖς; Luke xii. 24, 27 κατανοήσατε τοὺς
κόρακας...τὰ κρίνα, xx. 23 κατανοήσας δὲ αὐτῶν τὴν πανουργίαν; Acts
vii. 31, 32, xi. 6 εἰς ἣν ἀτενίσας κατενόουν καὶ εἶδον: Rom. iv. 19; Heb.
iii. 1 κατανοήσατε τὸν ἀπόστολον κ.τ.λ.; x. 24 κατανοῶμεν ἀλλήλους,
'take careful note of.'

τὸ πρόσωπον τῆς γενέσεως αὐτοῦ.  *Vultum nativitatis suae*, V.
**The countenance** (*vultum* as expressive of character) **of his birth or**
**creation in the image of God** (see ch. iii. 9 and above, *v.* 18); that
is to say, as the next clause shews, his real self or personality (κατενόησεν γὰρ ἑαυτόν).  Comp. ἐπὶ τῆς ἐν τῷ κατόπτρῳ μορφῆς ἡ εἰκὼν πρὸς
τὸ ἀρχέτυπον σχηματίζεται, Greg. Nyssen, quoted in Suicer.  Comp.
the later use of πρόσωπον to signify the Persons or ὑποστάσεις of the
blessed Trinity.

For the thought comp.

> "As when a painter poring on a face
> Divinely, through all hindrance finds the man
> Behind it, and so paints him that his face,
> The shape and colour of a mind and life,
> Lives for his children ever at its best
> And fullest."  (Tennyson.)

ἐν ἐσόπτρῳ.  A mirror of polished metal.

24.  ἀπελήλυθεν καὶ εὐθέως ἐπελάθετο ὁποῖος ἦν.  The tenses are
used with great exactness: the perfect denotes immediate succession
and enduring result, 'he has gone and is still away'; comp. *terra*
*tremit, fugere ferae*, Virg. *Georg.* I. 330.  The aorist denotes the single
instantaneous act of forgetting.  For similar exact uses of these
tenses in combination, comp. Luke iv. 18 ἔχρισέν με (a single eternal
act) εὐαγγελίσασθαι, ἀπέσταλκέν με (continued result) κηρύξαι: Heb. ii.
14 ἐπεὶ τὰ παιδία κεκοινώνηκεν σαρκὸς καὶ αἵματος καὶ αὐτὸς μετέσχεν (at
His incarnation) τῶν αὐτῶν.  See Winer, III. § xl. 6, where other
instances are given.

25.  παρακύψας.  First of stooping or inclining to one side (not stooping *down*), either with a verb of looking, or absolutely as here: παρακύψας
βλέπει τὰ ὀθόνια, Luke xxiv. 12; παρακύψας βλέπει κείμενα τὰ ὀθόνια,
John xx. 5; ὡς οὖν ἔκλαιεν παρέκυψεν εἰς τὸ μνημεῖον, ib. 11; εἰς ἃ
ἐπιθυμοῦσιν οἱ ἄγγελοι παρακύψαι, 1 Pet. i. 12; see also Gen. xxvi. 8;
Prov. vii. 6.  Though the strict meaning of παρακύπτειν is to glance
sideways or 'to peep,' as ἄφρων ἀπὸ θύρας παρακύπτει εἰς οἰκίαν, Ecclus.
xxi. 23, the context sometimes, as here, carries with it the sense of
intently gazing.  See Dr Field, *Otium Norvicense*, on Luke xxiv. 12
and on this passage.

εἰς νόμον τέλειον τὸν τῆς ἐλευθερίας, **into a perfect law, namely**
**the law of liberty.**  The absence of the article before νόμον is
noticeable.  The conception is first stated generally, a perfect law;
the article introduces a limitation defining that perfect law to be the

law of liberty.  It is an idiom which secures attention to the anarthrous
noun.  See Winer III. § xx. 4 and Green p. 34, and note the following
examples: εἰρήνην ἀφίημι ὑμῖν, εἰρήνην τὴν ἐμὴν δίδωμι ὑμῖν, John xiv.
27; εἰ γὰρ ἐδόθη νόμος ὁ δυνάμενος ζωοποιῆσαι, Gal. iii. 21, where see
Ellicott; ἐν πίστει ζῶ τῇ τοῦ υἱοῦ τοῦ θεοῦ, Gal. ii. 20.

τὸν τῆς ἐλευθερίας.  The freedom of the law of Christ is contrasted
with the bondage to minute precepts which characterized the developed
Mosaic system: τῇ ἐλευθερίᾳ ἡμᾶς Χριστὸς ἠλευθέρωσεν· στήκετε οὖν καὶ
μὴ πάλιν ζυγῷ δουλείας ἐνέχεσθε, Gal. v. 1; γνώσεσθε τὴν ἀλήθειαν καὶ
ἡ ἀλήθεια ἐλευθερώσει ὑμᾶς, John viii. 32; comp. with this λόγῳ
ἀληθείας supra v. 18; ἐὰν οὖν ὁ υἱὸς ὑμᾶς ἐλευθερώσῃ ὄντως ἐλεύθεροι
ἔσεσθε, John viii. 36.  See also Rom. viii. 15.  Christians are children
of God, *liberi* not *servi*.  Comp. *cui servire regnare est*, 'whose service
is perfect freedom.'  Collect for Peace, from Sacramentary of Gelasius.
The law of Christ then is called a perfect law because it is final and
complete, as distinct from the Mosaic law which was transitory and
imperfect; it is called a law of liberty because it is the expression
of a Father's love for his children, not of a Master's law for slaves.

καὶ παραμείνας.  The secret of Christian service is constancy, fixed-
ness on the ideal self discovered in the perfect law: ὡς ἠγάπησα τὸν
νόμον σου, κύριε, ὅλην τὴν ἡμέραν μελέτη μού ἐστιν, Ps. cxix. 97.

ἀκροατὴς ἐπιλησμονῆς, a forgetful hearer.  A Hebrew construction
frequent in N.T., as πάθη ἀτιμίας, Rom. i. 26; κριτὴς τῆς ἀδικίας, Luke
xviii. 6; ὁ οἰκονόμος τῆς ἀδικίας, Luke xvi. 8.  The idiom is partly due
to the vividness of Oriental speech, partly to the comparative paucity
of adjectives in Hebrew.  There are however parallels in the classics:
μέλαινα δ' ἄστρων...εὐφρόνῃ, 'starry night,' Soph. *El.* 19; λευκῆς χιόνος
πτέρυγι, *Ant.* 114, 'a snowy wing'; Winer, P. III. § 34 *b*; Green, p. 90;
Donaldson, *Greek Gram.* 454.
ἐπιλησμονή not classical, and here only in N.T.

ποιητὴς ἔργου.  The condition of abiding in the law of liberty is
activity in the exercise of it.  Hence the transition to true worship or
service.

μακάριος ἐν τῇ ποιήσει αὐτοῦ.  See John viii. 31—34, the thought
of which passage underlies this, ἐὰν ὑμεῖς μείνητε ἐν τῷ λόγῳ τῷ ἐμῷ
ἀληθῶς μαθηταί μού ἐστε, καὶ γνώσεσθε τὴν ἀλήθειαν, καὶ ἡ ἀλήθεια
ἐλευθερώσει ὑμᾶς...ὁ ποιῶν τὴν ἁμαρτίαν (comp. with ἐν τῇ ποιήσει αὐτοῦ)
δοῦλός ἐστιν.  Sin and righteousness are regarded as creations.  If the
'maker' keeps his eye fixed on the model—abiding in that steadfast
gaze—he will be happy in his making, as every artist or maker of
things true and beautiful knows.  His making will be true to his
γένεσις.

ποίησις.  Here only in N.T.  Comp. καὶ ἐν πάσῃ σοφίᾳ ποίησις
νόμου, Ecclus. xix. 20.

26.  εἴ τις δοκεῖ, is thought to be, has the reputation (δόξα) of
being.

μὴ χαλιναγωγῶν. μὴ not οὐ, because the sentence is hypothetical, 'if he does not bridle &c.' It may be noticed however that in Modern Greek μή is invariably used with participles, and that there is a tendency to this use in the N.T. It is the grammatical expression of a more subjective method of stating facts. See Winer, P. III. § lv. 5. Among instances where the explanation on classical principles is difficult are: μὴ ἔχοντος αὐτοῦ ἀποδοῦναι ἐκέλευσεν αὐτὸν ὁ κύριος αὐτοῦ πραθῆναι κ.τ.λ., Matt. xviii. 25; ὅταν γὰρ ἔθνη τὰ μὴ νόμον ἔχοντα φύσει τὰ τοῦ νόμου ποιῶσιν, Rom. ii. 14; καὶ ἦν ἡμέρας τρεῖς μὴ βλέπων, καὶ οὐκ ἔφαγεν οὐδὲ ἔπιεν, Acts ix. 9.

χαλιναγωγεῖν. Only here and iii. 2 in N.T., and elsewhere only in late Greek authors. Comp. ἀχάλινον κεκτημένοι τὸ στόμα, Plato *de Legg.* 701 c; ἀχαλίνων στομάτων | ἀνόμου τ' ἀφροσύνας | τὸ τέλος δυστυχία, Eur. *Bacch.* 385—387.

**27.  θρησκεία.**  ἅπ. λεγ. in N.T. *Cultus*, religion in its external aspect, the outward observance of religious rites as opposed to εὐσέβεια or piety.  "St James is not here affirming, as we sometimes hear, these offices to be the sum total, nor yet the great essentials of true religion, but declares them to be the body, the θρησκεία, of which godliness or the love of God is the informing soul." Trench, *N.T. Synonyms.* Here St James reflects the most enlightened spirit of ancient prophecy: see especially Is. i. 13—17; Micah vi. 7, 8; and comp. Matt. xxiii. 23.
There is a special interest in this definition of θρησκεία by St James, whose assiduity in the θρησκεία of Judaism earned for him the title of ὁ δίκαιος. For the classical use of the word comp. Herod. II. 18 ἀχθόμενοι τῇ περὶ τὰ ἱρὰ θρησκηίην (τῶν Αἰγυπτίων), and II. 37 ἄλλας τε θρησκηίας ἐπιτελέουσι μυρίας.

**ἐπισκέπτεσθαι ὀρφανοὺς καὶ χήρας.** *Visitare pupillos et viduas in tribulatione eorum,* V.; κρίνατε ὀρφανῷ καὶ δικαιώσατε χήραν, Is. i. 17. The care of widows was one of the earliest notes of the Church, it went on side by side with the continuous worship in the temple. See Acts vi. 1; 1 Tim. v. 3. It is a mark of the divine loving-kindness, Ps. lxviii. 5, cxlvi. 9; and on the other hand the helplessness of the orphan and widow made them at all times victims of oppression: Ps. xciv. 6; Is. x. 2; Jer. vii. 6, xxii. 3; Zech. vii. 10; Ezek. xxii. 7; Mal. iii. 5. The Pharisees, who made a boast of θρησκεία, devoured widows' houses, Matt. xxiii. 14.

**ἄσπιλον.** See 1 Tim. vi. 14 τηρῆσαί σε τὴν ἐντολὴν ἄσπιλον: 1 Pet. i. 19 ἀμνοῦ ἀμώμου καὶ ἀσπίλου Χριστοῦ: and 2 Pet. iii. 14 ἄσπιλοι καὶ ἀμώμητοι. Comp. Eph. v. 27 ἵνα παραστήσῃ αὐτὸς ἑαυτῷ ἔνδοξον τὴν ἐκκλησίαν, μὴ ἔχουσαν σπίλον ἢ ῥυτίδα ἤ τι τῶν τοιούτων, ἀλλ' ἵνα ᾖ ἁγία καὶ ἄμωμος. σπίλος belongs to later Greek: Lob. *Phryn.* 28 τοῦτο φυλάττου λέγε δὲ κηλίς.

**κόσμου.** Originally, order, εὖ κατὰ κόσμον, Hom. *Il.* x. 472 and frequently in Classical Greek: Herod., Thuc., Plat. and the poets, order in government, conduct, dress. So ornament, 1 Pet. iii. 3 ὁ ἔξωθεν ἐμπλοκῆς τριχῶν...κόσμος: possibly the meaning of the word in ch. iii. 6. Then applied by Pythagoras and his followers to the

order of the Universe, as opposed to chaos, hence the world. So
Plato, *Gorg.* p. 508 φασὶν δὲ σοφοὶ καὶ οὐρανὸν καὶ γῆν καὶ θεοὺς καὶ
ἀνθρώπους τὴν κοινωνίαν συνέχειν καὶ φιλίαν καὶ κοσμιότητα καὶ σωφρο-
σύνην καὶ δικαιότητα καὶ τὸ ὅλον τοῦτο διὰ ταῦτα κόσμον καλοῦσιν.
Comp. Plin. *H. N.* II. 3 *Quem κόσμον Graeci nomine ornamenti adpella-
verunt, eum nos perfecta absolutaque elegantia mundum.* Comp. also
Tertullian, *Lib. Apol.* c. xvii. *Deus, qui totam molem istam...de nihilo
expressit in ornamentum majestatis suae: unde et Graeci nomen mundo
κόσμον accommodaverunt.* This sense does not appear in the Canonical books of the O.T., but in the Book of Wisdom we find εἰδέναι
σύστασιν κόσμου, vii. 17; καὶ κτίσασα τὸν κόσμον ἐξ ἀμόρφου ὕλης, xi. 17.
This is also a N.T. use: ἀπὸ καταβολῆς κόσμου, Matt. xxv. 34; Luke
xi. 50; Hebr. iv. 3; πρὸ καταβολῆς κόσμου, 1 Pet. i. 20; ὁ κόσμος δι'
αὐτοῦ ἐγένετο, John i. 10. But in the N.T. κόσμος has the further
significations of: (α) <u>the world of men and women into which we are
born, and in which we live</u>: ὑμεῖς ἐστε τὸ φῶς τοῦ κόσμου, Matt. v. 14;
ὁ δὲ ἀγρός ἐστιν ὁ κόσμος, Matt. xiii. 38; ἐρχόμενον εἰς τὸν κόσμον, John
i. 9. (β) The world as opposed to God, the wicked world: ἡ βασιλεία ἡ ἐμὴ οὐκ ἔστιν ἐκ τοῦ κόσμου τούτου, John xviii. 36; ὁ τοῦ κόσμου
ἄρχων, John xiv. 30; οὐ τὸ πνεῦμα τοῦ κόσμου ἐλάβομεν, 1 Cor. ii. 12;
οἱ χρώμενοι κόσμῳ τούτῳ, 1 Cor. vii. 31; with this comp. πρὸς τοὺς κοσμο-
κράτορας τοῦ σκότους τοῦ αἰῶνος τούτου, Eph. vi. 12.

# CHAPTER II.

**2.** τὴν omitted before συναγωγὴν with ℵ*BC: AKLP and almost
all the later authorities insert the article.

**3.** σὺ στῆθι ἐκεῖ ἢ κάθου. B places ἐκεῖ after κάθου, so also ff, an
O. L. codex. The T. R. has ὧδε after κάθου with ℵC²KLP and many
versions: the omission of ὧδε is supported by ABC* ff and V.

**4.** οὐ διεκρίθητε with ℵAB²C and most cursives. B* omits οὐ, so
also ff. KLP and others have καὶ οὐ.

**5.** τῷ κόσμῳ with ℵA*BC*. The T. R. τοῦ κόσμου τούτου has very
slight support; τοῦ κόσμου appears in A²C²KLP and other authorities.
It is an instance of the more difficult giving place to the easier
reading.

**13.** The reading varies between ἀνέλεος ℵABCK, ἀνίλεως L and many
other MSS. and Fathers, and ἀνέλεως and ἀνήλεως in a few codices.

**19.** ὅτι εἷς ἐστὶν ὁ θεός; the reading of ℵA, the Vulgate, Peshitto
and other versions: εἷς ὁ θεός ἐστιν B: εἷς ὁ θεός, some versions: ὁ θεὸς
εἷς ἐστίν K²L.

**20.** ἀργή, supported by BC*, some cursives, O. L. (*vacua*) and some
other versions. On the other hand νεκρά is read in ℵAC², later uncials,
the Vulgate and several other versions. But the tendency to bring
this verse into agreement with *v.* 26 probably accounts for νεκρά.

**22.** συνήργει, so W. H. with ℵ*BCKLP and the Vulgate (coope-
rabatur): συνεργεῖ, Tischendorf with ℵA and O. L. (communicat).

**1—4.** The Subject of θρησκεία naturally leads to the Thought of the συναγωγή, closely connected with which is the spiritual Danger of προσωπολημψία, against which St James now warns his Brethren.

**1. ἀδελφοί μου,** the name itself is a protest against the sin of προσωπολημψία.

**μή...ἔχετε** is pointed interrogatively by Westcott and Hort. This construction however is regularly used only where a negative answer is expected, and even if there are exceptions to the rule, the imperative is more forcible and more characteristic of St James' style. See Winer, III. 67, 3 *b*.

**ἐν προσωπολημψίαις, with respect of persons.** Do not let those personal distinctions and differences continue to find a place in religious life. The plural denotes the different ways in which προσωπολημψία shews itself, the various acts and instances of deference to persons. See note i. 17. The compounds προσωπολημψία, προσωπολημπτεῖν, προσωπολήμπτης are first found in the N.T. They are among the earliest purely Christian words.—πρόσωπον λαμβάνειν is a Hebraism נָשָׂא פָנִים, lit. to lift the face (opposed to making the countenance fall); hence to be favourable to: translated by ἐθαύμασά σου τὸ πρόσωπον, Gen. xix. 21: hence in N.T. always in a bad sense of shewing favour or preference to persons on account of external advantages, rank, wealth, power: οὐ λαμβάνεις πρόσωπον οὐδενός, Luke xx. 21, in parallels οὐ βλέπεις εἰς πρόσωπον ἀνθρώπων, Matt. xxii. 16, Mark xii. 14; comp. οὐ γὰρ προσωπολήμπτης ὁ θεός, Acts x. 34; θαυμάζοντες πρόσωπα, Jude 16. For προσωπολημψία itself, see Rom. ii. 11; Eph. vi. 9; Col. iii. 25.

**τὴν πίστιν τοῦ κυρίου** κ.τ.λ., **the faith in the Lord Jesus,** that faith of which He is the object, in virtue of which the disciples were called οἱ πιστεύοντες.

**τῆς δόξης.** Comp. Hebr. xii. 11 where δικαιοσύνης has the same emphatic position qualifying the whole phrase. For the expression see 1 Cor. ii. 8 οὐκ ἂν τὸν κύριον τῆς δόξης ἐσταύρωσαν, and comp. John i. 14 ἐθεασάμεθα τὴν δόξαν αὐτοῦ, δόξαν ὡς μονογενοῦς παρὰ Πατρός. See also John ii. 11, xvii. 5, 22, 24. In the LXX. δόξα is used of the Shekinah or glorious manifestation of Jehovah in the tabernacle, e.g. καὶ δόξης Κυρίου ἐπλήσθη ἡ σκηνή, Ex. xl. 35—a signification closely connected with the use of the word by St John: see Bp Westcott on John i. 14 and comp. Book of Enoch, ch. xli., 'my eyes beheld all the sinners who denied the Lord of glory.' The construction of τῆς δόξης with πίστιν, which is possibly suggested by the marginal reading in W. H., has the support of some interpreters, who render: (*a*) belief in the glory of the Lord Jesus or (*b*) faith proceeding from the Lord Jesus in the glory (about to be revealed). The expression however of πίστις Ἰησ. Χρ. varied sometimes by the construction of εἰς or ἐν is so usual (see Rom. iii. 22; Gal. ii. 16; Col. ii. 5) that it is natural to take these words together and to regard τῆς δόξης as added with special reference to the subject under discussion.

**2. ἐὰν γὰρ εἰσέλθῃ.** ἐάν is virtually equivalent to ὅταν. The supposed case is presented vividly and distinctly, Goodwin, p. 102.

**εἰς συναγωγὴν ὑμῶν, into a synagogue** (or assembly) **of yours.** It is natural to suppose that the first Christians would take the name of Synagogue to designate their place of assembly for worship interchangeably with ἐκκλησία, which afterwards came to be the prevalent expression. It is at any rate clear that the συναγωγή here mentioned is a Christian and not a Jewish place of assembly. It is used in a distinctively Christian sense in Herm. *Past.* M. xi. 9 συναγωγὴν ἀνδρῶν δικαίων, and Epiphanius says of the Ebionites, συναγωγὴν οὗτοι καλοῦσι τὴν ἑαυτῶν ἐκκλησίαν, Lightfoot, *Phil.* p. 190. Like any other synagogue among the Jews its doors would be open to any Jew or proselyte who chose to enter. And from what St James says it appears to have been a grave spiritual danger and temptation for the poor Christian communities of the Dispersion to welcome with special honour a wealthy unconverted Jew who may have been prompted by curiosity or sympathy to enter their assembly. See Lightfoot, *Phil. loc. cit.* and Hort's *Judaistic Christianity*, p. 150.

**χρυσοδακτύλιος, wearing a gold ring or rings.** As luxury advanced the wearing of rings became increasingly the fashion. Rings were worn on all except the middle finger (Plin. *H. N.* xxxiii. 6). See Wetstein, who quotes Lucian, *Nigrin.* 21 οἱ πλουτοῦντες αὐτοὶ καὶ τὰς πορφυρίδας προφαίνοντες καὶ τοὺς δακτυλίους προτείνοντες; Aelian, *V. H.* III. 9, δακτυλίους πολλοὺς φέρων ἐκαλλύνετο ἐπὶ τούτῳ; Seneca, *N. Q.* VII. 31, Exornamus annulis digitos et in omni articulo gemma disponitur; Mart. xi. 60, Senos Charinus omnibus digitis gerit nec nocte ponit annulos nec dum lavatur. Comp. also Juv. *Sat.* VII. 139, Ciceroni nemo ducentos | nunc dederit nummos nisi fulserit annulus ingens. Note the *ingens;* it would be seen at a glance. Rings were even hired to give the appearance of wealth: ideo conducta Paulus agebat | Sardonyche, Juv. *Sat.* VII. 143. G. F. Watts in his impressive picture, 'He had great possessions,' has rightly noted this indication of great wealth. According to Clemens Alex., who forbids luxury in Christians, a special exception is made for the ring which was considered necessary for the purpose of sealing, *Paed.* III. 11—57 f. This however is clearly distinct from the ostentatious use of rings referred to by St James.

**ἐν ἐσθῆτι λαμπρᾷ.** See Luke xxiii. 11; Acts x. 30.

**3. ἐπιβλέψητε.** ἐπί indicates an earnest, fixed look. The rich man at once attracts attention.

**σὺ κάθου ὧδε καλῶς. Sit thou here in a good place.** The classical phrase is ἐν καλῷ. Dr Field, *Otium Norv.*, quotes ἄγει μέ τις λαβὼν εἰς τὸ θέατρον, καθίσας ἐν καλῷ, Alciph. *Ep.* III. 20. Comp. Matt. xxiii. 6 φιλοῦσιν...τὰς πρωτοκαθεδρίας ἐν ταῖς συναγωγαῖς and Mark xii. 39; Luke xi. 43, xx. 46.

**κάθου.** See Veitch *sub voc.* κάθημαι. This form for the more classical κάθησο occurs in the Comic writers of the classical period and in late prose, as here and Ps. cx. 1 (cited Matt. xxii. 44 and elsewhere). The use of a popular and vernacular form not used in literature is a touch of reality.

ὑπὸ τὸ ὑποπόδιόν μου, the words are now placed in the mouth of one person, perhaps the ἀρχισυνάγωγος.

**4. οὐ διεκρίθητε.** For reading see critical notes. **Did ye not make a distinction among yourselves** (though you are ἀδελφοί), and thereby shewed yourselves to be judges whose reasonings are evil? διεκρίθητε though passive in form has here a middle or intransitive meaning. This appears from the two other passages in the N.T. where the same form occurs, Matt. xxi. 21; Mark xi. 23. Compare the prevailing N.T. form ἀπεκρίθη in place of the far rarer ἀπεκρίνατο, which last occurs four times only in the synoptic gospels, and three of these are in the parallel accounts of the Passion.

There is a tendency in later Greek to the disuse of middle forms. In Modern Greek the middle voice has ceased to exist. There are also instances in Hellenistic Greek of recurrence to original forms, and "the aorist stems in -η and -θη appear to have originally had an intransitive sense of which the passive sense was a growth or adaptation." Monro's *Hom. Gram.* § 44.

But apart from these arguments from the history of language the passive rendering fails here to give good sense.

**διαλογισμῶν πονηρῶν.** See on ἀκροατὴς ἐπιλησμονῆς i. 25. διαλογισμοί, reasonings, never in a good sense in N.T., διαλογισμοὶ πονηροί, Matt. xv. 19; οἱ διαλ. οἱ κακοί, Mark vii. 21. See also Rom. xiv. 1; Phil. ii. 14; 1 Tim. ii. 8.

**5—14.** The Royal Law of Love is infringed by the unjust and scornful treatment of the poor described in the preceding section, and thus the whole law is broken.

**5. ἀκούσατε** emphasizes the important reasoning which follows; comp. our Lord's frequent formula ὁ ἔχων ὦτα ἀκούειν ἀκουέτω.

**ἐξελέξατο.** Comp. 1 Cor. i. 26—28 βλέπετε γὰρ τὴν κλῆσιν ὑμῶν, ἀδελφοί, ὅτι οὐ πολλοὶ σοφοὶ κατὰ σάρκα, οὐ πολλοὶ δυνατοί, οὐ πολλοὶ εὐγενεῖς· ἀλλὰ τὰ μωρὰ τοῦ κόσμου ἐξελέξατο ὁ θεός, ἵνα καταισχύνῃ τοὺς σοφούς, καὶ τὰ ἀσθενῆ τοῦ κόσμου ἐξελέξατο ὁ θεός, ἵνα καταισχύνῃ τὰ ἰσχυρά· καὶ τὰ ἀγενῆ τοῦ κόσμου καὶ τὰ ἐξουθενημένα ἐξελέξατο ὁ θεός, κ.τ.λ. But the statement rests immediately on the first beatitude: Μακάριοι οἱ πτωχοί, ὅτι ὑμετέρα ἐστὶν ἡ βασιλεία τοῦ θεοῦ, Luke vi. 20. In Acts ii. 39 the Godward side of the thought is expressed: καὶ πᾶσι τοῖς εἰς μακρὰν ὅσους ἂν προσκαλέσηται Κύριος ὁ θεὸς ἡμῶν. Comp. also διὰ τοὺς ἐκλεκτοὺς οὓς ἐξελέξατο, Mar. xiii. 20, and ἐκλεκτοί frequently as those chosen out to do the work of Christ in the world. So St Paul is σκεῦος ἐκλογῆς, Acts ix. 15.

**τῷ κόσμῳ** (for the reading see critical notes), **in respect of the world,** in the world's regard. Comp. ἀστεῖος τῷ θεῷ, Acts vii. 20; δυνατὰ τῷ θεῷ, 2 Cor. x. 4; νικᾷν πᾶσι τοῖς κριταῖς, Aristoph. *Aves,* 445; θεοῖσιν οὗτοι κἀνδράσιν ῥιψάσπιδες, Aristoph. *Pax* 1186, 'in the judgment of.'

ἐμοὶ γὰρ ὅστις ἄδικος ὢν σοφὸς λέγειν | πέφυκε πλείστην ζημίαν ὀφλισκάνει,
Eur. *Med.* 580, Jelf 600, Winer, III. § xxxi. 4 *a*.

For κόσμος see on i. 27.

**πλουσίους ἐν πίστει**, i.e. not that their riches consist in faith, but
that faith is the sphere or region in which they are rich, in which
their riches lie, they are rich as being οἱ πιστεύοντες. In fact ἐν πίστει
qualifies πλουσίους much as τῷ κόσμῳ qualifies πτώχους. See Beyschlag *ad loc.* and Bp Westcott on Heb. xi. 2 ἐν ταύτῃ γὰρ ἐμαρτυρή-
θησαν οἱ πρεσβύτεροι. The expression is to be distinguished from
πλούσιος ὢν ἐν ἐλέει, Ephes. ii. 4, where the genitive would be required
in the classical idiom, as πλούσιος κακῶν, Eur. *Or.* 394.

**ἧς ἐπηγγείλατο.** The reference may be to an ἄγραφον or unrecorded
saying of the Lord's, possibly of the Risen Lord to St James himself.
But the words of the first beatitude cited above are the words of a
promise, see also Matt. xxv. 34. For the attraction of ἧς into the case
of the antecedent comp. Acts i. 1 περὶ πάντων ὧν ἤρξατο ὁ Ἰησοῦς ποιεῖν
τε καὶ διδάσκειν.

**6. ἠτιμάσατε.** The aorist points to the particular instance cited
by the Apostle. You dishonoured the poor man—deprived him of his
due τιμή or rank and dignity in the kingdom of heaven. The more
technical term in this sense is ἀτιμόω.

**οὐχ οἱ πλούσιοι** κ.τ.λ. Not only did you degrade those whom Christ
honoured, but you honoured those who have shewn themselves un-
worthy.

**καταδυναστεύουσιν ὑμῶν, lord it over you,** oppress you. See
Acts x. 38 τοὺς καταδυναστευομένους ὑπὸ τοῦ διαβόλου, the only other
passage where the word occurs in N.T., but comp. κατακυριεύειν, Matt.
xx. 25, Mark x. 42, Acts xix. 16, 1 Pet. v. 3, and κατεξουσιάζειν, Matt.
xx. 25, Mark x. 42.

The oppression of the poor by the unprincipled rich was an inveterate
evil among the Israelites denounced from first to last by the Prophets.
The widening breach between the Jews and Christians tended to
deepen this hostility. See Pss. x., xi. and cxl. 12, 13. See also Cheyne
on Isaiah, liii. 9.

**αὐτοί,** with its proper sense of contrast, 'they on their part' in contrast with you who place them in the best seats of the synagogue.

**ἕλκουσιν, drag with violence.** εἷλκον αὐτὸν ἔξω τοῦ ἱεροῦ, Acts xxi.
30. Comp. also Acts ix. 1 ὅπως ἐάν τινας εὕρῃ τῆς ὁδοῦ ὄντας, ἄνδρας τε
καὶ γυναῖκας, δεδεμένους ἀγάγῃ εἰς Ἱερουσαλήμ.

**εἰς κριτήρια.** See 1 Cor. vi. 2, 4; also Matt. x. 17, Acts ix. 2,
xxvi. 11. These were not heathen tribunals but Jewish courts which
were recognised and permitted under the Roman government.

**7. τὸ καλὸν ὄνομα.** Not the name of 'Christian,' as some have
thought, but the name of Jesus Christ into [or in] which they had
been baptized; see the first instance of baptism, Acts ii. 38, βαπτισθήτω
ἕκαστος ὑμῶν ἐν τῷ ὀνόματι Ἰησοῦ Χριστοῦ εἰς ἄφεσιν τῶν ἁμαρτιῶν ὑμῶν.

Usually εἰς τὸ ὄνομα, Matt. xxviii. 19; Acts viii. 16; 1 Cor. i. 15, and frequently.

The use of the word βλασφημεῖν implies the divine character of the name.

τὸ ἐπικληθὲν ἐφ' ὑμᾶς, **called** *or* **invoked upon you** at baptism. Comp. Jer. xiv. 9 καὶ τὸ ὄνομά σου ἐπικέκληται ἐφ' ἡμᾶς. See also Deut. xxviii. 10; 2 Chron. vi. 33, vii. 14; Amos ix. 12. These instances associate with the expression the thoughts of ownership and service. A freedman bore his master's name and soldiers that of their general, especially the bodyguard of an emperor, as Augustiani, Commodiani. To these may be added Sebastianus, a soldier in the bodyguard of Diocletian (Σέβαστος being the Greek equivalent of Augustus). So Christiani, soldiers of Christ the King.

**8.** μέντοι, rare in N.T.; 5 times in St John; also 2 Tim. ii. 19; Jude 8. It introduces a concession. **If however ye fulfil the royal law** (which you transgressed by dishonouring the poor through προσωπολημψία) **ye do well.**

νόμον...βασιλικόν. The position of βασιλικόν is emphatic, and distinguishes the law of Christ, the βασιλεύς, from the Mosaic law. Compare Plato, *Ep.* p. 1297 A εἰς βασιλέως δ' εἶδος πειρᾶσθαι μεταβάλλειν καὶ δουλεῦσαι νόμοις βασιλικοῖς, and 2 Macc. iii. 13 δι' ἃς εἶχε βασιλικὰς ἐντολάς, i.e. the laws or commands which a king makes and issues, the meaning here and not, as has been suggested, 'the law which even kings obey.' The expression does not occur elsewhere in the N.T., but it is natural that the thought of the βασιλεία, the kingdom, or, as it would mean to a contemporary, the empire of Christ, should be especially present with the Apostle, who was himself of the royal line of David. It is a phrase which bears upon it the stamp of an original writer summing up a leading point of Christian teaching, and not by any means one likely to have been invented by a late writer.

ἀγαπήσεις τὸν πλησίον σου ὡς σεαυτόν. See Levit. xix. 18, and Matt. xix. 19, and comp. Rom. xiii. 9 τὸ γὰρ οὐ μοιχεύσεις..., καὶ εἴ τις ἑτέρα ἐντολή, ἐν τῷ λόγῳ τούτῳ ἀνακεφαλαιοῦται, ἐν τῷ Ἀγαπήσεις τὸν πλησίον σου ὡς σεαυτόν κ.τ.λ.

καλῶς ποιεῖτε, ye do well, i.e. you are right, comp. Aristoph. *Plut.* 859 καλῶς τοίνυν ποιῶν ἀπόλλυται. So, "Di bene fecerunt inopis me quodque pusilli | finxerunt animi," Hor. *Sat.* I. 4. 17. See also Acts xv. 29 ἐξ ὧν διατηροῦντες ἑαυτοὺς εὖ πράξετε.

**9.** τοῦ νόμου. Here the law of Christ which makes no distinction between rich and poor.

**10.** Regarded as a whole law is the expression of the divine will; therefore infraction of the law in one particular is transgression of the divine will, and so a transgression of the whole law. The instances cited are cases of transgressing the Mosaic law, but the principle is of universal application. It is a different principle from that taught in the Rabbinical schools, according to which each particular act of obedience to each law has its assigned reward. The law was not

treated as a whole but as a series of separate enactments. "Whosoever fulfils only *one* law, good is appointed to him, his days are prolonged and he will inherit the land." Kiddushin i, 10, quoted by
Schürer, *Gesch. des jüd. Volkes*, II. § 28 (Eng. Trans. Div. II. Vol. II.
p. 92).

On the other hand Wetstein *ad loc.* quotes sayings agreeing with
St James' teaching, e.g. Si faciat omnia unum vero omittat omnium et
singulorum reus est, Sabbat. f. 70. 2; again R. Johanan dicit, omnis
qui dicit: Totam legem ego in me recipio praeter verbum unum, hic
sermonem Domini sprevit, et praecepta ejus irrita fecit. One false note
destroys the harmony, and a broken link destroys the chain. For our
Lord's word on this see Matt. v. 19.

ὅστις ... τηρήσῃ, πταίσῃ. In Classical Greek ὅστις ἄν would
be usual. The omission of ἄν however removes the indeterminate
character of the expression; it is conceived as an actual case. Comp.
Hom. *Od.* VIII. 523 f. ὡς δὲ γυνὴ κλαίῃσι φίλον πόσιν ἀμφιπεσοῦσα | ὅς
τε ἑῆς πρόσθεν πόλιος λαῶν τε πέσῃσιν, Soph. *Oed. Col.* 395, γέροντα
δ᾽ ὀρθοῦν φλαῦρον ὃς νέος πέσῃ, *Ant.* 1025, ἐπεὶ δ᾽ ἁμαρτῇ. So also in
prose Thuc. IV. 17, ἐπιχώριον ὂν ἡμῖν οὗ μὲν βραχεῖς ἀρκῶσι μὴ πολλοῖς
χρῆσθαι. See Campbell, *Soph.*, *Essay on Lang.* § 27 and Goodwin,
§ 62, n. 3.

πάντων ἔνοχος. Comp. ἔνοχος θανάτου, Matt. xxvi. 66; ἔνοχος τοῦ
σώματος καὶ τοῦ αἵματος τοῦ κυρίου, 1 Cor. xi. 27. ἔνοχος bound or held,
from ἐνέχεσθαι: πάντων is a genitive of cause. The construction
follows that of verbs of prosecuting and sentencing: (Μιλτιάδεα) οἱ
ἐχθροὶ ἐδίωξαν τυραννίδος τῆς ἐν Χερσονήσῳ, Hdt. VI. 104; οὐχ ἁλίσκεται
ψευδομαρτυριῶν, Arist. *Rhet.* I. 15. 17, Jelf § 501. See also Winer
(253) III. xxx. *d* who connects the construction with verbs of taking
hold of &c., where the Greek idiom requires a genitive, as: τὰ κρείσσονα
καὶ ἐχόμενα σωτηρίας, Hebr. vi. 9.

**11.** εἰ δὲ οὐ μοιχεύεις. This use of οὐ for μή in the protasis of a
conditional sentence is not infrequent in the N.T., especially when
there is an antithesis between a negative and affirmative sentence
as here. As Dr Moulton notes on Winer, p. 601, the expression is
equivalent to εἰ οὐ μοιχεύων ἔσῃ, φονεύων δέ. εἰ οὐ μοιχεύεις = 'if thou
art guiltless of adultery.' Comp. εἰ τοὺς θανόντας οὐκ ἐᾷς θάπτειν,
Soph. *Aj.* 1131; εἰ ἀποστῆναι ᾽Αθηναίων οὐκ ἠθελήσαμεν, Thuc. III. 55;
εἰ ἄλλοις οὐκ εἰμὶ ἀπόστολος ἀλλά γε ὑμῖν εἰμι, 1 Cor. ix. 2.

In Modern Greek ἐὰν δέν (the modern equivalent to οὐ) is the
regular idiom.

**12.** διὰ νόμου ἐλευθερίας μέλλοντες κρίνεσθαι. See note i. 25.

**13.** ἡ γὰρ κρίσις κ.τ.λ. The judgment implied by κρίνεσθαι διὰ νόμ.
ἐλευθ. is pitiless to him who shews no pity. But neglect of the poor,
or absence of ἔλεος, is implied in deference to the rich or προσωπολημψία. The law of liberty condemns such distinction. Therefore the
προσωπολήμπτης will find no mercy under that law the principle of
which is ἔλεος. But even divine compassion does not extend to him
who has no compassion on his fellow-creatures, the lesson of the

parable of the unmerciful servant, Matt. xviii. 23—35. ἔλεος the contrary principle rejoiceth over judgment because there is nothing for judgment to condemn, ἔλεος like ἀγάπη being the fulfilling of the law. ἐλεημοσύνη indeed. is nearly equivalent to δικαιοσύνη, see the various readings St Matt. vi. 1 and comp. Dan. iv. 27 τὰς ἁμαρτίας σου ἐν ἐλεημοσύναις (בְּצִדְקָה) λύτρωσαι καὶ τὰς ἀδικίας ἐν οἰκτιρμοῖς πενήτων. ἀνέλεος for the classical ἀνελεής or the more purely Attic form ἀνηλεής, in Homer νηλεής, see Lob. *Phryn.* 711. For the reading here see crit. notes.

**14—26. The relation between πίστις and ἔργα:**—a subject suggested by the preceding paragraph, but also probably by one of the questions referred to St James for solution. Such questions were frequently put to Rabbis as to our Lord (see Matt. xviii. 21, xix. 3, xxii. 17, 36). So St Paul decides the relations between πίστις, ἐλπίς and ἀγάπη 1 Cor. xiii., assigning the leading position to ἀγάπη which is closely akin to ἔλεος.

Probably as a reaction from justification by works of the law a fallacy had sprung up among the Jewish Christians that faith in Christ existing as an inactive principle, a mere speculative belief, would suffice without works. St James shews what an impossible position this is. ἔλεος is regarded as the practical result and test of πίστις as it is in Matt. xxv. 34—40, a passage probably in the Apostle's mind here. The works of which St James speaks are works of πίστις not of the Mosaic law. Such ἔργα Christ himself sets forth as required in the Christian life in the Sermon on the Mount and in such passages as Matt. vii. 20, ἀπὸ τῶν καρπῶν αὐτῶν ἐπιγνώσεσθε αὐτούς; Matt. xxvi. 10, γνοὺς δὲ ὁ Ἰησοῦς εἶπεν αὐτοῖς, Τί κόπους παρέχετε τῇ γυναικί; ἔργον γὰρ καλὸν ἠργάσατο εἰς ἐμέ, and others. It is noticeable also that when our Lord enjoins keeping of the commandments Matt. xix. 18—20 the instances of observances are taken from the second table only, comp. with this Rom. xiii. 8 ὁ γὰρ ἀγαπῶν τὸν ἕτερον νόμον πεπλήρωκεν. St James's teaching here is the teaching of Christ and of St Paul.

**15. ἀδελφὸς ἢ ἀδελφή,** a recurring reminder of the relationship of the disciples to one another.

**γυμνοὶ ὑπάρχωσιν κ.τ.λ.,** comp. Matt. xxv. 35, 36. In later Judaism the duty of almsgiving was vividly realised. This is one of the post-exile religious ideas which strongly influenced thought at this period. See Tobit iv. 8 ff. where the Hebr. text has: 'Every one who occupieth himself in alms shall behold the face of God, as it is written, I will behold thy face by almsgiving,' Ps. xvii. 15, almsgiving being as elsewhere substituted for righteousness. So *Khasidim*, the pious, are those who exercise *Khesed*, mercy.

St James's one injunction to St Paul when he recognised his mission to the Gentiles was 'to remember the poor': μόνον τῶν πτωχῶν ἵνα μνημονεύωμεν, Gal. ii. 9, and the Church over which he presided proved its first enthusiasm by acts of charity.

With the Stoics ἔλεος was reckoned among the defects or vices: it

was a disturbing element that broke in on the philosophic calm: ὁ
ἀπειθῶν τῇ θείᾳ διοικήσει ἔστω ταπεινός, ἔστω δοῦλος, λυπείσθω, φθονείτου,
ἐλείτω, Epict. Diss. III. 24. 43.  Comp. Virgil's picture of the happy
man; among his blessings is the absence of pity: neque ille | aut doluit
miserans inopem, Georg. II. 498.

τῆς ἐφημέρου τροφῆς, of the day's supply of food, as distinguished from τῆς καθ' ἡμέραν τροφῆς.  Field, Otium Norv., ἀπῆλθεν ἐκ
τῆς οἰκίας μόνος...ἄδουλος, ἄπορος, οὐδὲ τὴν ἐφήμερον ὁ δύστηνος ἐκ τῶν ἑαυτοῦ χρημάτων τροφὴν (ne unius quidem diei viaticum) ἐπαγόμενος, Dion.
Hal. Ant. VIII. 41 (Wetstein).

16.  χορτάζεσθε, from χόρτος, see note i. 11, and for the verb note
on Matt. v. 6 in this series.  First of cattle, 'to feed,' βοσκημάτων δίκην
...βόσκονται χορταζόμενοι, Plato, Rep. 586: then, as a coarse comic
word, of man, 'to eat.'  In later Greek χορτάζειν means to satisfy, so
frequently in synoptic gospels; elsewhere in N.T. only here and John
vi. 26; Phil. iv. 12; Rev. xix. 21.

17.  οὕτως καὶ ἡ πίστις κ.τ.λ.  The conclusion is drawn by analogy.
It is inconceivable that ἔλεος, pity, or compassion, can exist without
results, so is the conception of a faith without works an impossible one.
νεκρὰ καθ' ἑαυτήν, dead in itself, right through itself, thoroughly
dead, ineffective and non-existent.  Works are a condition and
evidence of life.  But these are very different from the works of the
law, minute observances each separately meritorious against which St
Paul's argument is directed.

18.  ἀλλ' ἐρεῖ τις.  The objector denoted by τις is virtually St James.
The ἀλλά is adversative to vv. 15, 16.  Shew me the faith without
works, i.e. Shew me a faith which is consistent with standing aloof
and bidding the hungry begone and feed himself and the naked clothe
himself.  Such faith is indeed a thing inconceivable.  But I will shew
you my faith as evidenced and proved by works of ἔλεος.

ἐκ τῶν ἔργων, as an inference or deduction from its works.

19.  The ineffectiveness of faith regarded as merely intellectual
assent is shewn by the example of belief in the unity of God, a belief
which even devils hold.

ὅτι εἷς ἐστὶν ὁ θεός, that God is one.  The central belief of Judaism,
Deut. vi. 4 ἄκουε, Ἰσραήλ, Κύριος ὁ θεὸς ἡμῶν Κύριος εἷς ἐστιν, the fundamental principle of faith.  For reading see crit. notes.

καλῶς ποιεῖς, thou art right.  See above, v. 8.

τὰ δαιμόνια, the evil spirits who by their submission to the word of
Christ recognised the One true God.  δαιμόνιον is the neuter of the
adj. δαιμόνιος and means literally that which proceeds from a δαίμων
or god.  εἰ μή τι δαιμόνιον εἴη, 'unless there were some hindrance
from the gods,' Xen. Mem. I. 3. 5.  So Demosthenes, Phil. III. § 54,
speaks of the divine power or force which seems to be hurrying on the
Hellenic race to destruction: ἐπελήλυθε καὶ τοῦτο φοβεῖσθαι μή τι δαιμόνιον τὰ πράγματα ἐλαύνῃ.  The δαιμόνιον of Socrates is the divine

warning voice which apart from his own reasoning faculties checked him from entering on dangerous enterprises. See Xen. *Mem.* I. 1. 2. It is defined Plut. *Symp.* 202 D πᾶν τὸ δαιμόνιον μεταξύ ἐστι θεοῦ τε καὶ θνητοῦ...ἑρμηνεῦον καὶ διαπορθμεῦον θεοῖς τὰ παρ' ἀνθρώπων καὶ ἀνθρώποις τὰ παρὰ θεῶν. Hence δαιμόνια are deities of an inferior order. One of the accusations against Socrates is, καινὰ δαιμόνια εἰσφέρειν, Xen. *Mem.* I. 1. 2, comp. Acts xvii. 18 ξένων δαιμονίων δοκεῖ καταγγελεὺς εἶναι. In the LXX. δαιμόνια is used to designate the false gods of the surrounding nations : Deut. xxxii. 17 ἔθυσαν δαιμονίοις καὶ οὐ θεῷ, a sense attributed by some to the word in this passage; but certainly not on good grounds, for how could faith in the true God be predicated of them?

In N.T. language τὸ δαιμόνιον is the unseen evil force or influence (comp. δαιμονίη ὁρμή, Hdt. VII. 18) which, gaining possession of a man, like a separate personality, impelled him to evil and afflicted him with disease. See note on S. Matt. ix. 33.

φρίσσουσιν. ἅπ. λεγ. in N.T.; properly to be rough, to bristle, then to shudder with fear: in Plutarch especially of awe in the presence of a god.
A faith which involves 'shuddering fear' is widely removed from the justifying faith of St Paul which brings peace, Rom. v. 1, and which is closely allied with that perfect love which casts out all fear, 1 John iv. 18.

**20.  ὦ ἄνθρωπε κενέ.** A comparison with Matt. v. 22 will shew that the first generation of Christians did not observe obedience to the letter, ῥακά in that passage being probably literally equivalent to κενέ here.

ὅτι ἡ πίστις χωρὶς τῶν ἔργων ἀργή ἐστιν. On the surface a verbal argument; for ἀργή (ἀ and ἔργον) is synonymous with χωρὶς τῶν ἔργων. But ἀργή carries with it a moral stigma, πᾶν ῥῆμα ἀργόν (where πονηρόν is a variant), Matt. xii. 36; οὐκ ἀργοὺς οὐδὲ ἀκάρπους, 2 Pet. i. 8.
The argument is this: the ἄνθρωπος κενός might appeal to the faith of Abraham as an example of faith without works, faith purely and simply in the One true God. St James shews that even then justification was a result not of an inactive belief but of works in which faith was manifested, and which implies a great deal more than an intellectual assent to a proposition. It implies that grasp of unseen realities and that instinctive love and trust in God which go to form the conception of faith in the Epistle to the Hebrews, the leading and inspiring characteristic of the heroes of Israel.

**21.  ἐδικαιώθη.** The strict meaning of δικαιοῦν is to make δίκαιος, so to justify or acquit. The further meaning 'to regard as righteous' is not etymologically justifiable and rests on supposed theological necessity. But the theology of this Epistle and indeed of the N.T. generally points to the possibility of τελειότης by an exact conformity to God's will such as Abraham exhibited.

ἀνενέγκας, comp. Gen. xxii. 9 ᾠκοδόμησεν ἐκεῖ Ἀβραὰμ τὸ θυσιαστήριον,
xxii. 13 ἀνήνεγκεν εἰς ὁλοκάρπωσιν ἀντὶ Ἰσαάκ, and so frequently of the
sacrifices of the old covenant.  In N.T. of the sacrifice of Christ:
τοῦτο γὰρ ἐποίησεν ἐφάπαξ ἑαυτὸν ἀνενέγκας (al. προσενέγκας), Heb. vii.
27 ; ἁμαρτίας ἡμῶν αὐτὸς ἀνήνεγκεν, 1 Pet. ii. 24 : of spiritual sacrifices,
ἀνενέγκαι πνευματικὰς θυσίας εὐπροσδέκτους θεῷ διὰ Ἰησοῦ Χριστοῦ, 1
Pet. ii. 5.  In liturgical language the ἀναφορά in the Eastern Church,
answering to the Canon of the Western Church, signified the second
portion of the Eucharistic service in which the consecration of the
Elements and the Communion are included.

θυσιαστήριον, the altar of Jehovah is carefully distinguished from
βωμός an altar of false gods both in LXX. and in N.T. where
βωμός occurs once only, Acts xvii. 23 βωμὸν ἐν ᾧ ἐπεγέγραπτο ἀγνώστῳ
θεῷ.

22.  ἡ πίστις συνήργει, faith was all along cooperating with.  The
works were an exercise of faith, and the result of them was perfection
of faith.  So Gideon was stronger in faith after the exercise of his
faith.  For the principle comp. the Aristotelian doctrine, ἐκ τῶν
ὁμοίων ἐνεργειῶν αἱ ἕξεις γίγνονται, Eth. Nic. II. i. 7.

23.  ἐπίστευσεν δὲ Ἀβραὰμ κ.τ.λ.  The quotation is from the LXX.
of Gen. xv. 6.  The example of Abraham's faith is cited Eccl. xliv. 20,
21 and 1 Macc. ii. 52 and in N.T. Rom. iv. 3, 9, 22 ; Gal. iii. 6.  The
prominence given to this illustration is another instance of the influence of post-exile thought in the N.T.  The faith of Abraham
became a leading topic with Philo and the Alexandrian school as well
as with Rabbinical writers at the Christian era.  See Bp Lightfoot,
Galatians, p. 156 f.

ἐλογίσθη αὐτῷ εἰς δικαιοσύνην, was reckoned or counted to him for
righteousness.  That is according to divine reckoning Abraham's
faith was righteousness.  There is no need to seek any other meaning
in the words than their exact and literal sense.  St Paul quotes the
words (Rom. iv. 3, 9, 22 ; Gal. iii. 6) to prove justification by faith,
St James quotes them to prove justification by works which spring
from faith and are inseparably connected with it.

εἰς δικαιοσύνην.  In some instances of this use of εἰς in the N.T. it
can be illustrated from the classics (Winer III. p. 229, xxix. a).  In
others where it is more clearly influenced by the Hebrew idiom with
ל εἰς still retains its proper sense denoting aim or result or the state
into which a thing passes; comp. the German machen zu.  Instances
are ἔσονται οἱ δύο εἰς σάρκα μίαν, Matt. xix. 5; αἱ γλῶσσαι εἰς σημεῖόν
εἰσιν, 1 Cor. xiv. 22; ἡ ἀκροβυστία αὐτοῦ εἰς περιτομὴν λογισθήσεται,
Rom. ii. 26.  See Green's Grammar, p. 212.

φίλος θεοῦ ἐκλήθη.  The precise expression is not found in the
LXX.; but comp. Is. xli. 8 σπέρμα Ἀβραὰμ ὃν ἠγάπησα, semen Abra-
ham amici mei, V., and 2 Chron. xx. 7 Ἀβραὰμ τῷ ἠγαπημένῳ σου:
Hebr. אֹהֲבִי : 'thy friend,' R.V.

ἐκλήθη. καλεῖσθαι is not merely equivalent to the substantive verb, but implies (1) prestige, as ὁ πᾶσι κλεινὸς Οἰδίπους καλούμενος, Soph. *Oed. R.* 8; (2) permanence in a class, τάδε γὰρ ἄλυτα κεκλήσεται, Soph. *El.* 230. See Jebb on the last passage and Ellendt's Lex. *sub voc.*; (3) recognition by others, comp. Luke i. 76; Rom. ix. 26.

**24. ὁρᾶτε.** Note the change to the plural from πιστεύεις...βλέπεις ...θέλεις. The conclusion is addressed to the brethren, no longer to the ἄνθρωπος κενός.

**25. 'Ραὰβ ἡ πόρνη.** See Heb. xi. 31.

ὑποδεξαμένη, having *secretly* (ὑπό) received them as guests. In Hebrews the simple verb δεξαμένη is used.

ἐκβαλοῦσα expresses energetic action, eagerness and impatience in sending them at once. See Matt. ix. 38 ὅπως ἐκβάλῃ ἐργάτας εἰς τὸν θερισμὸν αὐτοῦ. Mark i. 12 καὶ εὐθὺς τὸ πνεῦμα αὐτὸν ἐκβάλλει εἰς τὴν ἔρημον, xi. 15 ἤρξατο ἐκβάλλειν τοὺς πωλοῦντας κ.τ.λ.

**26. ὥσπερ τὸ σῶμα χωρὶς πνεύματος** κ.τ.λ. The illustration is important. The union of faith and works is as close as the union of body and spirit. In each case the union is that which we call life. Separation of the two elements means death. Body (σῶμα) and spirit (πνεῦμα) is an exhaustive division of the human individual. Sometimes indeed man is regarded as consisting of spirit, soul (ψυχή) and body, as 1 Thess. v. 23. But in this passage and elsewhere as Rom. viii. 9 ff., where body or flesh (σάρξ) and spirit are spoken of as alone constituting the human entity, ψυχή is included in πνεῦμα, which is divinely infused life in its highest manifestation by virtue of which man became a living soul: καὶ ἐνεφύσησεν εἰς τὸ πρόσωπον αὐτοῦ πνοὴν ζωῆς· καὶ ἐγένετο ὁ ἄνθρωπος εἰς ψυχὴν ζῶσαν, Gen. ii. 7. Comp. πᾶσα σὰρξ ἐν ᾗ ἐστὶν πνεῦμα ζωῆς, Gen. vi. 17. The ψυχή though including all lower forms of life is in its perfect state one with πνεῦμα. Bodily life and spiritual life are made of one high principle of life. See Delitzsch, *System of Biblical Psychology*, p. 231 f. (Eng. Trans.). Life consists in movement and energy; but these under present conditions are impossible without σῶμα. So faith is inconceivable without works, and works without faith.

## CHAPTER III.

**3. εἰ δὲ** with אABC (ἴδε) KL and many others, also O.L. and Vulgate (si autem). ἰδού is read in a few cursives and has the authority of several versions.

**5. μεγάλα αὐχεῖ** with ABC*P; μεγαλαυχεῖ in אC²KL and later MSS. ἡλίκον, for ὀλίγον of T.R., with אA²BCP; ὀλίγον, a change to an easier reading, has a good deal of later support, A*ᵛⁱᵈC²KL &c.

**6. καὶ ἡ γλῶσσα:** so אᶜABCKLP &c. Tischendorf omits καὶ on the authority of א*, and on the same unsupported authority reads καὶ σπιλοῦσα for ἡ σπιλοῦσα below.

**8.** ἀκατάστατον with אABP, Old Latin and Vulgate &c. ἀκατάσχε-τον of the T.R. is read in CKL and many later MSS.

**9.** κύριον with אABCP, Old Latin and other versions; KL and a majority of later authorities have θεόν. But it is more probable that θεὸν should have been substituted for κύριον, than that the reverse should have happened.

**12.** οὔτε ἁλυκὸν γλυκὺ ποιῆσαι ὕδωρ with א (οὐδεὲ) ABD, Old Latin and Vulgate. The T.R. has the support of KLP and later MS. authority and some versions in reading οὐδεμία πηγὴ ἁλυκὸν καὶ γλυκὺ ποιῆσαι ὕδωρ. The reading in the text is an instance of the rule that a reading is to be preferred out of which all the rest may have been derived, although it could not have been derived from any of them.

**17.** The insertion of καὶ in T. R. before ἀνυπόκριτος is against the best authority.

---

**1.** A FURTHER TEMPTATION OR SPIRITUAL DANGER CONNECTED WITH THE SYNAGOGUE IS AMBITION FOR THE OFFICE OF TEACHER OR RABBI.

**2—12.** FROM THIS THOUGHT OF THE TEACHING OFFICE AND ITS RESPONSIBILITIES AND FAILURES THERE IS A NATURAL TRANSITION TO THE USE AND GOVERNMENT OF THE TONGUE. Yet so passionate and agitated is the rebuke, that we may imagine it to have been occasioned by an actual experience of gross slander or grievous inconsistency of conduct.

**13—18.** BUT BESIDES THE EFFECT AND DANGERS OF SPEECH, THE TOPIC OF TEACHING SUGGESTS ANOTHER POINT—THE POSSESSION AND USE OF WISDOM. HENCE THE DISTINCTION BETWEEN THE TRUE WISDOM AND THE FALSE WISDOM.

**1.** Two results are noted from the intemperate or unconsidered use of language: (1) The swiftness with which the evil spreads from an insignificant beginning. (2) The vast influence of words, which have large issues. A chance word which gives pain or which stimulates may influence a life. The thought of the irretrievable character of the word once spoken comes out in the Homeric phrase ποῖόν σε ἔπος φύγεν ἔρκος ὀδόντων *Il.* IV. 350 and frequently. Comp. Virgil's account of *fama*—a thing spoken.

μὴ πολλοὶ διδάσκαλοι γίνεσθε, **do not become many** (of you), do not put yourselves under instruction with the view of being, **teachers** or *Rabbis.* The temptation to become a διδάσκαλος was great; for to no other class of the community were higher honours paid. "To speak with the teacher, to invite him to be the guest, to marry his daughter, Israel was taught to consider the highest honour. The young men were expected to count it their glory to carry the Rabbi's burdens, to bring his water, to load his ass." Hausrath, *N. T. Times* I. 105, Eng. Trans. Rabbi ben Joezer said: "Let thine house be a meeting-house for the wise; and powder thyself in the dust of their feet, and drink their words with thirstiness." Pirke Aboth, I. 4, quoted by Hausrath.

In these circumstances to become a Rabbi was the ambition of every Israelite of leisure and ability. Even married men and those advanced in life became disciples in the synagogue schools, in order to obtain this dignity. Our Lord foresaw this danger for the Christian Church which St James denounces, Matt. xxiii. 5—8. Note especially *v.* 8 εἷς γάρ ἐστιν ὑμῶν ὁ διδάσκαλος, πάντες δὲ ὑμεῖς ἀδελφοί ἐστε, a word which St James seems to recall here by the introduction of ἀδελφοί μου.

We learn from Acts xiii. 1, 1 Cor. xii. 28 and Eph. iv. 11 that the office of διδάσκαλος was recognised in the Christian Church or synagogue.

**μεῖζον κρίμα, a severer judgment,** a keener censure, than those who are not teachers. See Mark xii. 40 and Luke xx. 47, οὗτοι λήμψονται περισσότερον κρίμα, the context of which brings it into close connexion with this passage.

κρίμα is in itself a neutral word—a judgment or decision which may be either of acquittal or condemnation, ὧν τὸ κρίμα ἔνδικόν ἐστιν, Rom. iii. 8, whose judgment or verdict, here of condemnation, is just. οἱ δὲ ἀνθεστηκότες ἑαυτοῖς κρίμα λήμψονται, Rom. xiii. 2, sentence of condemnation human and divine. ὁ γὰρ ἐσθίων καὶ πίνων κρίμα ἑαυτῷ ἐσθίει καὶ πίνει μὴ διακρίνων τὸ σῶμα, 1 Cor. xi. 29, where the context, especially *v.* 32, shews that 'damnation' or even 'condemnation' is too strong a word. κρίμα is here a divine judgment that disciplines and corrects in this world.

As regards the accent the only authority for κρῖμα is the length of the first syllable in a single passage, Aesch. *Supp.* 397. κρίμα is rightly preferred. See Dr Vaughan on Romans ii. 2 and Dr Moulton's note, Winer p. 57 (II. vi. 2).

λημψόμεθα, the use of the 1st person plural implies the authority of St James as himself a διδάσκαλος.

**2. πολλά,** in many ways apart from speech.

εἴ τις ἐν λόγῳ οὐ πταίει. Comp. γλώσσῃ σὺ δεινός· ἄνδρα δ᾽ οὐδέν᾽ εἶδ᾽ ἐγὼ | δίκαιον ὅστις ἐξ ἅπαντος εὖ λέγει. | KP. χωρὶς τό τ᾽ εἰπεῖν πολλὰ καὶ τὰ καίρια, Soph. *Oed. Col.* 806—808; si volumus aequi omnium rerum judices esse...hoc primum nobis suadeamus neminem nostrum esse sine culpa, Seneca *de Ira* LI. 27; ἄνθρωπος οὐκ ἔστι δίκαιος ἐν τῇ γῇ ὃς ποιήσει ἀγαθὸν καὶ οὐχ ἁμαρτήσεται, Eccles. vii. 20.

For the use of οὐ after εἰ, see note ii. 11.

**τέλειος,** see note i. 4. The respect in which he is τέλειος is defined by the following clause δυνατός—σῶμα. Control over the tongue implies perfect control over the whole body.

For χαλιναγωγῆσαι, see i. 26. The word suggests the illustration which follows.

**3. εἰ δὲ τῶν ἵππων** κ.τ.λ. A man's tongue or speech is regarded as a force distinct from himself, just as his body is. If he can bring his tongue under control, he can bring his body under control; just as one who controls the horse's mouth or the ship's helm guides the whole horse or ship. τὸ σῶμα, the body, including its members, forces and affections. Comp. Rom. vi. 12 μὴ οὖν βασιλευέτω ἡ ἁμαρτία ἐν τῷ θνητῷ ὑμῶν σώματι εἰς τὸ ὑπακούειν ταῖς ἐπιθυμίαις αὐτοῦ κ.τ.λ. See also Rom. vii. 23; 1 Cor. ix. 27.

**τῶν ἵππων** depends directly on τὰ στόματα not on τοὺς χαλινούς. **If we put their bits into horses' mouths** &c. καὶ marks the apodosis. For the thought comp. Soph. *Ant.* 483 σμικρῷ χαλινῷ δ' οἶδα τοὺς θυμουμένους | ἵππους καταρτυθέντας.

**μετάγομεν,** drive or lead in different directions, μετά implies change of place.

**4. ἰδού,** in later Greek little more than a vivid particle of transition.

**ὑπό,** generally used of personal agency: ch. i. 14 is hardly an exception to this. Comp. 1 Cor. vi. 12 ἀλλ' οὐκ ἐγὼ ἐξουσιασθήσομαι ὑπό τινος. Col. ii. 18 εἰκῇ φυσιούμενος ὑπὸ τοῦ νοὸς τῆς σαρκὸς αὐτοῦ.

**μετάγεται.** Singular according to the rule where the subject is regarded as a class: contrast with this ch. ii. 19 τὰ δαιμόνια πιστεύουσιν καὶ φρίσσουσιν, where τὰ δαιμόνια are regarded as separate personal agencies.

**ὁρμή,** *voluntas* O.L., *impetus dirigentis* V., **impulse,** will, desire of the steersman. In N.T. only here and Acts xiv. 5, where it probably bears the same meaning: see Page on that passage.

**5. μεγάλα αὐχεῖ, boasteth great things.** There is no thought of an unfounded boast. The achievements on which the tongue prides itself are real achievements.

**ἰδοὺ ἡλίκον πῦρ** κ.τ.λ.: a third similitude. The tongue is like a spark that sets on fire a mighty forest.

**ἡλίκον, how small.** Like *quantulus* in Latin, ἡλίκος has both meanings, 'how great,' 'how small.' The *var. lect.* ὀλίγον points to the latter signification here. Alford compares Lucian, *Hermot.* 5 παπαῖ, ὦ 'Ερμότιμε, ἡλίκους ἡμᾶς ἀποφαίνεις, οὐδὲ κατὰ τοὺς πυγμαίους ἐκείνους, ἀλλὰ χαμαιπετεῖς παντάπασιν ἐν χρῷ τῆς γῆς.

**ἡλίκην ὕλην ἀνάπτει,** *in quam magna silva incendium fecit,* O.L., *quam magnam silvam incendit* V.; 'how great a matter' A.V.; 'how much wood' R.V.; 'how great a forest' R.V. *marg.* The A.V. rendering 'matter,' i.e., a mass of materials, timber, firewood, etc., is a frequent and classical meaning of ὕλη from Homer downwards: *Od.* v. 257 πολλὴν δ' ἐπεχεύατο ὕλην (shipbuilding material), so ὕλη ναυπηγησίμη Plato *Legg.* 705 c. But the prevailing use of the word in the sense of forest, and the aptness and frequency of the illustration, are in favour of that interpretation here: comp. *Il.* xi. 155 f. ὡς δ' ὅτε πῦρ ἀΐδηλον ἐν ἀξύλῳ ἐμπέσῃ ὕλῃ· | πάντῃ τ' εἰλυφόων ἄνεμος φέρει, οἱ δέ τε θάμνοι | πρόρριζοι πίπτουσιν ἐπειγόμενοι πυρὸς ὁρμῇ. Pind. *Pyth.* iii. 36 πολλὰν δ' ὄρει πῦρ ἐξ ἑνὸς | σπέρματος ἐνθορὸν ἀΐστωσεν ὕλαν. Plut. *Symp.* viii. p. 730 E τὸ πῦρ τὴν ὕλην ἐξ ἧς ἀνήφθη μητέρα καὶ πατέρα οὖσαν ἤσθιε. Ps. lxxxii. (LXX.) 14 ὡσεὶ πῦρ ὃ διαφλέξει δρυμόν, ὡσεὶ φλὸξ κατακαύσαι ὄρη. See

also Virg. *Georg.* II. 303, *Aen.* II. 304, x. 405, XII. 521. The passage
in the Georgic indicates the hidden, unnoticed beginning; in *Aen.* II.
the terror; in x. the swift progress; in II. and XII. the violence and
destructive fury. Comp. also Lucr. v. 1243 f. ignis ubi ingentes
silvas ardore cremarat...quacunque e causa flammeus ardor | horribili
sonitu silvas exederat altis | ab radicibus et terram percoxerat igni.

6. **καὶ ἡ γλῶσσα πῦρ.** For the general sense of the difficult passage
which follows, comp. Prov. xvi. 24—30, especially the expressions:
ἐπὶ δὲ τῶν ἑαυτοῦ χειλέων θησαυρίζει πῦρ, v. 27; λαμπτῆρα δόλου πυρσεύσει
κακοῖς (not in Hebr.), v. 28; κάμινός ἐστι κακίας (not in Hebr.), v. 30:
and Ecclus. xxviii. 10—26, especially ψίθυρον καὶ δίγλωσσον καταράσασθε,
πολλοὺς γὰρ εἰρηνεύοντας ἀπώλεσαν. γλῶσσα τρητὴ πολλοὺς ἐσάλευσε καὶ
διέστησεν αὐτοὺς ἀπὸ ἔθνους εἰς ἔθνος, καὶ πόλεις ὀχυρὰς καθεῖλε, καὶ οἰκίας
μεγιστάνων κατέστρεψε, vv. 13, 14.

A consideration of the structure of the sentence, the poetical form
in which the thoughts are cast, also throws light on the meaning.
From this it appears that the first thought is resumed and expounded
in the last two lines, while the centre doublet contains a parallelism
in itself. The effect is that of an underground flame concealed for a
while, then breaking out afresh. Thus φλογίζουσα and φλογιζομένη
refer to πῦρ, and σπιλοῦσα to κόσμος, though grammatically these
participles are in agreement with γλῶσσα. A somewhat similar relation
between the beginning and end of a clause may be noted in ch. ii.
5 ἀγαπητοὶ...τοῖς ἀγαπῶσιν αὐτόν. The subjoined arrangement of the
words may assist the reader:

καὶ ἡ γλῶσσα πῦρ,
ὁ κόσμος τῆς ἀδικίας, ἡ γλῶσσα καθίσταται ἐν τοῖς μέλεσιν ἡμῶν,
ἡ σπιλοῦσα ὅλον τὸ σῶμα
καὶ φλογίζουσα τὸν τροχὸν τῆς γενέσεως
καὶ φλογιζομένη ὑπὸ τῆς γεέννης.

**ὁ κόσμος τῆς ἀδικίας,** *universitas iniquitatis* V., i.e. the sum
total of iniquity. 'The world of iniquity' R.V., 'that world...' R.V.
*marg.* This rendering, adopted by most editors ancient and modern,
is open to question, (a) from the abruptness and difficulty of the
expression itself, (b) from its want of relation to what follows, (c) from
the presence of the article, (d) from the want of N.T. parallels for this
signification. In the O.T., Prov. xvii. 6 is cited as the only instance:
τοῦ πιστοῦ ὅλος ὁ κόσμος χρημάτων. The expression occurs in the LXX.
only, not in the Hebr. It is true that as Beyschlag remarks κόσμος is
used to translate צָבָא; but in these passages it refers to the *order* of
the heavenly host, not to the number or mass of it.

But ὁ κόσμος τῆς ἀδικίας may also be rendered 'the adornment' or 'em-
bellishment' of iniquity,' that which gives it its fair outward show and
yet conceals its inner foulness, the tongue or speech "robed to allure and
fanged to rend and slay" (W. Watson). Comp. "Vice no longer made
repulsive by grossness, but toned down by superficial refinements and
decked in the tinsel of false chivalry." Bp Stubbs, *Const. Hist.* II.
336. In favour of this rendering it may be urged (a) that it offers no

strain on the sense of this passage, but falls in naturally with the
context: (b) that it is the prevailing meaning of κόσμος in the O.T.
and is so used in 1 Pet. iii. 3, ὁ ἔξωθεν ἐμπλοκῆς τριχῶν καὶ περιθέσεως
χρυσίων ἢ ἐνδύσεως ἱματίων κόσμος: (c) that the guile and deceitfulness
of the tongue, though the most obvious and dangerous evils of speech,
if not included in this expression would be absent from St James'
description. This is indeed the predominant meaning of 'to gloze'
and 'gloss,' words directly derived from γλῶσσα: "glozing the evil
that is in the world" Jer. Taylor: "so glozed the tempter" Milton:
"lay these glozes by" Shakspere: "a false glozing paradise" South.
Comp. with this Eur. Troad. 981 μὴ ἀμαθεῖς ποίει θεὰς | τὸ σὸν κακὸν
κοσμοῦσα: Med. 576 εὖ μὲν τούσδ᾽ ἐκόσμησας λόγους: Ion 834 οἱ συντι-
θέντες τἄδικ᾽ εἶτα κοσμοῦσι | κοσμοῦσι. See also Cramer's Catena ad loc.
ὡσανεὶ ἔλεγεν, ὁ τῆς εὐγλωττίας πυρσός, ὅταν τοὺς μεγάλα πταίοντας
κοσμεῖ, ἐγκαλλώπισμα δοκεῖ τῆς ἀδικίας. χρὴ τοιγαροῦν τῇ δεινότητι
κεχρῆσθαι, οὐ πρὸς τὸ τὴν ἀδικίαν κοσμεῖν ἀλλὰ πρὸς τὸ τὴν ἀρετὴν σεμνύειν,
τὴν καὶ χωρὶς λόγων ὑπέρλαμπρον. Comp. also 1 Thess. ii. 5 οὔτε γάρ
ποτε ἐν λόγῳ κολακίας ἐγενήθημεν, καθὼς οἴδατε, οὔτε προφάσει πλεονεξίας,
and in Latin: Aen. IV. 172 conjugium vocat, hoc praetexit nomine
culpam; Ov. Met. VII. 69 speciosaque nomina culpae | imponis. Comp.
also Pss. v. 9 (with this Matt. xxiii. 29), xii. 2, xxviii. 3, lxii. 4; Is. v.
20; Jer. ix. 8. The sentence thus interpreted might have been written ἡ γλῶσσα...κοσμοῦσα τὴν ἀδικίαν καὶ σπιλοῦσα ὅλον τὸ σῶμα. The
evil tongue adorns and embellishes iniquity and yet it defiles and
stains the whole body or personality of a man.

σπιλοῦν from the post-classical σπίλος, a stain, for which the classical word is κηλίς: Lob. Phryn. 28.

With φλογίζουσα there is a return to the metaphor of πῦρ. φλογίζουσα is ἅπ. λεγ. in N.T.

τὸν τροχὸν τῆς γενέσεως, rotam nativitatis V. τροχός, a wheel, is
to be distinguished from τρόχος, a course. Comp. ἐκ τρόχων πεπαυμένοι
Eur. Med. 46, and σύριγγες τ᾽ ἄνω τροχῶν ἐπήδων, Eur. Hipp. 1235.
Here τὸν τροχὸν τῆς γενέσεως is the wheel or revolution of a man's life
to which he was destined from his γένεσις, that for which he was
created in the image of God, the natural life in the highest sense,
comp. Tennyson's "I was born to other things," In Mem. cxx. Or, in
a wider sense, the world's divinely appointed course. This ordered
life of the individual or of society the tongue has often set aflame by
speech that curses (see below v. 9) or stirs passion or suggests evil or
creates slander and suspicion. On such words and their results,
tragedies like Othello and Romola are founded. The metaphor suggests fierce and violent disturbance and ruin, φλόξ being often used of
fire in its destructive aspect: Ζηνὸς ἄγρυπνον βέλος | καταιβάτης κεραυνὸς
ἐκπνέων φλόγα, Aesch. P. V. 359: ναυσὶν ἐμβαλεῖν φλόγα, Eur. Rh.
120: τὰν φόνιον ἔχετε φλόγα, Eur. Troad. 1318.

For this sense of τροχὸς comp. τροχὸς ἅρματος γὰρ οἷα βίοτος τρέχει
κυλισθεὶς Anacreon, IV. 7.

Some have seen in this passage a reference to the astrological
use of γένεσις. Comp. Lat. 'nativitas' and Eng. 'nativity' in such

expressions as 'to cast a man's nativity'—his destined life. The
Clementine Homilies shew how prevalent such thoughts were in early
times.

**φλογιζομένη ὑπὸ τῆς γεέννης.** Gehenna, valley of Hinnom, or of
the sons of Hinnom, a valley to the south of Jerusalem, where in the
days of Ahaz children were made to pass through fire to Moloch.
Hence in after times accursed and regarded as the earthly type of the
place of torment for the ungodly. See Matt. v. 22 τὴν γέενναν τοῦ
πυρός. Comp. also Book of Enoch, ch. liii., 'I beheld a deep valley
burning with fire; to this valley they brought monarchs and the
mighty.'

For the poetical form of the whole of this passage see Bishop Jebb's
*Sacred Literature*, § 14.

**7. γάρ** introduces a further fact in illustration of the preceding
thought—the indomitable character of the tongue. *v.* 7 is subordinate
to *v.* 8; and might have been expressed by a concessive clause, 'for
though all creatures are subject to man, yet cannot he tame the
tongue.'

**ἑρπετῶν.** Heb. רֶמֶשׂ. Gen. i. 24, 25; Acts x. 12; Rom. i. 23.

**δαμάζεται καὶ δεδάμασται.** The act is characterised as not only
present, but as past with abiding result.

**τῇ φύσει τῇ ἀνθρωπίνῃ.** The dative is here instrumental. Note
how St James exalts the dignity of man's nature. He recognises an
original and inherent superiority in that nature over the lower
animals.

Comp. Soph. *Antig.* 332 ff. πολλὰ τὰ δεινὰ κοὐδὲν ἀνθρώπου δεινότερον
πέλει | ...κουφονόων τε φῦλον ὀρνίθων ἀμφιβαλὼν ἄγει | καὶ θηρῶν ἀγρίων
ἔθνη, πόντου τ' εἰναλίαν φύσιν | σπείραισι δικτυοκλώστοις | περιφραδὴς
ἀνήρ.

**8. ἀκατάστατον, restless, disquieted.** ἀκατάσχετον, uncontrolled, un-
ruly. For the reading see critical notes. For the thought comp. Hesiod,
Ἔργα 761 δεινὴν δὲ βροτῶν ὑπαλεύεο φήμην· | φήμη γάρ τε κακὴ πέλεται
κούφη μὲν ἀεῖραι | ῥεῖα μάλ' ἀργαλέη δὲ φέρειν χαλεπὴ δ' ἀποθέσθαι. |
φήμη δ' οὔτις πάμπαν ἀπόλλυται ἥν τινα πολλοὶ | λαοὶ φημίζουσι· θεός νύ
τις ἐστὶ καὶ αὐτή.

**μεστὴ ἰοῦ θανατοφόρου,** comp. Ps. cxli. 3 ἰὸς ἀσπίδων ὑπὸ τὰ χείλη
αὐτῶν.

**9. ἐν αὐτῇ.** The instrumental use of ἐν in N.T. is generally to be
attributed to a Hebraism, introduced from the LXX., or due to the
writer's familiarity with the Semitic idiom: e.g. εἰ πατάξομεν ἐν μαχαίρῃ;
Luke xxii. 49: ἐὰν ὁμολογήσῃς ἐν τῷ στόματί σου, Rom. x. 9:
ἀποκτεῖναι ἐν τῇ ῥομφαίᾳ, Rev. vi. 8. But in many instances this use
of ἐν may be explained on classical principles: comp. ἐν τίνι ἁλισθή-
σεται; (in what, &c.) Matt. v. 13, and ἐν φόνῳ μαχαίρης ἀπέθανον (in
slaughter of the sword) Heb. xi. 37, with δῆσαι ἐν πέδαις Xen. *An.* IV. 3.
8, καθικόμενον ἐν τῇ ῥάβδῳ Lucian *Dial. Mort.* 23. 3. See Winer 485,
and specially Dr Moulton's note 3.

τὸν κύριον καὶ πατέρα. κύριον has here the O.T. sense of Jehovah. The collocation is unusual. God is regarded in His power and in His love (Beyschlag).

τοὺς ἀνθρώπους τοὺς καθ᾽ ὁμοίωσιν θεοῦ γεγονότας. Comp. ποιήσωμεν ἄνθρωπον κατ᾽ εἰκόνα ἡμετέραν καὶ καθ᾽ ὁμοίωσιν, Gen. i. 26. This designation conveys the gravity of the sin of cursing; it is a sin against God Himself. "Remanet nobilitas" Bengel; the image of God is not lost even through sin.

εὐλογοῦμεν...καταρώμεθα. Comp. Philo *de Decal.* p. 196 οὐ γὰρ ὅσιον δι᾽ οὗ στόματος τὸ ἱερώτατον ὄνομα προφέρεται διὰ τούτου φθέγγεσθαί τι τῶν αἰσχρῶν.

10, οὐ χρή. χρή here only in N.T.: **it is not right or fitting**. It is not the same as δεῖ, which implies moral obligation, duty. Here the unfitness or incongruity is expressed.

11. μήτι ἡ πηγὴ κ.τ.λ. An argument from natural analogy. This inconsistency of blessing and cursing with the same mouth is unnatural. We are reminded of Aristotle's argument against usury—the unnaturalness of 'barren metal' bearing, having offspring (τόκος) as it were.

ἡ πηγή, the article generalises. Comp. *Od.* IV. 406 πικρὸν ἀποπνείουσαι ἁλὸς πολυβενθέος ὀδμήν: Herod. IV. 52 ἐκδιδοῖ γὰρ ἐς αὐτὸι κρήνη πικρή: *Geor.* II. 238 "salsa etiam tellus et quae perhibetur amara."

12. συκῆ ἐλαίας ποιῆσαι κ.τ.λ. Comp. Matt. vii. 16, 17, where the thought is similar but not quite parallel.

ἁλυκὸν (ὕδωρ). So θερμόν, Aristoph. *Nub.* 1040: and in Latir *frigida, calida, gelida (aqua)*. In LXX. ἁλυκός is always used of the Salt Sea (never called the Dead Sea in the Bible), e.g. ἔσται ἡ διέξοδος θάλασσα ἡ ἁλυκή Numb. xxxiv. 12: ἕως θαλάσσης Ἀραβὰ θαλάσσης ἁλυκῆς Deut. iii. 17.

13—18. Another line of thought, also springing from the topic of teaching (v. 1), is the right use of wisdom and knowledge (v. 13), contrasted with a perverted use of them (v. 14). Then follows a description of the false wisdom (vv. 15, 16) and the true wisdom (vv. 17, 18).

For a further treatment of σοφία in its N.T. sense, and of the distinction here drawn by St James between ἡ ἄνωθεν σοφία and that designated as ἐπίγειος, ψυχική, δαιμονιώδης, see Introduction, p. xxxviii. Here it will suffice to say that ἡ ἄνωθεν σοφία is that beautiful conception of wisdom or *Chokmah*, which had sprung up among the Jews after the return from Babylon, and which is embodied chiefly in the books of Wisdom, Ecclesiasticus, Proverbs and Job. By the contrasted earthly σοφία appears to be meant not Hellenic or Græco-Roman philosophy, degraded though it was on its practical side at this epoch, but rather the principles of the Zealots: that conception of the kingdom of God and consequent plan of life which Josephus himself terms a φιλοσοφία (*Ant.* XVIII. 1. 1) and which by its passionate and misguided zeal and mundane view of the destiny of Israel precisely answers to this description.

**13.  τίς σοφὸς καὶ ἐπιστήμων.**  St James is here thinking of σοφία and ἐπιστήμη as practical systems of life.  σοφία as well as πίστις and ἔλεος must have its ἔργα.  Comp. Eph. v. 15 βλέπετε οὖν ἀκριβῶς πῶς περιπατεῖτε μὴ ὡς ἄσοφοι ἀλλ᾽ ὡς σοφοί, where the Apostle indicates a philosophy of life.  σοφία, ἀκρίβεια and ἐπιστήμη are closely connected terms: see Aristotle *Eth. Nic.* I. vii. 18.  Comp. Ecclus. xvi. 26 ἐν ἀκριβείᾳ ἐπαγγελῶ ἐπιστήμην.  σοφὸς καὶ ἐπιστήμων are also connected Deut. i. 13, 15, iv. 6: ὅτε ἑαυτοῖς ἄνδρας σοφοὺς καὶ ἐπιστήμονας καὶ συνετοὺς εἰς τὰς φυλὰς ὑμῶν.  Comp. Is. xxxiii. 6 σοφία καὶ ἐπιστήμη καὶ εὐσέβεια πρὸς τὸν Κύριον, Dan. i. 20 καὶ ἐν παντὶ ῥήματι σοφίας καὶ ἐπιστήμης ὧν ἐζήτησε παρ᾽ αὐτῶν ὁ βασιλεὺς κ.τ.λ.

σοφός, as in Classical Greek, is used of practical skill (thus Oholiab and Bezalel and his fellow-craftsmen are σοφοὶ τῇ διανοίᾳ Ex. xxxvi. 1, 4, 8; comp. Arist. *Eth. Nic.* VI. 7 where the *Margitis* is cited : τὸν δ᾽ οὔτ᾽ ἄρ σκαπτῆρα θεοὶ θέσαν οὔτ᾽ ἀροτῆρα | οὔτ᾽ ἄλλως τι σοφόν) as well as of supreme and heavenly wisdom.  If any distinction is to be drawn here ἐπιστήμων would refer to the trained and exact Rabbinical knowledge which would tempt its possessor to seek the office of a διδάσκαλος, *v.* 1.

**ἐκ τῆς καλῆς ἀναστροφῆς.**  ἀναστροφή lit. a turning back; of a ship returning for a second attack, διέκπλοι δὲ οὐκ εἰσὶν οὐδὲ ἀναστροφαί, Thuc. II. 89.  So of a horse wheeling round, Xen. *Mag. Eq.* 3. 14, hence from the notion of turning about in a place, a habitation, δαιμόνων ἀναστροφή, Aesch. *Eum.* 23.  Then later, as here, a mode of life, in old English 'conversation.'  Comp. Polyb. IV. 89 ὁ Φίλιππος κατά τε τὴν λοιπὴν ἀναστροφὴν καὶ κατὰ τὰς πράξεις τεθαυμασμένος.  So in Apocr. ἴσθι πεπαιδευμένος ἐν πάσῃ ἀναστροφῇ σου, Tob. iv. 14 and 2 Macc. v. 8, and in N.T. τὴν ἐμὴν ποτε ἀναστροφὴν ἐν τῷ Ἰουδαϊσμῷ, Gal. i. 13 ; in two other passages of the Pauline Epp. Eph. iv. 22, 1 Tim. iv. 12, and eight times in 1 and 2 Peter, in Heb. xiii. 7 τὴν ἔκβασιν τῆς ἀναστροφῆς, the issue of their life.  ἀναστροφή is therefore the life of movement and action.  The life of Christian Wisdom and of 'Zeal' are contrasted in their outcome.  καλός as a philosophical term is associated with that which is ideally perfect in life or art.  ἡ καλὴ ἀναστροφή is therefore the perfect life of action.

**ἐν πραΰτητι σοφίας, in mildness of wisdom**, gentleness which is characterised by wisdom.  Comp. *mitis sapientia Laeli.*  See ch. i. 21.  The gentleness of wisdom is perhaps emphasized in contrast to the asperity of philosophic discussion, but here it is more especially opposed to the rivalry of religious parties among the Jews and to that fierce and fanatical spirit indicated by ζῆλος.  In a good sense ζῆλος is used of passionate devotion to the cause of Jehovah, ὁ ζῆλος κυρίου τῶν δυνάμεων ποιήσει ταῦτα, 2 Kings xix. 31 ; ὁ ζῆλος τοῦ οἴκου σου κατέφαγέν με, Ps. lxviii. 9 cited by our Lord, John ii. 17, the only passage where the word occurs in the Gospels.  But comp. Σίμωνα τὸν καλούμενον ζηλωτήν, Luke vi. 15 and the parallel καναναῖος from the Hebrew (קִנְאָה) equivalent to ζῆλος. Thus like other elements in Jewish life 'zeal' was turned to account in the kingdom of God. The zealots derived their tenets from the signal instances of zeal in the O.T. such as that of Phinehas Numb. xxv. 7, 11 or of Jehu 2 K. x. 16. Then by a natural transition the word became associated with the thought of contention and strife: comp. ἔριδι καὶ ζήλῳ, Rom. xiii. 13; ζῆλος καὶ ἔρις καὶ διχοστασίαι, 1 Cor. iii. 3; θυμοὶ ἐριθίαι, 2 Cor. xii. 20; ἔρεις ζῆλοι θυμοί, Gal. v. 20. St Paul however recognises its good side as a characteristic of Israel: ζῆλον θεοῦ ἔχουσιν· ἀλλ' οὐ κατ' ἐπίγνωσιν, Rom. x. 2.

**14.　ζῆλον πικρόν,** in strong contrast to πραΰτητι σοφίας.

**ἐριθείαν** (ἐριθίαν W. H.), **party spirit,** intrigue, contention. The derivation is from ἔριθος, a day labourer; ἐν δ' ἐτίθει τέμενος βαθυλήιον· ἔνθα δ' ἔριθοι | ἤμων ὀξείας δρεπάνας ἐν χερσὶν ἔχοντες, *Il.* xviii. 550; πότνι' 'Αθηναία, ποῖαί σφ' ἐπόνασαν ἔριθοι, Theocr. *Id.* xv. 80. ἐριθεία rare in classics, see Arist. *Pol.* viii. (v.) 2. 6 where it is used in the derived sense of party spirit or faction. Aristotle also uses the verb ἐριθεύεσθαι, *Pol.* viii. (v.) 3. 9, comp. Polyb. x. 22. 9; ἐριθεύεσθαι τοὺς νέους, to inveigle the young men into party measures. Not in LXX., in N.T. see Rom. ii. 8, τοῖς δὲ ἐξ ἐριθίας, Gal. v. 20, Phil. i. 17 οἱ δὲ ἐξ ἐριθίας, ii. 3 μηδὲν κατ' ἐριθίαν.

Curtius, *Etym.* § 343, refers ἔριθος to the root αρ- the fundamental meaning of which is movement in direction of something with a view to attainment, as in ἀρέσθαι, ἄρνυμαι, μίσθαρνος. The last word explains ἔριθος, earning wages, and also ἐριθία in the sense of struggle for party ends &c. It may be added that there is no etymological connexion between ἐριθεία and ἔρις.

**εἰ δὲ ζῆλον πικρὸν ἔχετε.** If you have (as you have in fact) bitter zeal (πικρόν emphatic by position, and added because zeal is not in itself evil), do not go on glorying and lying against the truth, i.e. the truth which heavenly wisdom shews—the truth of Christ, the Christian faith. Bitter emulation and contentiousness are absolutely inconsistent with the truth as Christ taught it. St James therefore calls upon the brotherhood to give up that life of emulation and quarrelling and show by a true and noble life what the heavenly σοφία is. The warning is addressed to zealots, whether converted or unconverted Jews (St James had influence with both). The spirit of misdirected zeal, already a danger in the Church, developed into the Judaistic opposition to St Paul. The tendency was to boast of the privileges of Israel: comp. Rom. iv. 1, 2; 2 Cor. xi. 18 ff.

**15.　αὕτη** (σοφία), this false wisdom indicated above, the fanaticism of the zealot.

**ἐπίγειος.** Comp. εἰ τὰ ἐπίγεια εἶπον ὑμῖν καὶ οὐ πιστεύετε, πῶς ἐὰν εἴπω ὑμῖν τὰ ἐπουράνια πιστεύσετε; John iii. 12: τὰ ἐπίγεια φρονοῦντες, Phil. iii. 19, see also 1 Cor. xv. 40; 2 Cor. v. 1; Phil. ii. 10. As applied to σοφία, ἐπίγειος denotes a wisdom which is limited by earthly conceptions.

ψυχική. ψυχικός is used in N.T. in distinction from πνευματικός, to indicate the lower animal life in contrast with the higher spiritual life. Comp. ψυχικὸς δὲ ἄνθρωπος οὐ δέχεται τὰ τοῦ πνεύματος τοῦ θεοῦ, 1 Cor. ii. 14: σπείρεται σῶμα ψυχικόν, ἐγείρεται σῶμα πνευματικόν, 1 Cor. xv. 44: οὗτοί εἰσιν...ψυχικοὶ πνεῦμα μὴ ἔχοντες, Jud. 19. Taken absolutely both in the classics and in Hellenistic Greek ψυχή signifies life in all its degrees and modes from the lowest vegetative life to the highest spiritual existence. This extent of meaning gives force to the expression: ὃς γὰρ ἂν θέλῃ τὴν ψυχὴν αὐτοῦ σῶσαι, Matt. xvi. 25.

δαιμονιώδης, here only in N.T. In its extreme phase the desperate resistance to foreign power or to any infringement of the national religion exhibited characteristics which closely approached the phenomena of demoniacal possession.

The false σοφία looked to a time of material prosperity and to the satisfaction of desire.

16. ἀκαταστασία, opposed to the εἰρήνη of the heavenly wisdom and especially characteristic of the zealots. Comp. οὐ γάρ ἐστιν ἀκαταστασίας ὁ θεός, ἀλλ' εἰρήνης, 1 Cor. xiv. 33.

πᾶν φαῦλον πρᾶγμα, comp. πᾶς γὰρ ὁ φαῦλα πράσσων μισεῖ τὸ φῶς, John iii. 20: ἐκπορεύσονται...οἱ τὰ φαῦλα πράξαντες εἰς ἀνάστασιν κρίσεως, John v. 29.

17. ἡ ἄνωθεν σοφία, the heavenly wisdom, the supreme excellence of the religious life, in which the child Jesus kept advancing, προέκοπτεν τῇ σοφίᾳ, Luke ii. 52, which was manifest in His manhood, πόθεν τούτῳ ἡ σοφία αὕτη; Matt. xiii. 54, and which guided His life, Matt. xi. 19. It is described with enthusiasm 4 Macc. i. 16 ff.; Ecclus. li. 13 ff. See on i. 5 and Introduction. Comp. Book of Enoch ch. xlii., 'wisdom found not a place on earth where she could inhabit; her dwelling therefore is in heaven.'

ἐπιεικής, from εἰκός, reasonable, fair, equitable. Arist. Eth. N. v. xiv. 8 says of the ἐπιεικής, ὁ μὴ ἀκριβοδίκαιος ἐπὶ τὸ χεῖρον ἀλλ' ἐλαττωτικός, καίπερ ἔχων τὸν νόμον βοηθόν, comp. Soph. O. C. 1125 f. ἐπεὶ τό γ' εὐσεβὲς | μόνοις παρ' ὑμῖν εὗρον ἀνθρώπων ἐγώ | καὶ τοὐπιεικὲς καὶ τὸ μὴ ψευδοστομεῖν. In the N.T. ἐπιείκεια is noted as a leading characteristic of Christians, τὸ ἐπιεικὲς ὑμῶν γνωσθήτω πᾶσιν ἀνθρώποις, Phil. iv. 5: it is required of a bishop to be ἐπιεικῆ, ἄμαχον, 1 Tim. iii. 4: of Christians generally ἀμάχους εἶναι, ἐπιεικεῖς, Tit. iii. 2. Like πραότης it is manifested in Christ Himself, παρακαλῶ ὑμᾶς διὰ τῆς πραότητος καὶ ἐπιεικείας τοῦ χριστοῦ, 2 Cor. x. 1. Juvenal expresses the thought in the line: "mitem animum ac mores modicis erroribus aequos," Sat. xiv. 15.

εὐπειθής, here only in N.T., suadibilis V., 'easy to be intreated' R.V., open to persuasion, the opposite of headstrong or obstinate.

ἀδιάκριτος, also ἅπ. λεγ. in N.T., non judicans V., 'without variance' R.V., 'doubtfulness or partiality' R.V. marg.

The various meanings are determined by the different senses of διακρίνεσθαι: and as the prevailing signification of the verb both in this epistle (i. 6 bis and possibly ii. 4) and elsewhere frequently (as

Acts x. 20, Rom. xiv. 23) is 'to doubt,' and as St James lays special stress on the sin of διψυχία, and as our Lord expressly rebukes the ὀλιγόπιστοι, the rendering in R. V. *marg.* 'without doubtfulness' is to be preferred to that given in the text.

ἀνυπόκριτος, comp. 1 Pet. i. 22 τὰς ψυχὰς ὑμῶν ἡγνικότες ἐν τῇ ὑπακοῇ τῆς ἀληθείας διὰ πνεύματος εἰς φιλαδελφίαν ἀνυπόκριτον—a quotation which illustrates εὐπειθής in this connexion. See also 2 Cor. vi. 6; 1 Tim. i. 5; 2 Tim. i. 5; and note our Lord's frequent denunciation of hypocrisy.

18. καρπὸς δὲ δικαιοσύνης κ.τ.λ. δικαιοσύνης gen. of apposition, the fruit which consists of righteousness. The connecting thought between this and the preceding paragraph centres in δικαιοσύνη, which is regarded as the supreme aim and crown of the Christian life: comp. 2 Tim. iv. 8 ὁ τῆς δικαιοσύνης στέφανος, and Matt. v. 6, where δικαιοσύνη occupies the central and culminating point of the beatitudes. In 4 Maccab. i. 18 δικαιοσύνη is noted as one of the ἰδέαι of σοφία. Bitter zeal and heavenly wisdom were alike sowing seed and the harvest was drawing on. But only for those who are now making peace (comp. μακάριοι οἱ εἰρηνοποιοί Matt. v. 9) is the fruit of righteousness being sown in peace. For the zealots whose policy was resistance and war there would be a harvest of contention and hatred. Here too wisdom was justified by its results (ἀπὸ τῶν ἔργων αὐτῆς). Zeal came to a bitter end at the siege of Jerusalem, while the true faith of Christ won its victory of peace.

τοῖς ποιοῦσιν, a *dativus commodi.*


# CHAPTER IV.

4. The omission of μοιχοὶ καί is supported by א*AB and some important versions. Old Latin *fornicatores,* Vulgate *adulteri.* The words are included in אᶜKLP and later authorities.

5. κατῴκισεν with אAB: κατῴκησεν KLP and a preponderance of later evidence. The variation arises from itacism, or confusion of form from similarity of sound, a frequent source of error.

12. καὶ κριτής with אABP and most versions: KL and others omit.

ὁ κρίνων with אABP: ὃς κρίνεις KL and the later mss.

τὸν πλησίον on the same evidence, as against τὸν ἕτερον.

14. τὸ τῆς αὔριον with אKL, several versions and Fathers: τὰ τῆς αὔριον AP and some cursives. The reading τῆς αὔριον only is found in B and adopted from that great authority by Westcott and Hort.

ἔστε with B and several versions: moreover AKP have ἔσται, probably by itacism for ἔστε: ἔστιν is read in L and is supported by the Old Latin and Vulgate (*vapor est*).

Ch. IV.   1—12.   The Struggle against the Desires of the Flesh
which are the Cause of evil Contention.

**1.**   πόθεν πόλεμοι καὶ πόθεν μάχαι ἐν ὑμῖν; The transition to this
paragraph is immediately suggested by εἰρήνην (iii. 18). But the
thought follows naturally on the whole preceding section, especially on
the clause, εἰ δὲ ζῆλον πικρὸν ἔχετε, κ.τ.λ. (iii. 14).

πόλεμοι...μάχαι, *bella et lites*, V., *unde pugnae et unde rixae in vobis*,
O.L.  Both these expressions appear to refer to private contention
rather than to international wars. The conjunction occurs in Homer:
ἀεὶ γάρ τοι ἔρις τε φίλη πόλεμοί τε μάχαι τε ('frays and feuds,' Purves)
*Il.* I. 177. So also πολεμίζειν ἠδὲ μάχεσθαι, *Il.* III. 435, where the
scholiast notes: μάχεται μέν τις καὶ λόγοις...πολεμεῖν δὲ λόγοις οὐ
λέγεται. There is no etymological objection to this sense of private
quarrel, the root πελ. meaning to strike, hence πλήσσω, πέλας,
πλησίον.

Beyschlag distinguishes: "πόλεμος der chronische Unfrieden, μάχη
der acute."

ἐκ denotes the remoter and ultimate source, ἀπό the nearer and
immediate source—quarrels and contentions may be traced back to
pleasures as their ultimate cause.

τῶν στρατευομένων, that are campaigning in your members. ἡδοναί
are like soldiers on the march; each man wishes his own ἡδοναί—here
equivalent to ἐπιθυμίαι—to gain the victory; hence the 'frays and
feuds.' For στρατεύεσθαι comp. Luke iii. 14; 1 Cor. ix. 7; 1 Pet. ii. 11:
in this last passage the σαρκικαὶ ἐπιθυμίαι are described as an external
force at war with the soul: τῶν σαρκικῶν ἐπιθυμιῶν αἵτινες στρατεύονται
κατὰ τῆς ψυχῆς. Comp. Plat. *Phaedo* p. 66 c, καὶ γὰρ πολέμους καὶ
στάσεις καὶ μάχας οὐδὲν ἄλλο παρέχει ἢ τὸ σῶμα καὶ αἱ τούτου ἐπιθυμίαι.
Cic. *de Fin.* I. 13 Ex cupiditatibus odia, discidia, discordiae, se-
ditiones, bella nascuntur.

ἡδονή in N.T. always in a bad sense as a danger to the spiritual life,
Luke viii. 14; Tit. iii. 3; 2 Pet. ii. 13.

**2 and 3.**   These two verses are among the examples of poetical
form in this epistle: ζηλοῦτε is an advance on ἐπιθυμεῖτε as οὐ δύνασθε
ἐπιτυχεῖν is an advance on οὐκ ἔχετε.

**2.**   ἐπιθυμεῖτε, καὶ οὐκ ἔχετε. The zealot's aims are disappointed;
his means, murder, perverted zeal, quarrels and contentions, lead to
nothing.  With οὐκ ἔχετε the argument is resumed and expanded by
an explanation. Mere desire (ἐπιθυμία) without prayer achieves nothing. There is a kind of asking (αἰτεῖτε) which is not true prayer
because its object is perverted. For effectiveness of prayer the desire
must be rightly directed, otherwise granted prayer will be no blessing.
There is such a thing as "to know the anguish of the granted prayer."

φονεύετε καὶ ζηλοῦτε, equivalent to a single term. The ζῆλος
involved the φόνος.

**3.**   αἰτεῖτε...αἰτεῖσθε. The active and middle seem to be used
indiscriminately as in the case of some other verbs, as ἀκούω and

ἀκούομαι, ἰδεῖν and ἰδέσθαι, φλέγειν and φλέγεσθαι. Clyde, § 31 d.
Comp. also Luke xv. 6 and 9, συγκαλεῖ...συγκαλεῖται, ADE al. plu.:
the cause of this being that the older form in -μαι has never been
quite displaced by the newer form in -ω. This is the more to be
expected in a verb of petition which necessarily implies the force of a
middle, viz. that the action is done in some way for or towards oneself,
or in one's own interest. Monro, p. 8; Jelf, § 368.

αἰτεῖτε however may be preferred on account of λαμβάνετε, and the
two middles αἰτεῖσθαι and αἰτεῖσθε connect the clauses in which they
are used.

As Trench points out, αἰτεῖν (*Lat.* petere) in N.T. always retains
its proper sense of begging from a superior. Thus our Lord never
uses αἰτεῖν or αἰτεῖσθαι of Himself in respect of what He seeks on
behalf of His disciples from God. The word employed is always
ἐρωτᾶν (*Lat.* rogare), an asking, that is, upon equal terms. John xiv.
16, xvi. 26, xvii. 9, 15, 20. See Trench, *N.T. Syn. sub voc.*

**ἐν ἡδοναῖς.** Not *upon* but *in* your pleasures.

**4. μοιχαλίδες,** for the omission of μοιχοὶ καί see crit. notes. The
address is still to men. But the feminine form and the abruptness of
the appeal indicate scorn and indignation. Comp. the Homeric expression: Ἀχαιΐδες οὐκέτ' Ἀχαιοί, *Il.* II. 235, and Virgil's "O vere
Phrygiae neque enim Phryges," *Aen.* IX. 617. The feminine μοιχαλίδες is accounted for partly because the image present to St James'
mind is that which is most frequent in the O.T., the wife's unfaithful-
ness to her husband, partly because the lapse into pleasure even
though accompanied by crimes of violence is essentially effeminate.
It is for this association of sins that the prophet Amos rebukes the
women of Israel—"the kine of Bashan," δαμάλεις τῆς Βασανίτιδος, Amos
iv. 1 f. Juvenal too has noted the same moral fact, softness and cruelty
go together : Juv. *Sat.* VI. 219 ff., Pone crucem servo, &c. Tischendorf *ad loc.* illustrates this use of the feminine form by the word
ποταγωγίδες employed by Aristotle and Plutarch in the sense of
μηνυταί, informers, who were probably men not women.

**οἴδατε,** note the late form here and comp. ἴστε, i. 19.

**ἡ φιλία τοῦ κόσμου ἔχθρα τοῦ θεοῦ ἐστίν.** Comp. Matt. vi. 24 οὐδεὶς
δύναται δυσὶ κυρίοις δουλεύειν...οὐ δύνασθε θεῷ δουλεύειν καὶ μαμωνᾷ,
Matt. xii. 30 ὁ μὴ ὢν μετ' ἐμοῦ κατ' ἐμοῦ ἐστίν, καὶ ὁ μὴ συνάγων μετ'
ἐμοῦ σκορπίζει, Rom. viii. 7 τὸ φρόνημα τῆς σαρκὸς ἔχθρα εἰς θεόν...οἱ δὲ
ἐν σαρκὶ ὄντες θεῷ ἀρέσαι οὐ δύνανται.

**ὃς ἐὰν οὖν βουληθῇ** κ.τ.λ. Even the very wish for the world's friendship constitutes enmity with God. It is a thought essentially akin to
the spirit of the Sermon on the Mount: see especially Matt. v. 22, 28.

**5. ἡ γραφὴ λέγει.** The citation which follows is from an unknown
source, but the form in which it is made gives the words an authority
equal to that of the O.T. Comp. John ii. 22 ἐπίστευσαν τῇ γραφῇ,
vii. 38 καθὼς εἶπεν ἡ γραφή, Rom. iv. 3 τί γὰρ ἡ γραφὴ λέγει; and so
frequently. Resch (*Agrapha*, log. 54, p. 256) supposes that this
passage is strictly parallel to Gal. v. 17 ἡ γὰρ σὰρξ ἐπιθυμεῖ κατὰ τοῦ

πνεύματος, τὸ δὲ πνεῦμα κατὰ τῆς σαρκός. He accounts for the variation
by supposing a common Hebrew original with a variation of reading
in the copies from which St Paul and St James respectively quoted.
Or perhaps the variation is in the rendering of the same Hebrew
or Aramaic original. It may be that πρὸς φθόνον is an intended
change of expression from κατὰ σαρκός. For φθόνος is precisely
that element of σάρξ, that work of the flesh, which would be excited
by disappointed desire. (See the enumeration Gal. v. 19—21.) It is
the feeling excited in a man of perverted mind on seeing another
obtain the good thing sought by himself. φθόνος sums up the bad
side of ζῆλος with which it is associated in Plat. *Phileb.* p. 47 E,
and 50 B, and elsewhere. πρός is very usual in this sense of
hostility: πρὸς Τρῶας μάχεσθαι, *Il.* XVII. 471: ἐγένετο γογγυσμὸς
τῶν Ἑλληνιστῶν πρὸς τοὺς Ἑβραίους, Acts vi. 1: πρᾶγμα ἔχων πρὸς
τὸν ἕτερον, 1 Cor. vi. 1: ἡ πάλη πρὸς αἷμα καὶ σάρκα, Eph. vi. 12,
and frequently.

ὃ κατῴκισεν, which (God) placed, caused to dwell, or, κατῴκησεν,
which dwelt. Comp. ὑμεῖς δὲ οὐκ ἐστὲ ἐν σαρκὶ ἀλλὰ ἐν πνεύματι,
εἴπερ πνεῦμα θεοῦ οἰκεῖ ἐν ὑμῖν, Rom. viii. 9: οὐκ οἴδατε ὅτι ναὸς θεοῦ
ἐστὲ καὶ τὸ πνεῦμα τοῦ θεοῦ ἐν ὑμῖν οἰκεῖ; 1 Cor. iii. 16.

ἐπιποθεῖ, earnestly longs, answering to ἐπιθυμεῖ in Gal. v. 17, if
Resch's theory be correct. ἐπί has an intensive force, implying
direction and so earnestness of aim.

If this view be taken the sense would be: Doth scripture say in
vain: Earnestly doth the Spirit which God caused to dwell within us
long against envy? envy being the predominant note of the friendship with the world which is enmity against God.

Other interpretations are however given to this difficult passage.
πρὸς φθόνον is connected with ἐπιποθεῖ which (a) stands absolutely
'yearns even unto jealous envy,' or (b) has for its object πνεῦμα ὃ
κατῴκισεν ἐν ἡμῖν, 'yearneth for the spirit which' &c. or (c) governs
ἡμᾶς understood, 'yearneth for us.'

This adverbial use of πρὸς φθόνον (though no other examples are
given) can be justified by such expressions as πρὸς ὀργήν, πρὸς βίαν,
πρὸς χάριν &c., and perhaps all these interpretations give a more
natural meaning to ἐπιποθεῖ. The connexion would then be a
strengthening of the thought of the preceding words. To friendship
with the world is opposed God's jealous love for us, which can bear no
rival.

Whatever interpretation be given it must be borne in mind (1) that
the passage is a quotation and therefore (a) it would suggest to
St James' readers more than it states; (b) it is intended to recall
teaching, and therefore would not appear so abrupt as it does to
modern readers. (2) It has direct reference to the immediately
preceding words which express an antagonism between friendship
with the world and friendship with God, and more expressly between
a human wish (βούλησις) for friendship with the world and friendship
with God. This statement is strengthened by an appeal to scripture
which asserts (a) an inner struggle of the divine Spirit against envy

and jealousy which are especially characteristic of the φιλία τοῦ
κόσμου, or (b) according to the second interpretation, the jealous
longing for us on the part of the Spirit which God Himself caused to
dwell within us.

As regards punctuation it is best perhaps to place the interrogative
point at λέγει, or at any rate to regard the quotation itself as a
categorical statement.

**6. μείζονα δὲ δίδωσιν χάριν. But (God) giveth greater grace.** These
words are also obscure. Either (a) a larger favour, even than the
indwelling Spirit, for He contends against the proud, who represent
the φιλία τοῦ κόσμου, and gives grace to the humble who have re-
nounced that friendship, (b) or more grace than the world gives,
(c) or more than is lost through hostility to the world.

**διὸ λέγει, because of which fact the Spirit of God saith.** The
quotation which follows is verbatim from Prov. iii. 34, except that
ὁ θεός replaces κύριος of the LXX.: see 1 Pet. v. 5, where the same quotation is made. It is interesting to comp. Luke i. 51, 52 διεσκόρπισεν
ὑπερηφάνους διανοίᾳ καρδίας αὐτῶν...καὶ ὕψωσεν ταπεινούς. Note the
occurrence of the leading words, ὑπερηφάνους and ταπεινούς. The
thought is the same. It is one that entered into that atmosphere of
religious life in which the Holy Family lived and which St James
shared.

**ἀντιτάσσεται, ranges himself against,** comp. ἀντιτάξομαι κτενῶν
σε, Eur. *Phoen.* 622: ἀθρόᾳ μὲν οὐδαμοῦ τῇ δυνάμει ἀντετάξαντο, Thuc.
IV. 55. It is a word which suggests the image of the Christian warfare
so frequent with St Paul. Comp. the formula used in renunciation
at Baptism συντάσσομαί σοι Χρίστε· ἀποτάσσομαί σοι Σατανᾶ (Bingham's
*Antiq.*, Vol. IV. xi. vii. § 2), and Acts xiii. 48 ὅσοι ἦσαν τεταγμένοι εἰς
ζωὴν αἰώνιον.

**7. ὑποτάγητε οὖν τῷ θεῷ.** Therefore, in this warfare, take God's
side, place yourself under Him as Captain. Polyb. uses οἱ ὑποταττό-
μενοι or ὑποτεταγμένοι for 'subjects.'

The passage which follows is another example of regularly constructed Hebrew poetry.

**ὑποτάγητε, ἀντίστητε κ.τ.λ.** The aorist imperative denotes instantaneous, not continued action, and is therefore used in urgent
entreaty or command; comp. the eager request, σῶσον, ἀπολλύμεθα,
Matt. viii. 25, and the aorists in the Lord's Prayer.

**τῷ διαβόλῳ.** διάβολος is strictly a rendering of the Hebrew word
שָׂטָן, of which Σατανᾶς is a transliteration, and means literally 'an
adversary,' from διαβάλλειν and ἐνδιαβάλλειν, to meet, oppose: comp.
Numb. xxii. 22 ἀνέστη ὁ ἄγγελος τοῦ θεοῦ διαβαλεῖν αἱ. ἐνδιαβάλλειν
αὐτόν, and Numb. xxii. 32 ἐγὼ ἐξῆλθον εἰς διαβολήν σου, also Zech. iii.
1 καὶ ὁ διάβολος εἱστήκει ἐκ δεξιῶν αὐτοῦ τοῦ ἀντικεῖσθαι αὐτῷ, where see
the Hebr. text. To this original meaning of the word the classical
force of διαβάλλειν and its derivatives added the ideas of (a) deceiving,
(b) calumniating, (c) accusing. In Rev. xx. 2 we find both the Greek
and Hebrew forms—ὅς ἐστιν διάβολος καὶ Σατανᾶς—a proof that the

meanings of the two words, synonymous at first, had already been severed, and one among many instances of the influence of translation on religious ideas.

Comp. Eph. iv. 27 μηδὲ δίδοτε τόπον τῷ διαβόλῳ, and vi. 11 πρὸς τὸ δύνασθαι ὑμᾶς στῆναι πρὸς τὰς μεθοδίας τοῦ διαβόλου, 1 Pet. v. 8 ὁ ἀντίδικος ὑμῶν διάβολος...ᾦ ἀντίστητε στερεοὶ τῇ πίστει.

**8. καθαρίσατε χεῖρας κ.τ.λ.** Comp. Ps. xxiv. 4 ἀθῶος χερσὶ καὶ καθαρὸς τῇ καρδίᾳ κ.τ.λ. and 1 Pet. i. 22 τὰς ψυχὰς ὑμῶν ἡγνικότες ἐν τῇ ὑπακοῇ τῆς ἀληθείας.

**ἁμαρτωλοί...δίψυχοι.** Those addressed in this paragraph are either worldly men outside the Christian brotherhood, or else those of the brethren who had become worldly. Laughter and joy are now characteristic of them.

**9. εἰς κατήφειαν,** 'to heaviness,' R.V., or dejection. κατήφεια, defined to be a mixture of shame and grief, lit. with downcast eye, perhaps from κατά and φάος, but deriv. uncertain. This is the natural expression of the painfulness of shame: "There is no outrage," says Hawthorne, "more flagrant than to forbid the culprit to hide his face for shame, as it was the essence of this punishment (the pillory) to do." It is a Homeric word: δυσμενέσιν μὲν χάρμα κατηφείην δέ σοι αὐτῷ, Il. III. 51, also Thuc. VII. 75 κατήφεια δέ τις ἅμα καὶ κατάμεμψις σφῶν αὐτῶν πολλὴ ἦν, Plut. Aemil. p. 267 A κατήφεια δὲ τὸ στρατόπεδον κατεῖχεν. For the thought comp. Prov. xiv. 13 τελευταῖα δὲ χαρὰ (al. χαρᾶς) εἰς πένθος ἔρχεται, and Jer. xvi. 9 καταλύω ἐκ τοῦ τόπου τούτου φωνὴν χαρᾶς καὶ φωνὴν εὐφροσύνης.

**10. ταπεινώθητε,** passive form with middle sense. See Monro, Hom. Grammar, § 44, where it is shewn that aorists in -ην and -θην had originally an intransitive sense of which the passive sense was a growth or adaptation. Comp. ἐχάρην, ἐδυνάσθην, ἀπεκρίθην.

**11. μὴ καταλαλεῖτε ἀλλήλων.** The argument reverts to the main subject. It is a last thought on the evils of the tongue. It is a warning against evil speaking and slandering. The mention of the law however points to a particular kind of evil-speaking. This law is, according to Beyschlag and others, the law of love, the νόμος βασιλικός mentioned above ch. ii. 8. But then the question arises how does a man speaking against his brother speak against the law, or judge the law? Certainly if he is guilty of slander he transgresses the law. But how does he become a νομοθέτης and a κρίτης? It is said indeed that in slandering a brother a man's conduct becomes a practical criticism and condemnation of the law of love. He enacts as it were a law opposed to the law of love; whereas his duty is simply to obey the law of love and to abstain from evil-speaking and slander. This explanation however is not wholly satisfactory.

But if the law be understood of the Mosaic law a more natural explanation suggests itself. It is probable that the question of the observance of the Mosaic law had already been mooted in the brotherhood. The earliest rule in the primitive Church was observance of the law as St James himself and even St Paul observed it. But some

Jewish Christians had from the first foreseen the transitory character of the law. And among these some, we may imagine, inspired by the thought of Christian liberty, would press their views with needless zeal, speaking against their brethren whose conscience led them to observe the law. These would be rightly regarded as judging the law; just as one who censures a statesman censures his policy.

To such as these St James now addresses himself. He is not as yet prepared for this great revolution. If the law is to be changed, it is for the one only Lawgiver and Judge to change it. It is not for the individual Christian to anticipate the change which time would bring.

12. νομοθέτης. ἅπ. λεγ. in N.T., quite classical and used in a special sense at Athens. For the verb comp. Ps. xxvii. 11 νομοθέτησόν με, κύριε, ἐν τῇ ὁδῷ σου.

ὁ δυνάμενος σῶσαι καὶ ἀπολέσαι. See Matt. x. 28 τὸν δυνάμενον καὶ ψυχὴν καὶ σῶμα ἀπολέσαι ἐν γεέννῃ.

σὺ δὲ τίς εἶ, ὁ κρίνων τὸν πλησίον; St James' teaching here, as so frequently, is based on the Sermon on the Mount. See Matt. vii. 1 μὴ κρίνετε ἵνα μὴ κριθῆτε.

## 13—17. The Temptations of Wealth.

The address is still probably to the brethren, some of whom engaged in business have not learnt to recognise God's law and His will in commercial projects and plans. Comp. Ecclus. xxvi. 29 μόλις ἐξελεῖται ἔμπορος ἀπὸ πλημμελείας, καὶ οὐ δικαιωθήσεται κάπηλος ἀπὸ ἁμαρτίας.

13. ἄγε νῦν οἱ λέγοντες. ἄγε like φέρε, ἴθι, ἰδού and in Modern Greek ἄς for ἄφες, is used with singular and plural subject alike, often to strengthen the imperative : ἀλλ' ἄγε δή τινα μάντιν ἐρείομεν, Hom. *Il.* i. 62: ἀλλ' ἴθι, ταῦτα δ' ὄπισθεν ἀρεσσόμεθ', *Il.* iv. 362. Monro, *Hom. Gram.* § 327. See also Goodwin § 84. *Age* is used in the same way in Latin : age nunc, comparate, Cic. *pro Mil.* 21 : ergo age, care pàter, cervici imponere nostrae, Virg. *Aen.* ii. 707.

The picture of commercial activity which follows illustrates "the Semite's born instinct for trading" (G. A. Smith, *Isaiah* i. 289). "The Semite was always a trader" (Budge, *Babylonian Life and History*, p. 150). But though the carrying trade of the ancient world was in the hands of the Semite race, the Jew did not at first take to trading. The spirit of commercial enterprise flourished for a time under Phoenician influence in the reign of Solomon. But the attempt to revive it in the joint reigns of Jehoshaphat and Ahaziah ended disastrously (2 Chron. xx. 37). The Hebrew genius for trade was first developed during the Captivity. Recent discoveries in the neighbourhood of Babylon have brought to light documents which testify to very extensive commercial transactions in which the Hebrew settlers in Babylonia would probably take part. Indeed the name of Egibi, the title of a leading firm in the reign of Nebuchadnezzar, has been identified with the name of Jacob. But this conclusion "is not certain at present," Budge, *Babylonian Life and History*, p. 117. In the gospels banking and trade transactions are referred to in the parables of the talents, of the minae, and of the merchant seeking goodly

pearls. The case of the son who took his portion and went off to seek
his fortune in a far country was probably a not unusual incident in
Jewish life. In Rev. xviii. 10—14 there is a striking description of
the trade of Babylon. In early days trade was provided for: "Thou
shalt lend unto many nations and shalt not borrow," Deut. xxviii. 12.
"They strike hands with the children of strangers" (make contracts
with the sons of aliens, Cheyne), Is. ii. 6, alluding to commercial
activity in the reigns of Jotham and Uzziah. The prophets were
opposed to foreign trade: "He is a trafficker...he loveth to oppress,"
Hos. xii. 1, 7, 8. In Ezek. xvi. 26 trade is called harlotry from its
venal and merely mercenary spirit. See Nahum iii. 4 f., Is. xxiii. 17,
and Is. lvii. 17, "For the iniquity of his covetousness I smote him."

The language which the Jew spoke, Aramaic, was the language of
trade, and the number of scattered Jewish settlements in all the principal cities of the world greatly favoured commercial intercourse.
"There is abundant evidence in the Mishnah that the Jews travelled
far by sea and land." Media, Italy, Spain, Alexandria, Naharden and
Greece are mentioned as countries which they visited. Regulations
are given in the Mishnah for use on board ship and on journeys. In
the Mishnah also trades are mentioned in which the Jews engaged,
among them traffic in silk, satin, vases of gold and other metals,
mirrors, &c., and even in slaves. There are a few restrictions—fir
cones, figs, incense, myrtles, sacred to Venus, and other things could
not be sold because connected with idolatrous rites. See Art. by
Major Conder, *Palestine Expl. F. Statement*, Jan. 1894. It is hardly
necessary to add that the trading instinct is still eminently characteristic of the race, and the jealousy to which it gives rise is at the root
of the Juden-hetze of the present day.

τήνδε τὴν πόλιν, this city, of which the speaker is then thinking.
See Green, *Gram.* p. 125, and Winer p. 201 n. 3.

ποιήσομεν. Comp. Acts xviii. 23 ποιήσας χρόνον τινά, 2 Cor. xi. 25
νυχθήμερον ἐν τῷ βυθῷ πεποίηκα. So also Acts xv. 33, xx. 3. So also
*facere* in Latin: Apameae quinque dies morati...Ionii decem fecimus,
Cic. *ad Atticum* v. 20, and Hebr. עָשָׂה, see Eccl. vi. 12.

ἐμπορευσόμεθα. ἐμπορεύεσθαι is first used of travel simply: ξένην
ἐπὶ γαῖαν ἐμπορεύσεται, Soph. *Oed. Tyr.* 456 ; of soldiers marching:
Polybius, see Schweigh. *Lex. Polyb. sub voc.*; then very commonly with
the added notion of travelling for business, like the Hebr. סָחַר, here
only in that sense in N.T. Then from the frequency of tricks and
deception in trade, to cheat, deceive: καὶ ἐν πλεονεξίᾳ πλαστοῖς λόγοις
ὑμᾶς ἐμπορεύσονται, 2 Pet. ii. 3. Comp. πολλά τινα πρὸς ταύτην τὴν
ὑπόθεσιν ἐμπορεύων καὶ μεθοδευόμενος, Polyb. xxxviii. 4. 10.

κερδήσομεν. For this rare form of the future see references in
Veitch, *sub voc.*

14. οἵτινες οὐκ ἐπίστασθε τὸ τῆς αὔριον κ.τ.λ. For reading see
crit. notes. *Qui ignoratis quid sit in crastinum; quae enim est vita
vestra ? Vapor est ad modicum parens* &c. V., Whereas ye know not
what shall be on the morrow. What is your life?—R.V., translating

the reading adopted by Westcott and Hort, 'ye know not on the morrow what your life shall be.'

ἀτμὶς γάρ ἐστε.  Ps. cii. 3 ἐξέλιπον ὡσεὶ καπνὸς αἱ ἡμέραι μου.

πρὸς ὀλίγον φαινομένη.  Comp. the story of Paulinus and the Pagan priest Coifi at the court of Edwin, King of Deira, c. 626, unus passerum domum citissime pervolaverit, qui cum per unum ostium ingrediens, mox per aliud exierit. Ita haec vita hominum ad modicum apparet; quid autem sequatur, quidve processerit, prorsus ignoramus, Bede, *H. E.* II. 13. See also Bright, *Early English Church History*, p. 116, and Wordsworth's *Eccl. Sonnets*, No. 16.

16.  νῦν δέ, but now, as it is.

ἐν ταῖς ἀλαζονείαις ὑμῶν, in your boastful or presumptuous talk, or your false pretensions.  ἀλαζ. from ἀλαζών lit. a wanderer, then of a boastful pretender. Aristotle defines the ἀλαζών as ὁ μείζω τῶν ὑπαρχόντων προσποιούμενος, *Eth. N.* IV. vii. 10 ('a man who pretends to have greater things than he possesses'), adding according to the probable reading εἰ δ᾽ ἕνεκά τινος ὁ μὲν δόξης ἢ τιμῆς οὐ λίαν ψαλτὸς ὁ ἀλάζων, ὁ δὲ ἀργυρίου ἢ ὅσα εἰς ἀργύριον ἀσχημονέστερος. It is probably with this last reference in the word that the Apostle uses it.  ἀλαζονείαις would thus signify the deception used to increase the value of goods—the tricks of trade.

Perhaps however ἐν ἀλαζονείαις is simply the presumptuous talk which forms plans and projects without reference to God's will.

17.  εἰδότι οὖν καλὸν ποιεῖν, if a man knows how to do what is right and honest and does it not, to him such a course is sin.


# CHAPTER V.

9.  κριθῆτε with all the chief mss.  κατακριθῆτε has very slight support.

11.  ὑπομείναντας אBP, Old Latin and Vulgate, ὑπομένοντας KL and several versions—the distinction is important, see below.

16.  τὰς ἁμαρτίας with אABP, several cursives, Fathers and versions apparently; Old Latin and Vulgate have *peccata*.  τὰ παραπτώματα KL and some of the Fathers.

---

1—6.  The thought of trade suggests the thought of wealth, as in Rev. xviii. 15 οἱ ἔμποροι τούτων πλουτήσαντες ἀπ᾽ αὐτῆς.

The rich men who are here addressed are outside 'the brotherhood.' This appears clearly both from the character of the address and from the acts ascribed to them, and also from the absence of appeal to any Christian principle, and from the marked contrast to the paragraph which follows, in which 'the brotherhood' is again addressed.

The prosperity of the wicked is the insoluble problem of the O.T. Two answers are suggested here:—(a) the perishable character of that

on which their prosperity rests; (*b*) the future retribution. Comp.
Zeph. i. 12, 14, 18; Job xx., especially *vv.* 18, 19; Ps. xii. 5; Prov. xiv.
31; Eccl. v. 8; Ezek. xviii. 18; Amos iv. 1, 2.

The picture of the rich oppressor and the persecuted poor is conceived in the spirit of Hebrew prophecy, and it is true to the religious
life of the Holy Family.    See Luke i. 53 πεινῶντας ἐνέπλησεν ἀγαθῶν,
καὶ πλουτοῦντας ἐξαπέστειλε κενούς. It has been in all ages the temptation
of irresponsible wealth to oppress and persecute. It was among the
evil signs of the times in the pre-exile period, Mic. ii. 2, Amos iii.
10, 11, 15, and again broke out after the return, Neh. v. 1—13.
Possibly this keen and cruel trade spirit was an immediate result of
Babylonian influence. In the Chaldean tablets the 'cry' of the poor
against the oppressor is frequently expressed. The slave trade, perhaps the most extensive business in the ancient world, directly tended
to heartlessness and oppression; and lending money on usury for
agricultural purposes was another process tending to the same result:
Ezek. xviii. 8, 17, xxii. 12; Is. iii. 14, 15.

1.   ἄγε.   See above, iv. 13.

ὀλολύζοντες κ.τ.λ.   Comp. Luke vi. 24, 25, a passage closely related
to this.   Comp. Is. xiii. 6 ὀλολύζετε· ἐγγὺς γὰρ ἡμέρα κυρίου, where there
is the same connexion as here with the day of judgment.

ταῖς ἐπερχομέναις, which are now coming upon you in succession
(ἐπί).

2.   σέσηπεν...γέγονεν...κατίωται.   The tense implies that the case
indicated by ταλαιπωρίαις is already present.   The tarnishing of the
gold and silver is an accomplished fact.   The words bring out the
thought that the wealth wrung from the poor by injustice and cruelty
is of no service to the rich man himself: 'putrescit in arca.'

ὁ πλοῦτος, corresponding in poetical parallelism to τὰ ἱμάτια, wealth
in Oriental countries consisting largely of garments: comp. Acts xx.
33 ἀργυρίου ἢ χρυσίου ἢ ἱματισμοῦ οὐδενὸς ἐπεθύμησα.

σητόβρωτα here only in N.T.   Comp. Job xiii. 28 ὥσπερ ἱμάτιον
σητόβρωτον.   The word is not elsewhere found.   For the thought see
Matt. vi. 19, 20 μὴ θησαυρίζετε ὑμῖν θησαυροὺς ἐπὶ τῆς γῆς, ὅπου σὴς καὶ
βρῶσις ἀφανίζει, κ.τ.λ. and comp. Hor. *Sat.* II. 3. 119 cui stragula
vestis | blattarum ac tinearum epulae putrescat in arca.   The word is
formed like σκωληκόβρωτος, Acts xii. 23.

3.   ὁ χρυσὸς ὑμῶν καὶ ὁ ἄργυρος κατίωται.   Arrian, *Epict.* IV.
6, ὡς ὁπλάρια ἐπικείμενα κατίωται.   The precious metals, gold and
silver, are not, strictly speaking, subject to rust, but to tarnish or
oxidisation, which does not destroy the metal: τοῦ χροίης καθύπερθε
μέλας οὐχ ἅπτεται ἰὸς | οὐδ' εὐρώς, αἰεὶ δ' ἄνθος ἔχει καθαρόν, Theogn.
451.   ὅτι Διὸς παῖς ὁ χρυσός· κεῖνον οὐ σὴς οὐδὲ κὶς δάπτει, Sappho,
fr. 142, Wharton.   The poetical image therefore must not be pressed
with prosaic precision.

ὁ ἰός, first, poison, connected with Lat. *virus*, from a root meaning
to work,—comp. 'works like poison in the blood'—then rust,

especially on iron and brass: σίδηρον γοῦν καὶ χαλκὸν καὶ τὰς τοιουτο-
τρόπους οὐσίας εὕροις ἂν ἀφανιζομένας, ἐξ ἑαυτῶν μὲν ὅταν ἑρπηνώδους νοσή-
ματος τρόπον ἰὸς ἐπιδραμὼν διαφάγοι, Phil. de Mundo, p. 610. 30.

**εἰς μαρτύριον ὑμῖν ἔσται**, for a witness against you. Comp. Matt.
xxiii. 31 μαρτυρεῖτε ἑαυτοῖς. The rust or tarnish of the hoarded gold
and silver is a symbol and witness of the destruction coming upon
you. Comp. Book of Enoch li., 'in those days men shall not be
saved by gold and by silver.'

**φάγεται**, eateth or will eat: comp. Ecclesiasticus xxxvi. 18 πᾶν βρῶμα
φάγεται κοιλία. It is a Hellenistic form not found in the classics. It
is used both of future and present time, and is of interest as supporting the theory of an original identity of the present and future forms.
Comp. ἔδομαι, πίομαι, and see Clyde § 33 and Lob. Phryn. 327 and 348.

**τὰς σάρκας**, pl. Comp. 2 Kings ix. 36 καταφάγονται οἱ κύνες τὰς
σάρκας τῆς Ἰεζάβελ.

**ὡς πῦρ**, with φάγεται, R.V.; with ἐθησαυρίσατε, Westcott and Hort.
The connexion with ἐθησαυρίσατε is supported by two passages in the
O.T. (LXX.) Prov. xvi. 27 ἐπὶ δὲ τῶν ἑαυτοῦ χειλέων θησαυρίζει πῦρ.
In the Hebr., however, there is no word corresponding to θησαυρίζει,
and there may be a confusion between the Hebrew words צָבַר, 'to heap
up' (elsewhere used to translate θησαυρίζειν) and צָרַב, 'to be scorched.'
The rendering of the Hebr. text is: 'and in his lips there is a scorch-
ing fire.' The other passage is Micah vi. 10 μὴ πῦρ καὶ οἶκος ἀνόμου
θησαυρίζων θησαυροὺς ἀνόμους καὶ μετὰ ὕβρεως ἀδικίας; in this passage
πῦρ is not represented in the Hebrew. Its insertion is due to the
similarity of שֵׁא (ish), 'there is,' and שֵׁא (esh), 'fire.' The juxta-
position of the two words in the Greek text, especially in the first
passage quoted, however, may have suggested the expression in St
James. On the other hand it is more natural to take ὡς πῦρ with the
words which precede rather than those which follow, and this is the
view of most commentators.

**ἐν ἐσχάταις ἡμέραις**, in last days, days of crisis; the absence of
the article marks the general character of the expression, which does
not necessarily mean the end of the world. Comp. Gen. xlix. 1 τί
ἀπαντήσει ὑμῖν ἐπ' ἐσχάτων τῶν ἡμερῶν. Prov. xxxi. 25 εὐφράνθη
ἐν ἐσχάταις ἡμέραις, 'she laugheth at the time to come' R.V., Is. ii. 2
ἔσται ἐν ταῖς ἐσχάταις ἡμέραις ἐμφανὲς τὸ ὄρος Κυρίου, Micah iv. 1
(where the Hebrew is the same as in the last passage) καὶ ἔσται ἐπ'
ἐσχάτων τῶν ἡμερῶν ἐμφανὲς τὸ ὄρος Κυρίου, 2 Tim. iii. 1 ἐν ἐσχάταις
ἡμέραις ἐνστήσονται καιροὶ χαλεποί. Bishop Westcott on 1 St John ii. 18
ἐσχάτη ὥρα ἐστίν, points out that in all these passages the expression
points to a time of crisis in the definite future, in Gen. xlix. 1 to the
entrance into Canaan, in Is. ii. 2, Mic. iv. 1 to the restoration of
Israel. In St John the use of the article, ἐν τῇ ἐσχάτῃ ἡμέρᾳ, gives a
definite meaning, as xi. 24 οἶδα ὅτι ἀναστήσεται ἐν τῇ ἀναστάσει ἐν τῇ
ἐσχάτῃ ἡμέρᾳ. See also in the same gospel chs. vi. 39, 40, 44, 54,
vii. 37, xii. 48. But there is a sense in which each age is a 'last
day' or hour, and in each there are 'last days' to come.

**4. ἰδού:** here as frequently in N.T. a vivid transitional particle. The Jews were agriculturists long before they were traders. It would be a natural step, as they grew in wealth, to acquire land in the countries of the Dispersion. It is probable that the land which Barnabas sold was in Cyprus.

**ὁ μισθὸς τῶν ἐργατῶν.** Comp. Luke x. 7 ἄξιος ὁ ἐργάτης τοῦ μισθοῦ αὐτοῦ, and Levit. xix. 13, where the rule is given: οὐ μὴ κοιμηθήσεται ὁ μισθὸς τοῦ μισθωτοῦ παρὰ σοὶ ἕως πρωί. More fully Deut. xxiv. 14, 15 οὐκ ἀπαδικήσεις μισθὸν πένητος καὶ ἐνδεοῦς ἐκ τῶν ἀδελφῶν σου ἢ ἐκ τῶν προσηλύτων τῶν ἐν ταῖς πόλεσί σου· αὐθημερὸν ἀποδώσεις τὸν μισθὸν αὐτοῦ· οὐκ ἐπιδύσεται ὁ ἥλιος ἐπ' αὐτῷ, ὅτι πένης ἐστὶ καὶ ἐν αὐτῷ ἔχει τὴν ἐλπίδα, καὶ καταβοήσεται κατὰ σοῦ πρὸς Κύριον. St James' words enforce this passage from the law, and by a truly poetical touch transfer the cry for justice from the labourer to the wages unjustly withheld. Like the rust on the hoarded metal, the wage kept back by fraud cries for vengeance. For this poetical figure comp. Habak. ii. 11, Luke xix. 40; and for prophetic denunciation of the same violation of the law see Jer. xxii. 13 παρὰ τῷ πλησίον αὐτοῦ ἐργᾶται δωρεάν, καὶ τὸν μισθὸν αὐτοῦ οὐ μὴ ἀποδώσει αὐτῷ and Micah iii. 10.

**τῶν ἀμησάντων.** ἀμᾶν here only in N.T. for the more usual θερίζειν. It is used in the classics in poetry and late prose of (a) reaping, ἤμων ὀξείας δρεπάνας ἐν χερσὶν ἔχοντες Il. xviii. 551, and in middle of (b) gathering, ταλάροισιν ἀμησάμενος (γάλα) Od. ix. 247. Curtius regards (a) as the root-meaning, connecting it with Latin meto, but see Lid. and Scott sub voc. The tense marks that the wages were due.

**τὰς χώρας ὑμῶν,** fields, farm lands, χώρα in the singular meaning a farm or estate: οἱ ἐν τῇ χώρᾳ ἐργάται, Xen. Hier. x. 5.

**ἀφυστερημένος,** still kept back; the perfect part. denotes that the act continues in its effects to the time implied.

**ἀφ' ὑμῶν,** according to most editors to be taken with ἀφυστερημένος, but even in that case ἀπό would differ from ὑπό, indicating not the agent but the source of the injustice, 'on your part' or 'by your fraud.' Comp. Acts ii. 22 ἀποδεδειγμένον ἀπὸ τοῦ θεοῦ, where see Page. Luke xvii. 25 ἀποδοκιμασθῆναι ἀπὸ τῆς γενεᾶς ταύτης. In several passages the MSS. vary between ἀπό and ὑπό, as Mark viii. 31, Luke vi. 18, Acts iv. 36, Rom. xiii. 1. In Modern Greek ἀπό is regularly used of the agent, and in common speech with the accus., ἀπὸ τὸν θεὸν ἔγειναν τὰ πάντα, Corfe, Mod. Grk Gram. p. 142. Another interpretation, however, connects ἀφ' ὑμῶν with κράζει, the wage cries from you, with whom it is placed, οὐ μὴ κοιμηθήσεται παρὰ σοί (Hebr. lodge with thee), Levit. loc. cit. For this construction comp. Gen. iv. 10 φωνὴ αἵματος ...βοᾷ...ἐκ τῆς γῆς, Ex. ii. 23 ἀνέβη ἡ βοὴ αὐτῶν πρὸς τὸν θεὸν ἀπὸ τῶν ἔργων·

**κράζει,** frequently used of the appeal against injustice or of the cry for deliverance: Judges iv. 3 καὶ ἐκέκραξαν οἱ υἱοὶ Ἰσραὴλ πρὸς Κύριον, Ps. xxi. 5 πρὸς σὲ ἐκέκραξαν καὶ ἐσώθησαν. Comp. also Is. v. 7 ἔμεινα τοῦ ποιῆσαι κρίσιν ἐποίησε δὲ ἀνομίαν καὶ οὐ δικαιοσύνην ἀλλὰ κραυγήν, 'he looked...for righteousness but behold a cry' R.V. In the Hebr. there is a play on the contrasted words 'righteousness' and 'a cry.'

Κυρίου Σαβαώθ, here only in N.T.; in LXX. either untranslated as
here, or rendered by Κύριος παντοκράτωρ, 2 Sam. v. 10, vii. 27, or
κύριος τῶν δυνάμεων, Ps. xxiv. 10, Lord of hosts, either as commanding
the armies of Israel or as Lord of the heavenly powers.

εἰσελήλυθαν. This aoristic termination of the perfect occurs Luke
ix. 36, John xvii. 6, 7, Acts xvi. 36, and elsewhere in N.T. This
approach to uniformity in the forms of the aorist and perfect tenses
is one of the marks of the post-classical period. See Simcox, *The
Language of the N.T.*, p. 35.

5. ἐτρυφήσατε, **ye lived delicately.** The force of these aorists
should be observed; the whole past is reviewed as on a judgment day.
τρυφᾶν, here only in N.T. The strengthened form καταρυφᾶν is
beautifully used Ps. xxxvii. 4 κατατρύφησον τοῦ κυρίου, and 11 πραεῖς...
καταρυφήσουσιν ἐπὶ πλήθει εἰρήνης. Comp. also Is. lv. 2 ἀκούσατέ
μου καὶ φάγεσθε ἀγαθά, καὶ ἐντρυφήσει ἐν ἀγαθοῖς ἡ ψυχὴ ὑμῶν, and
Eur. *Ion* 1375 χρόνον γὰρ ὅν μ' ἐχρῆν ἐν ἀγκάλαις | μητρὸς τρυφῆσαι καί
τι τερφθῆναι βίου | ἀπεστερήθην φιλτάτης μητρὸς τροφῆς, Plato *Legg.*
695 D βασιλικὴ καὶ τρυφῶσα παιδεία.

The whole picture may be compared with the parables of Dives and
Lazarus, Luke xvi. 19 f., and the Rich Fool, Luke xii. 16 f.

ἐσπαταλήσατε, **ye lived a life of wantonness.** Comp. 1 Tim. v. 6
ἡ δὲ σπαταλῶσα ζῶσα τέθνηκεν, the only other passage where the
word occurs in N.T. ὃς κατασπαταλᾷ ἐκ παιδὸς οἰκέτης ἔσται, ἔσχατον δὲ
ὀδυνηθήσεται ἐφ' ἑαυτῷ, Prov. xxix. 21, is a mistranslation of the Hebr.
"He that delicately bringeth up his servant from a child shall have
him become a son at the last" R.V. ἐν πλησμονῇ ἄρτων καὶ ἐν εὐθηνίᾳ
ἐσπατάλων αὕτη (Sodom) καὶ αἱ θυγατέρες αὐτῆς, Ezek. xvi. 49, οἱ καθεύ-
δοντες ἐπὶ κλινῶν ἐλεφαντίνων καὶ κατασπαταλῶντες ἐπὶ ταῖς στρωμναῖς
αὐτῶν κ.τ.λ. Amos vi. 4. The word is well explained Clem. Alex. IV.,
*Strom.* p. 450 ὅσα σπαταλῶσα ἐπιθυμεῖ ἡ ψυχὴ ἡμῶν οὐκ ἀρκουμένη τοῖς
ἀναγκαίοις περιεργαζομένη δὲ τὴν χλιδήν.

ἐθρέψατε τὰς καρδίας ὑμῶν. καρδία (לֵב) is used in a wide sense in
Hebrew psychology. It is the centre or seat of the vital powers
generally, here in the lower physical sense of appetite. Comp. Jud.
xix. 5 στήρισον τὴν καρδίαν σου κλάσματι ἄρτου: Acts xiv. 17 ἐμπιπλῶν
τροφῆς καὶ εὐφροσύνης τὰς καρδίας ὑμῶν.

ἐν ἡμέρᾳ σφαγῆς. See Jer. xii. 3 ἅγνισον αὐτοὺς εἰς ἡμέραν σφαγῆς,
where the correct rendering of the Hebrew is: "pull them out like
sheep for the slaughter, and prepare them for the day of slaughter"
R.V. (The first clause is not represented in the LXX.) The context
in Jeremiah, a protest against the prosperity of the wicked, has a
close relation to this passage. St James reminds the evil rich man
that the day of retribution is at hand.

6. κατεδικάσατε, **ye condemned.** Another reference to the courts,
κριτήρια, ch. ii. 6, which were used as instruments of oppression.

ἐφονεύσατε τὸν δίκαιον, **ye slew the just one.** Either (a) some
special case of martyrdom is referred to, or (b) τὸν δίκαιον points to a
class, the article generalising. See Winer, p. 132 and comp. 2 Cor.

xii. 12 τὰ σημεῖα τοῦ ἀποστόλου, Matt. xii. 35 ὁ ἀγαθὸς ἄνθρωπος...ἐκ-
βάλλει ἀγαθά, or (c) by τὸν δίκαιον Jesus Christ is intended.  Comp.
Acts iii. 14 ὑμεῖς δὲ τὸν ἅγιον καὶ δίκαιον ἠρνήσασθε κ.τ.λ.  Of these (a)
appears to be the preferable interpretation.  One actual instance of
such cruelty and oppression best explains the vehement and indignant
protest of the apostle.  Such an incident may be explained by the
motives named in Wisdom of Solomon ii. 10—20 καταδυναστεύσωμεν
πένητα δίκαιον...ἐνεδρεύσωμεν τὸν δίκαιον ὅτι δύσχρηστος ἡμῖν ἐστι...κατα-
δικάσωμεν αὐτόν, ἔσται γὰρ αὐτοῦ ἐπισκοπὴ ἐκ λόγων αὐτοῦ.  The words
found a striking parallel in the death of James himself: Eus. H. E.
II. 23 καὶ ἔλεγον ἀλλήλοις· Λιθάσωμεν Ἰάκωβον τὸν δίκαιον.  καὶ ἤρξαντο
λιθάζειν αὐτόν, κ.τ.λ.  Plato Rep. 362 A describes the fate of the man
δοκῶν μὲν εἶναι ἄδικος διὰ βίου ὢν δὲ δίκαιος.  In the end μαστιγώσεται,
στρεβλώσεται...τελευτῶν πάντα κακὰ παθὼν ἀνασχινδυλευθήσεται.

οὐκ ἀντιτάσσεται ὑμῖν, **he resists you not.**  The non-resistance of
the innocent righteous is in the spirit of our Lord's words, Matt. v.
39 ff. ἐγὼ δὲ λέγω ὑμῖν μὴ ἀντιστῆναι τῷ πονηρῷ, κ.τ.λ.  Comp. also the
picture of the suffering servant of Jehovah, Is. liii. 7 ff. ὡς πρόβατον
ἐπὶ σφαγὴν ἤχθη, καὶ ὡς ἀμνὸς ἐναντίον τοῦ κείροντος ἄφωνος οὕτως οὐκ
ἀνοίγει τὸ στόμα.  Comp. Book of Enoch, ch. ciii., 'to those who
hate us have we humbled our neck; but they have shewn no compassion towards us.'  If the clause be pointed interrogatively the
meaning would be either (a) Doth not the Lord (ὁ κύριος understood)
oppose you? or (b) Doth not he oppose you by his testimony at the
judgment seat of Christ?

**7.**  The death of the righteous martyr raises once more the thought
of μακροθυμία, this time with hopes of the παρουσία.  The Book of
Enoch again has a parallel: 'Wait with patient hope; for formerly
you have been disgraced with evil and with affliction, but now shall
you shine like the luminaries of heaven.  You shall be seen and the
gates of heaven shall be opened to you.  Your cries have cried for
judgment and it has appeared to you,' ch. civ.

οὖν.  Therefore, because this grievous persecution is directed
against you.

ἕως τῆς παρουσίας τοῦ κυρίου.  The recognised expression for the
advent or presence of Christ.  In the gospels the use of παρουσία is
confined to our Lord's discourse in Matt. xxiv.  In St Paul's epistles
it occurs six times, in 1 and 2 Thess., and in 1 Cor. xv. 23 (in 1 Cor.
i. 8 the true reading is ἡμέρᾳ), it occurs in 2 Pet. three times, namely
i. 16, iii. 4 and 12, and 1 John ii. 28.  There is no LXX. authority
for the word.

Another Pauline word for the appearing of Christ is ἐπιφάνεια,
2 Thess. ii. 8, and five times in the Pastoral Epistles.

The whole expression ἕως τῆς παρ. not only marks the limit—the
terminus ad quem—but also suggests a reason for long-suffering.

ὁ γεωργός.  The metaphor suggests patience, toil, co-operation
(κοινωνία εἰς τὸ εὐαγγέλιον, Phil. i. 5), faith, reward.  ὡς ὁ ἀροτριῶν καὶ
πρόσελθε αὐτῇ (σοφία) καὶ ἀνάμενε τοὺς καρποὺς αὐτῆς, Ecclus. vi. 19.

τὸν τίμιον καρπὸν τῆς γῆς indicates the naturalness of the development till the end comes. The ripening of events, the parable of the Fig Tree, Matt. xxi. 19—22, of the Seed growing secretly, the Tares, the grain of Mustard Seed, the Hidden Leaven, Mark iv. 26, Matt. xiii. 24—35, teach the same lesson.

ἕως λάβῃ. For the omission of ἄν in this construction see Mark xiv. 32, Luke xv. 4 ἕως εὕρῃ αὐτό, xxii. 34 ἕως τρίς με ἀπαρνήσῃ εἰδέναι, 2 Thess. ii. 7 and Rev. vi. 11, xx. 5. When ἕως is followed by οὗ or ὅτου the sequence of the subjunctive is frequent. The construction is used of an event conceived as possible, but uncertain in regard to the time of its occurrence. See Winer, p. 387, Green, p. 166.

(ὑετὸν) πρόϊμον καὶ ὄψιμον. See Deut. xi. 14; Jer. v. 24; Joel ii. 23; Hos. vi. 3. In Hebrew the former rain is lit. 'sprinkling,' יוֹרֶה, the latter lit. 'gathered,' מַלְקוֹשׁ, from the gathering of the harvest. The former rain begins as a rule at the end of October or beginning of November, lasting often through January and February. By that time the ground is softened and ploughing made possible. The latter rains, on which the growth of the crop depends, fall in March and April. In 1885 the rainfall in Palestine was Jan. 7·79 in.; Feb. 2·90 in.; March 5·47 in.; April 6·52 in.; from May to Nov. less than 1 in.; in Dec. 6·27 in., *Pal. Expl. F. Quart. St.*, April, 1894. The fertility of Palestine is wholly dependent on the rainfall. "Its uncertainty caused it to be a special subject of prayer. At the present day Moslems, Christians and Jews unite in fasts, processions and prayers for the 'showers that water the earth,'" Thomson, *The Land and the Book*, p. 91. As contrasted with Egypt, which is 'watered with the foot,' Palestine is a land that 'drinketh water of the rain of heaven.' Hence 'rain in due season' is the promised reward of faithfulness in Israel, Deut. xi. 10—14.

8. ἡ παρουσία τοῦ κυρίου ἤγγικεν, a Christian watchword, cited in its Aramaic form Μαρὰν ἀθά, 1 Cor. xvi. 22, and Phil. iv. 5 τὸ ἐπιεικὲς ὑμῶν γνωσθήτω πᾶσιν ἀνθρώποις· ὁ κύριος ἐγγύς: where as here the παρουσία is a motive for forbearance and fairness of judgment; see below.

9. μὴ στενάζετε, a strengthened expression for μὴ καταλαλεῖτε, ch. iv. 11. Comp. Matt. vii. 1 μὴ κρίνετε ἵνα μὴ κριθῆτε: and see Phil. iv. 5.

κριτής κ.τ.λ. Note the same close connexion between slander and the presence of the Judge, ch. iv. 11. For κριτής in connexion with the παρουσία see Acts x. 42; 2 Tim. iv. 8; Heb. xii. 23. For the effect of the παρουσία on conduct see Matt. xxiv. 46—51; Luke xii. 40. With the phrase πρὸ τῶν θυρῶν comp. Matt. xxiv. 33 ἐγγύς ἐστιν ἐπὶ θύραις, Mark xiii. 29, Rev. iii. 20 ἕστηκα ἐπὶ τὴν θύραν.

10. κακοπαθείας, here only in N.T. Comp. *infra v.* 13 κακοπαθεῖν, 'to endure hardship'; and 2 Tim. ii. 3, 9, iv. 5.

μακροθυμίας, longsuffering, a late Greek word found in Plutarch, elsewhere only in LXX. and N.T., 10 times in St Paul's epistles, in Heb. vi. 12, and of divine longsuffering, 1 Pet. iii. 20 and 2 Pet. iii.

15.　Trench defines it as a "long holding out of the mind before it gives room to action or passion—generally passion." The μακρόθυμος is βραδὺς εἰς ὀργήν. Here it is endurance under persecution, a noble self-restraint which refuses to take vengeance, Matt. v. 22—24, 39—41. In 1 Macc. viii. 4 it is used of the Roman *patience* which conquered the world, κατεκράτησαν τοῦ τόπου παντὸς τῇ βουλῇ αὐτῶν καὶ μακροθυμίᾳ. For a description of the divine μακροθυμία (though the word itself does not occur in the passage) Trench refers to Wisdom xii. 20, 21.

οἳ ἐλάλησαν ἐν τῷ ὀνόματι Κυρίου, added to indicate a parallel between the prophets and the suffering Christians to whom St James writes, comp. Matt. v. 12. Like the prophets they are on the side of God against the world. Comp. Is. l. 10 πεποίθατε ἐπὶ τῷ ὀνόματι Κυρίου, Jer. xxiii. 25 προφητεύουσιν ἐπὶ τῷ ὀνόματί μου, Ezek. xvi. 14 ἐξῆλθέν σου ὄνομα ἐν τοῖς ἔθνεσι. By ὄνομα Κυρίου is meant that by which the Lord is known, every manifestation of Him, that which formed the basis and substance of the prophetic teaching.

11.　τοὺς ὑπομείναντας, those who endured, indicating special instances of endurance; τοὺς ὑπομένοντας would signify a class, generally 'those who endure.'

ὑπομονήν. See ch. i. 3 and also Trench *N. T. Synonyms*, Second Series.

τὸ τέλος Κυρίου, that which in the end Jehovah brought to pass for Job: ὁ γὰρ αὐτὸς ἠθέλησεν καὶ ἐποίησεν, Job xxiii. 13; comp. *v.* 7 of the same ch. ἐξαγάγοι δὲ εἰς τέλος τὸ κρίμα μου. For the genitive see Winer, pp. 309, 310. Others render this expression 'the end of the Lord Jesus,' the result of His sufferings. But such a reference would be less appropriate here, and if that meaning had been intended the expression would have been more explicit.

πολύσπλαγχνος. Here only in N.T., but σπλάγχνα, lit. the larger and more important internal organs, especially the heart, is frequently used in the sense of pity and compassion: Phil. i. 8 ἐπιποθῶ πάντας ὑμᾶς ἐν σπλάγχνοις Ἰησοῦ Χριστοῦ, where see Bp Lightfoot, Luke i. 78 σπλάγχνα ἐλέους, 'a compassionate heart,' Col. iii. 12 σπλ. οἰκτιρμῶν, Philemon 7 τὰ σπλ. τῶν ἁγίων ἀναπέπαυται διὰ σοῦ, and elsewhere. The verb σπλαγχνίζεσθαι is only found in the synoptic gospels, and is there used always to express the Lord's compassion as a motive for healing.

With this verse the epistle as a whole connected subject appears to end. What follows is in the nature and manner of a postscript. It contains special warnings needed for the Churches, which had not fallen into the preceding argument.

12.　πρὸ πάντων marks the importance of what follows.

μὴ ὀμνύετε κ.τ.λ. This emphatic rule is founded on the Lord's words, recorded by St Matthew only, v. 33 ff. μὴ ὀμόσαι ὅλως κ.τ.λ. Comp. xxiii. 16—22. The only oath enjoined in the Mosaic code is

that by which an accused person cleared himself from the charge, Ex.
xxii. 11; Lev. v. 1, vi. 3; Numb. v. 19—22.  Comp. Deut. vi. 13, x. 20;
Ps. lxiii. 11.  But such was the sanctity attached to an oath that it
could not be demanded on a trivial accusation ; a denial was sufficient
(τὸ ναὶ ναὶ καὶ τὸ οὒ οὔ), or the word *amen* or σὺ εἶπας (see Matt. xxvi.
63, 64) constituted an oath.  By a curious inconsistency an oath
taken by heaven, earth, Jerusalem or any other creature came to be
regarded as invalid (Mishnah, Shebuoth ɪv. 13, as cited by Dr Ginsburg,
Kitto's *Encyc.* under 'Oath'), compare our Lord's words, Matt. xxiii.
16—22.

So great was the fear of offending by a false oath that pious Jews
before the time of Christ discountenanced swearing altogether :
Ecclesiasticus xxiii. 9—11 ὅρκῳ μὴ ἐθίσῃς τὸ στόμα σου, καὶ ὀνομασίᾳ τοῦ
ἁγίου μὴ συνεθισθῇς...ἀνὴρ πολύορκος πλησθήσεται ἀνομίας, καὶ οὐκ ἀπο-
στήσεται ἀπὸ τοῦ οἴκου αὐτοῦ μάστιξ, κ.τ.λ.  The Pharisees avoided oaths
as much as possible, the Essenes entirely,—a rule which even Herod
was obliged to recognise by exempting the Essenes from the oath of
allegiance, Joseph. *Ant.* xv. 10. 4.  For the whole subject see Kitto's
*Encycl.*, under ' Oath.'

ἤτω.  For this rare form see Veitch *sub voc.* εἰμί.  In Plat.
*Rep.* 361 ἔστω is now read or ἴτω.

The construction with the accusative is more classical than the
idiom used Matt. v. 34, 35 ἐν τῷ οὐρανῷ...ἐν τῇ γῇ.

**13—20.**  Deeply important practical rules relating to (*a*) Prayer as
a force in life, (*b*) Intercessory prayer, (*c*) Confession, (*d*) Conversion.

**13.  κακοπαθεῖ.**  See above, *v.* 10.

**ψαλλέτω.**  The word implies the accompaniment of a musical
instrument.  For psalmody among the Jews see Bp Lightfoot's note
on Col. iii. 16.  He shews by quotation from Philo that it had reached
a high development at this epoch: ποιοῦσιν ᾄσματα καὶ ὕμνους εἰς θεὸν
διὰ παντοίων μέτρων καὶ μελῶν ἃ ῥυθμοῖς σεμνοτέροις ἀναγκαίως χαράτ-
τουσι, Philo, *de Vita Cont.* § 3 (ɪɪ. p. 476); πάννυχοι δὲ διατελέσαντες
ἐν ὕμνοις καὶ ᾠδαῖς, Philo *in Flacc.* 14 (ɪɪ. p. 535).  For the hymnody of
the first Christians see Acts iv. 24, xvi. 25, 1 Cor. xiv. 15, 26.  It is
probable that fragments of Christian hymns are to be found in the
epistles, as in Eph. v. 14 and 1 Tim. iii. 16.

**14.  ἀσθενεῖ, is sick,** a special form of the more general κακοπαθεῖ.
For the word see Matt. x. 8, Luke iv. 40.

Note the aorists προσκαλεσάσθω...προσευξάσθωσιν of single acts contrasted with προσευχέσθω and ψαλλέτω, the continuous exercise of
prayer and psalmody.

**τοὺς πρεσβυτέρους τῆς ἐκκλησίας,** probably the earliest mention in
the N.T. of the presbyters of the Church.  The term and the office
were undoubtedly in the first instance transferred from the Jewish to
the Christian Church.  The Jewish πρεσβύτεροι are frequently named
with the chief priests and scribes: together they constituted the San-
hedrin, Mark xiv. 53 οἱ ἀρχιερεῖς καὶ οἱ πρεσβύτεροι καὶ οἱ γραμματεῖς.

So in the Christian Church an important question is referred to 'the
Apostles and Presbyters' in Jerusalem, Acts xv. 6. Christian Presbyters are also mentioned, Acts xi. 30, xiv. 23, xv. 2, &c.

τῆς ἐκκλησίας, also a term which connects Christianity with
Judaism, comp. Matt. xviii. 17 ἐὰν δὲ παρακούσῃ αὐτῶν, εἰπὲ τῇ
ἐκκλησίᾳ, a direction which must have been understood in the first
instance to refer to the ruling body of the synagogue, the *collegium
presbyterorum*, but which could naturally be transferred to that Church
which our Lord calls τὴν ἐκκλησίαν μου, as distinct from the Jewish
Church. See note in this series on Matt. xvi. 18 and xviii. 17.

ἐπ' αὐτόν, over him. ἐπί denotes the direction of the act. Comp.
Luke xxiii. 28 μὴ κλαίετε ἐπ' ἐμέ, Acts xix. 13 ἐπεχείρησαν δέ τινες καὶ
τῶν περιερχομένων Ἰουδαίων ἐξορκιστῶν ὀνομάζειν ἐπὶ τοὺς ἔχοντας τὰ
πνεύματα τὰ πονηρὰ τὸ ὄνομα τοῦ κυρίου Ἰησοῦ, a passage which bears a
close relation to this. For besides the positive direction given for the
use of prayer and the ordinary remedies for sickness there is an
implicit warning against superstitious usages such as were practised
by Jewish exorcists, and which from the remotest ages had been
prevalent in Babylonia and other regions where the Jews were now
settled. The Kouyunjik gallery of the British Museum contains
many specimens of terra cotta tables (often bilingual, Accadian and
Assyrian) containing ceremonies and incantations for the sick; some
are against evil spirits, some for special diseases of the head or eyes.

ἀλείψαντες ἐλαίῳ. The remedial use of oil was very general in
ancient times, and is still prevalent in many countries. See Is. i. 6
οὐκ ἔστιν μάλαγμα ἐπιθεῖναι οὔτε ἔλαιον οὔτε καταδέσμους, Mark vi. 13
καὶ ἤλειφον ἐλαίῳ πολλοὺς ἀρρώστους καὶ ἐθεράπευον. Comp. also Luke
x. 34. The aorist participle is sometimes as here used to express an
action contemporaneous with the principal verb. See Monro, *Hom.
Gram.* p. 48, § 77. The anointing was to be accompanied with prayer.
The doctrine of extreme unction seems to have been based upon this
passage. But as leading Roman Catholic theologians have themselves seen (see Beyschlag *ad loc.*), St James is not here speaking of
those who are at the point of death, but of sick persons whose
recovery is contemplated.

ἐν τῷ ὀνόματι. Comp. Acts iii. 6 ἐν τῷ ὀνόματι Ἰησοῦ Χριστοῦ τοῦ
Ναζωραίου περιπάτει, and xix. 13, cited above.

**15.** εὐχὴ τῆς πίστεως. The prayer which is based upon faith,
which proceeds from faith. Comp. Matt. xxi. 22 καὶ πάντα ὅσα ἂν
αἰτήσητε ἐν τῇ προσευχῇ πιστεύοντες λήμψεσθε.

σώσει τὸν κάμνοντα. κάμνειν here and Heb. xii. 3 only in the sense
of being sick. σώσει, here in the sense of physical recovery as in
Matt. ix. 22, Mark v. 23, and John xi. 12. The difficulty that such
means have not been and could not be always efficacious in the
recovery of the sick is resolved by the consideration that prayer is
always subject to the condition of *deo volente*. Such a prayer
unanswered might well result in a higher σωτηρία than the recovery
of bodily health.

ἐγερεῖ αὐτόν ὁ κύριος. This also must refer to the raising from the bed of sickness—it is an expansion of σώσει. The unconditional promise is startling, but again ἐὰν ὁ κύριος θέλῃ is to be understood.

κἂν ἁμαρτίας ᾖ πεποιηκώς κ.τ.λ. The underlying thought here is that sin is the hindrance to recovery. For ἀφεθήσεται see Matt. xvi. 19, xviii. 18, and John xx. 23 ἄν τινων ἀφῆτε τὰς ἁμαρτίας ἀφέωνται αὐτοῖς· ἄν τινων κράτητε κεκράτηνται.

For the analytic form ᾖ πεποιηκώς see Winer III. xlv.

16. ἐξομολογεῖσθε ..ὅπως ἰαθῆτε. It is disputed whether ἰαθῆτε be used of physical healing or in a figurative sense. The context certainly points rather to the first explanation. St James urges the practice (note the present imperatives) of mutual confession and intercessory prayer as appointed means of recovery from sickness.

πολὺ ἰσχύει κ.τ.λ. In its primary sense this clause is to be taken with the preceding words. Prayer of a righteous man is a strong force, an effective remedy in its working. ἐνεργουμένη, middle not passive, as the following examples seem to shew: 2 Cor. i. 6 εἴτε παρακαλούμεθα, ὑπὲρ τῆς ὑμῶν παρακλήσεως τῆς ἐνεργουμένης ἐν ὑπομονῇ τῶν αὐτῶν παθημάτων ὧν καὶ ἡμεῖς πάσχομεν, iv. 12 ὁ θάνατος ἐν ἡμῖν ἐνεργεῖται, Eph. iii. 20 κατὰ τὴν δύναμιν τὴν ἐνεργουμένην ἐν ἡμῖν. See also Col. i. 29, 1 Thess. ii. 13, 2 Thess. ii. 7.

The participle may indicate either (a) the cause, or (b) the time of the effectiveness of the prayer; that is (a) through its working, or (b) while it is working, is in activity.

As an instance of such effective prayer, which must have been often present to St James' mind, see Acts xii. 12, when St Peter, delivered from prison, came to the house of Mary, οὗ ἦσαν ἱκανοὶ συνηθροισμένοι καὶ προσευχόμενοι. See v. 17 ἀπαγγείλατε Ἰακώβῳ καὶ τοῖς ἀδελφοῖς ταῦτα. St James' own practice strikingly agreed with his words here: μόνος εἰσήρχετο εἰς τὸν ναόν, ηὑρίσκετό τε κείμενος ἐπὶ τοῖς γόνασι, καὶ αἰτούμενος ὑπὲρ τοῦ λαοῦ ἄφεσιν, ὡς ἀπεσκληκέναι τὰ γόνατα αὐτοῦ δίκην καμήλου, Hegesip. ap. Eus. H. E. II. 23.

The great physician, Sir Andrew Clark, two days before his death, said in answer to a question: "Not value prayers! Prayer is that which moves more than medicine; prayer is all powerful: it is the basis of love. Pray for me always."

17. Ἡλίας. For the historical account see 1 Kings xvii., xviii. In those chapters, however, there is no mention made of the two prayers of Elijah; and the duration of the famine is there limited to less than three years, xviii. 1. In St Luke iv. 25 the account agrees with this, marking the tradition followed by the family at Nazareth.

ὁμοιοπαθὴς ἡμῖν, of like passions with us, constituted as we are. Therefore we may expect the like result to prayer. For ὁμοιοπαθής see Acts xiv. 15; and Plato *Tim.* 45 c, where it is used synonymously with συμφυής.

προσευχῇ προσηύξατο. One of the few Hebraisms in this epistle. Comp. Luke xxii. 15 ἐπιθυμίᾳ ἐπεθύμησα, Acts iv. 17 ἀπειλῇ ἀπειλησώμεθα, Matt. xv. 4 θανάτῳ τελευτάτω, and also Plat. *Sympos.* 195 B

φεύγων φυγῇ τὸ γῆρας, Soph. *Oed. R.* 65 ὕπνῳ εὕδοντα. See also
Ecclesiasticus xlviii. 1 ff. καὶ ἀνέστη Ἡλείας προφήτης ὡς πῦρ καὶ ὁ λόγος
αὐτοῦ ὡς λαμπὰς ἐκαίετο.

τοῦ μὴ βρέξαι. The genitive of aim or object, here corresponding
with the use of ἵνα after verbs of request or petition: as Matt. xiv. 36
παρεκάλουν αὐτὸν ἵνα μόνον ἅψωνται, and frequently. (*a*) For this
final use of τοῦ with the infinitive, comp. Matt. ii. 13 μέλλει γὰρ
Ἡρῴδης ζητεῖν τὸ παιδίον τοῦ ἀπολέσαι αὐτό, Luke xxiv. 29 εἰσῆλθεν τοῦ
μεῖναι σὺν αὐτοῖς. With this compare the use of the Latin gerund and
gerundive, e.g. Marii miserunt Romam oratores pacis petendae, Liv. ix.
45 (Madvig, § 417 obs. 5).

(*b*) It also expresses result, e.g. Luke xxiv. 16 οἱ ὀφθαλμοὶ αὐτῶν
ἐκρατοῦντο τοῦ μὴ ἐπιγνῶναι αὐτόν. This usage is closely connected
with the final use, for in Hebrew thought every result was regarded as
purposed and predetermined. See note on Matt. i. 22 in this series.

(*c*) It is used regularly after words constructed with a genitive, as
1 Cor. xvi. 4 ἐὰν ᾖ ἄξιον τοῦ κἀμὲ πορεύεσθαι.

(*d*) In some passages it appears (1) as the object of verbs where the
accusative would be required in Classical Greek, as 1 Cor. ii. 2 οὐ γὰρ
ἔκρινα τοῦ εἰδέναι τι ἐν ὑμῖν, or (2) as the subject of the verb, Acts x. 25
ὡς δὲ ἐγένετο τοῦ εἰσελθεῖν τὸν Πέτρον. In Ps. cvi. 23 (LXX.) there is
an instance of a triple use of this infinitive : καὶ εἶπε τοῦ ἐξολοθρεῦσαι
(objective) αὐτούς, εἰ μὴ Μωυσῆς ὁ ἐκλεκτὸς αὐτοῦ ἔστη ἐν τῇ θραύσει
ἐνώπιον αὐτοῦ τοῦ ἀποστρέψαι (final) ἀπὸ θυμοῦ ὀργῆς αὐτοῦ, τοῦ μὴ
ἐξολοθρεῦσαι (consecutive). These and similar expressions may indeed
be explained as extensions of recognised genitival uses, but it is better
to regard them as illustrating the gradual forgetfulness in language of
the origin of idioms. In illustration of this comp. the use in French
of the infinitive with *de* either as subject or object of a verb: e.g. il
est triste de vous voir,—on craint d'y aller ; the adoption of the
(Latin) accusative in the same language as the sole representative
of the Latin cases; sometimes the single case form which survives in
a modern language is the genitive, e.g. Romaic ὁποῦ or ποῦ, 'who.'
The extension of ἵνα (νά) with the subjunctive in Modern Greek to
the various uses of the infinitive is another instance of this generalising tendency. This extended use of τοῦ with the infinitive, however, is not more remarkable than that the Greek infinitive, originally
a dative expressing purpose, should come to be joined with a genitive
of the article and so revert to its original meaning. "The Greek
Infinitive is a *survival* from a period when the Dative of purpose or
consequence was one of the ordinary constructions of the language,"
Monro, *Hom. Gram.*, § 242. See note on χαίρειν, i. 1.

βρέξαι. In classics generally transitive. Very rare in this sense.

**18. ἐβλάστησεν**: in the other three passages of the N.T. where
βλαστάνω occurs, viz. Matt. xiii. 26, Mark iv. 27, Heb. ix. 4, it bears
an intransitive sense as usually in the classics.

**19. ἀδελφοί μου** introduces another and a last topic closely connected with prayer, namely Conversion.

τῆς ἀληθείας. The clause ἐάν τις ἐν ὑμῖν makes it clear that the truth spoken of is the Christian truth, the saving truth of the gospel, almost equivalent to ἡ πίστις. Comp. 1 Tim. vi. 10 ῥίζα γὰρ πάντων τῶν κακῶν ἐστὶν ἡ φιλαργυρία, ἧς τινες ὀρεγόμενοι ἀπεπλανήθησαν ἀπὸ τῆς πίστεως, 21 ἀντιθέσεις τῆς ψευδωνύμου γνώσεως, ἥν τινες ἐπαγγελλόμενοι περὶ τὴν πίστιν ἠστόχησαν, 2 Tim. ii. 18 οἵτινες περὶ τὴν ἀλήθειαν ἠστόχησαν, λέγοντες ἀνάστασιν ἤδη γεγονέναι, καὶ ἀνατρέπουσι τήν τινων πίστιν. Therefore the conversion spoken of here is not conversion from heathenism or Judaism, but from some perversion of the Christian truth or morality such as is indicated in the passages cited.

**20.** σώσει ψυχὴν αὐτοῦ ἐκ θανάτου, **shall save his soul** (i.e. the soul of the convert) **from death.**

καὶ καλύψει πλῆθος ἁμαρτιῶν. Comp. Prov. x. 12 'love covereth all transgressions' R.V., where καλύψει is a literal rendering of the Hebr. הְּכָבַּה, 'cover' in the sense of 'forgive.' The LXX. translation of the passage is incorrect, but it is accurately cited 1 Peter iv. 8 ἀγάπη καλύπτει πλῆθος ἁμαρτιῶν. Comp. 1 Cor. xiii. 7 (ἡ ἀγάπη) πάντα στέγει. The meaning here is, will cover the multitude of his convert's sins, i.e. bring him through repentance within the range of divine forgiveness. The reference is undoubtedly to the passage in Proverbs, and ἀγάπη is virtually in thought the subject of καλύψει. Such an act as conversion is the highest act of ἀγάπη.

St James himself had this blessedness of converting many: ὅσοι δὲ καὶ ἐπίστευσαν, διὰ Ἰάκωβον. πολλῶν οὖν καὶ τῶν ἀρχόντων πιστευόντων, ἢν θόρυβος τῶν Ἰουδαίων καὶ γραμματέων καὶ Φαρισαίων λεγόντων ὅτι κινδυνεύει πᾶς ὁ λαὸς Ἰησοῦν τὸν χριστὸν προσδοκᾶν, Hegesip. ap. Eus. *H. E.* ii. 23.

The abrupt termination of the Epistle may be accounted for by the character of the document. It may be regarded as a series of decisions on the duties, temptations and difficulties of the Christian life suggested by actual facts which had been brought to the Apostle's notice; hence it takes the form of a charge or message to the Churches rather than that of an epistle in the ordinary sense of the word. The message ended, the conclusion comes without the usual epistolary greetings.

# INDICES.

## I. GENERAL.

# II. GREEK.

σώζειν, 67
σῶμα, 39

ταπεινός, 16
ταπείνωσις, 16
τέλειος, 13, 25, 41
τέλος, 65
— *τροπή, 21
*τροχός, 44
*τρυφᾶν, 62

*ὕλη, 42
ὑπό, 39, 42
ὑπομονή, xli, 12

φάγεσθαι, 60
φθόνος, 53
*φιλία, 52

φίλος θεοῦ, 38
*φλογίζειν, 44, 45
*φρίσσειν, 37
φῶς, 19

χαίρειν, 11
*χαλιναγωγεῖν, 27, 41
χήρα, 27
χορτάζειν, 36
χόρτος, 16
— *χρή, 46
— *χρυσοδακτύλιος, 30
χρυσός, 59
χώρα, 61

ψάλλειν, 66
ψυχή, 49
ψυχικός, 49

\* Words used by St James only in N.T.

In addition to the above the following words used by St James are not found elsewhere in the N.T.: βρύειν, γέλως, ἐνάλιος, θρησκός, πικρός, προσωπολημπτεῖν, σήπειν, ἐξέλκειν, βοή, ἐπιτήδειος, ἔοικε, κατιοῦν, κατοικίζειν, κενῶς, μαραίνειν, ταλαιπωρεῖν, ὁμοίωσις, ταχύς. — Mayor's *St James*, cxci.

CAMBRIDGE : PRINTED BY J. & C. F. CLAY, AT THE UNIVERSITY PRESS.

# THE PITT PRESS SERIES.

## *COMPLETE LIST.*

### 1. GREEK.

| Author | Work | Editor | Price |
|---|---|---|---|
| Aeschylus | Prometheus Vinctus | Rackham | 2/6 |
| Aristophanes | Aves—Plutus—Ranae | Green | 3/6 *each* |
| ,, | Vespae | Graves | 3/6 |
| ,, | Nubes | ,, | 3/6 |
| Demosthenes | Olynthiacs | Glover | 2/6 |
| Euripides | Heracleidae | Beck & Headlam | 3/6 |
| ,, | Hercules Furens | Gray & Hutchinson | 2/- |
| ,, | Hippolytus | Hadley | 2/- |
| ,, | Iphigeneia in Aulis | Headlam | 2/6 |
| ,, | Medea | ,, | 2/6 |
| ,, | Hecuba | Hadley | 2/6 |
| ,, | Alcestis | ,, | 2/6 |
| ,, | Orestes | Wedd | 4/6 |
| Herodotus | Book V | Shuckburgh | 3/- |
| ,, | ,, VI, VIII, IX | ,, | 4/- *each* |
| ,, | ,, VIII 1—90, IX 1—89 | ,, | 2/6 *each* |
| Homer | Odyssey IX, X | Edwards | 2/6 *each* |
| ,, | ,, XXI | ,, | 2/- |
| ,, | ,, XI | Nairn | 2/- |
| ,, | Iliad VI, XXII, XXIII, XXIV | Edwards | 2/- *each* |
| Lucian | Somnium, Charon, etc. | Heitland | 3/6 |
| ,, | Menippus and Timon | Mackie | 3/6 |
| Plato | Apologia Socratis | Adam | 3/6 |
| ,, | Crito | ,, | 2/6 |
| ,, | Euthyphro | ,, | 2/6 |
| ,, | Protagoras | J. & A. M. Adam | 4/6 |
| Plutarch | Demosthenes | Holden | 4/6 |
| ,, | Gracchi | ,, | 6/- |
| ,, | Nicias | ,, | 5/- |
| ,, | Sulla | ,, | 6/- |
| ,, | Timoleon | ,, | 6/- |
| Sophocles | Oedipus Tyrannus | Jebb | 4/- |
| Thucydides | Book III | Spratt | 5/- |
| ,, | Book VII | Holden | 5/- |
| Xenophon | Agesilaus | Hailstone | 2/6 |
| ,, | Anabasis Vol. I. Text | Pretor | 3/- |
| ,, | ,, Vol. II. Notes | ,, | 4/6 |
| ,, | ,, I, II | ,, | 4/- |
| ,, | ,, I, III, IV, V | ,, | 2/- *each* |
| ,, | ,, II, VI, VII | ,, | 2/6 *each* |
| ,, | Hellenics I, II | Edwards | 3/6 |
| ,, | Cyropaedeia I, II (2 vols.) | Holden | 6/- |
| ,, | ,, III, IV, V | ,, | 5/- |
| ,, | ,, VI, VII, VIII | ,, | 5/- |

25000
13/8/00

1

## 2. LATIN.

| Author | Work | Editor | Price |
|---|---|---|---|
| **Caesar** | De Bello Gallico | | |
| | Com. I, III, VI, VIII | Peskett | 1/6 *each* |
| ,, | ,, II–III, and VII | ,, | 2/- *each* |
| ,, | ,, I–III | ,, | 3/- |
| ,, | ,, IV–V | ,, | 1/6 |
| ,, | De Bello Civili. Com. I | Peskett | 3/- |
| ,, | ,, ,, Com. III | ,, | 2/6 |
| **Cicero** | Actio Prima in C. Verrem | Cowie | 1/6 |
| ,, | De Amicitia | Reid | 3/6 |
| ,, | De Senectute | | 3/6 |
| ,, | De Officiis. Bk III | Holden | 2/- |
| ,, | Pro Lege Manilia | Nicol | 1/6 |
| ,, | Div. in Q. Caec. et Actio Prima in C. Verrem | Heitland & Cowie | 3/- |
| ,, | Ep. ad Atticum. Lib II | Pretor | 3/- |
| ,, | Philippica Secunda | Peskett | 3/6 |
| ,, | Pro Archia Poeta | Reid | 2/- |
| ,, | ,, Balbo | ,, | 1/6 |
| ,, | ,, Milone | ,, | 2/6 |
| ,, | ,, Murena | Heitland | 3/- |
| ,, | ,, Plancio | Holden | 4/6 |
| ,, | ,, Sulla | Reid | 3/6 |
| ,, | Somnium Scipionis | Pearman | 2/- |
| **Cornelius Nepos** | Four parts | Shuckburgh | 1/6 *each* |
| **Horace** | Epistles. Bk I | ,, | 2/6 |
| ,, | Odes and Epodes | Gow | 5/- |
| ,, | Odes. Books I, III | ,, | 2/- *each* |
| ,, | ,, Book II, IV | ,, | 1/6 *each* |
| ,, | Epodes | ,, | 1/6 |
| **Juvenal** | Satires | Duff | 5/- |
| **Livy** | Books IV, VI, IX, XXVII | Stephenson | 2/6 *each* |
| ,, | ,, V | Whibley | 2/6 |
| ,, | ,, XXI, XXII | Dimsdale | 2/6 *each* |
| **Lucan** | Pharsalia. Bk I | Heitland & Haskins | 1/6 |
| ,, | De Bello Civili. Bk VII | Postgate | 2/- |
| **Lucretius** | Book V | Duff | 2/- |
| **Ovid** | Fasti. Book VI | Sidgwick | 1/6 |
| ,, | Metamorphoses, Bk I | Dowdall | 1/6 |
| **Plautus** | Epidicus | Gray | 3/- |
| ,, | Stichus | Fennell | 2/6 |
| ,, | Trinummus | Gray | 3/6 |
| **Quintus Curtius** | Alexander in India | Heitland & Raven | 3/6 |
| **Tacitus** | Agricola and Germania | Stephenson | 3/- |
| ,, | Hist. Bk I | Davies | 2/6 |
| **Terence** | Hautontimorumenos | Gray | 3/- |
| **Vergil** | Aeneid I to XII | Sidgwick | 1/6 *each* |
| ,, | Bucolics | ,, | 1/6 |
| ,, | Georgics I, II, and III, IV | ,, | 2/- *each* |
| ,, | Complete Works, Vol. I, Text | ,, | 3/6 |
| ,, | ,, ,, Vol. II, Notes | ,, | 4/6 |

## 3. FRENCH.

| Author | Work | Editor | Price |
|---|---|---|---|
| **About** | Le Roi des Montagnes | Ropes | 2/- |
| **Biart** | Quand j'étais petit, Pts I, II | Boïelle | 2/- each |
| **Boileau** | L'Art Poétique | Nichol Smith | 2/6 |
| **Corneille** | La Suite du Menteur | Masson | 2/- |
| ,, | Polyeucte | Braunholtz | 2/- |
| **De Bonnechose** | Lazare Hoche | Colbeck | 2/- |
| ,, | Bertrand du Guesclin | Leathes | 2/- |
| ,, | ,, Part II (*With Vocabulary*) ,, | | 1/6 |
| **Delavigne** | Louis XI | Eve | 2/- |
| ,, | Les Enfants d'Edouard | ,, | 2/- |
| **De Lamartine** | Jeanne d'Arc | Clapin & Ropes | 1/6 |
| **De Vigny** | La Canne de Jonc | Eve | 1/6 |
| **Dumas** | La Fortune de D'Artagnan (*With Vocabulary*) | Ropes | 2/- |
| **Erckmann-Chatrian** | La Guerre | Clapin | 3/- |
| **Guizot** | Discours sur l'Histoire de la Révolution d'Angleterre | Eve | 2/6 |
| **Mme de Staël** | Le Directoire | Masson & Prothero | 2/- |
| ,, | Dix Années d'Exil | ,, | 2/- |
| **Malot** | Remi et ses Amis | Verrall | 2/- |
| ,, | Remi en Angleterre | ,, | 2/- |
| **Merimée** | Colomba | Ropes | 2/- |
| **Michelet** | Louis XI & Charles the Bold | | 2/6 |
| **Molière** | Le Bourgeois Gentilhomme | Clapin | 1/6 |
| ,, | L'École des Femmes | Saintsbury | 2/6 |
| ,, | Les Précieuses ridicules | Braunholtz | 2/- |
| ,, | ,, (*Abridged Edition*) | ,, | 1/- |
| ,, | Le Misanthrope | ,, | 2/6 |
| ,, | L'Avare | ,, | 2/6 |
| **Perrault** | Fairy Tales | Rippmann | 1/6 |
| **Piron** | La Métromanie | Masson | 2/- |
| **Ponsard** | Charlotte Corday | Ropes | 2/- |
| **Racine** | Les Plaideurs | Braunholtz | 2/- |
| ,, | ,, (*Abridged Edition*) | ,, | 1/- |
| ,, | Athalie | Eve | 2/- |
| **Saintine** | Picciola | Ropes | 2/- |
| **Scribe & Legouvé** | Bataille de Dames | Bull | 2/- |
| **Scribe** | Le Verre d'Eau | Colbeck | 2/- |
| **Sédaine** | Le Philosophe sans le savoir | Bull | 2/- |
| **Souvestre** | Un Philosophe sous les Toits | Eve | 2/- |
| ,, | Le Serf & Le Chevrier de Lorraine | Ropes | 2/- |
| ,, | Le Serf (*With Vocabulary*) | ,, | 1/6 |
| **Thierry** | Lettres sur l'histoire de France (XIII—XXIV) | Masson & Prothero | 2/6 |
| ,, | Récits des Temps Mérovingiens, I—III | Masson & Ropes | 3/- |
| **Villemain** | Lascaris ou les Grecs du XVe Siècle | Masson | 2/- |
| **Voltaire** | Histoire du Siècle de Louis XIV, in three parts | Masson & Prothero | 2/6 each |
| **Xavier de Maistre** | {La Jeune Sibérienne. Le Lépreux de la Cité d'Aoste} | Masson | 1/6 |

## 4. GERMAN.

| Author | Work | Editor | Price |
|---|---|---|---|
| Andersen | Six Fairy Tales | Rippmann | 2/6 |
| | Ballads on German History | Wagner | 2/- |
| Benedix | Dr Wespe | Breul | 3/- |
| Freytag | Der Staat Friedrichs des Grossen | Wagner | 2/- |
| | German Dactylic Poetry | ,, | 3/- |
| Goethe | Knabenjahre (1749—1761) | Wagner & Cartmell | 2/- |
| | Hermann und Dorothea | ,, ,, | 3/6 |
| ,, | Iphigenie | Breul | 3/6 |
| Grimm | Selected Tales | Rippmann | 3/- |
| Gutzkow | Zopf und Schwert | Wolstenholme | 3/6 |
| Hackländer | Der geheime Agent | E. L. Milner Barry | 3/- |
| Hauff | Das Bild des Kaisers | Breul | 3/- |
| ,, | Das Wirthshaus im Spessart | Schlottmann & Cartmell | 3/- |
| ,, | Die Karavane | Schlottmann | 3/- |
| Immermann | Der Oberhof | Wagner | 3/- |
| Klee | Die deutschen Heldensagen | Wolstenholme | 3/- |
| Kohlrausch | Das Jahr 1813 | ,, | 2/- |
| Lessing | Minna von Barnhelm | Wolstenholme | 3/- |
| Lessing & Gellert | Selected Fables | Breul | 3/- |
| Mendelssohn | Selected Letters | Sime | 3/- |
| Raumer | Der erste Kreuzzug | Wagner | 2/- |
| Riehl | Culturgeschichtliche Novellen | Wolstenholme | 3/- |
| ,, | Die Ganerben & Die Gerechtigkeit Gottes | ,, | 3/- |
| Schiller | Wilhelm Tell | Breul | 2/6 |
| ,, | ,, (Abridged Edition) | ,, | 1/6 |
| ,, | Geschichte des dreissigjährigen Kriegs Book III. | ,, | 3/- |
| ,, | Maria Stuart | ,, | 3/6 |
| ,, | Wallenstein I. (Lager and Piccolomini) | ,, | 3/6 |
| ,, | Wallenstein II. (Tod) | ,, | 3/6 |
| Uhland | Ernst, Herzog von Schwaben | Wolstenholme | 3/6 |

## 5. ENGLISH.

| Author | Work | Editor | Price |
|---|---|---|---|
| **Bacon** | History of the Reign of King Henry VII | Lumby | 3/- |
| ,, | Essays | West | 3/6 & 5/- |
| ,, | New Atlantis (*In the Press*) | G. C. M. Smith | |
| **Cowley** | Essays | Lumby | 4/- |
| **Earle** | Microcosmography | West | 3/- & 4/- |
| **Gray** | Poems | Tovey | 4/- & 5/- |
| **Lamb** | Tales from Shakespeare | Flather | 1/6 |
| **Macaulay** | Lord Clive | Innes | 1/6 |
| ,, | Warren Hastings | ,, | 1/6 |
| ,, | William Pitt and Earl of Chatham | ,, | 2/6 |
| ,, | Lays and other Poems | Flather | 1/6 |
| **Mayor** | A Sketch of Ancient Philosophy from Thales to Cicero | | 3/6 |
| **More** | History of King Richard III | Lumby | 3/6 |
| ,, | Utopia | ,, | 3/6 |
| **Milton** | Arcades and Comus | Verity | 3/- |
| ,, | Ode on the Nativity, L'Allegro, Il Penseroso & Lycidas | ,, | 2/6 |
| ,, | Samson Agonistes | ,, | 2/6 |
| ,, | Sonnets | ,, | 1/6 |
| ,, | Paradise Lost, six parts | ,, | 2/- *each* |
| **Pope** | Essay on Criticism | West | 2/- |
| **Scott** | Marmion | Masterman | 2/6 |
| ,, | Lady of the Lake | ,, | 2/6 |
| ,, | Lay of the last Minstrel | Flather | 2/- |
| ,, | Legend of Montrose | Simpson | 2/6 |
| ,, | Old Mortality | Nicklin | 2/6 |
| **Shakespeare** | A Midsummer-Night's Dream | Verity | 1/6 |
| ,, | Twelfth Night | ,, | 1/6 |
| ,, | Julius Caesar | ,, | 1/6 |
| ,, | The Tempest | ,, | 1/6 |
| ,, | King Lear | ,, | 1/6 |
| ,, | Merchant of Venice | ,, | 1/6 |
| ,, | King Richard II | ,, | 1/6 |
| ,, | As you Like it | ,, | 1/6 |
| **Shakespeare & Fletcher** | Two Noble Kinsmen | Skeat | 3/6 |
| **Sidney** | An Apologie for Poetrie | Shuckburgh | 3/- |
| **Wallace** | Outlines of the Philosophy of Aristotle | | 4/6 |
| **West** | Elements of English Grammar | | 2/6 |
| ,, | English Grammar for Beginners | | 1/- |
| **Carlos** | Short History of British India | | 1/- |
| **Mill** | Elementary Commercial Geography | | 1/6 |
| **Bartholomew** | Atlas of Commercial Geography | | 3/- |
| **Robinson** | Church Catechism Explained | | 2/- |

## 6. EDUCATIONAL SCIENCE.

| *Author* | *Work* | *Editor* | *Price* |
|---|---|---|---|
| Colbeck | Lectures on the Teaching of Modern Languages | | 2/- |
| Comenius | Life and Educational Works | Laurie | 3/6 |
| | Three Lectures on the Practice of Education | | |
| Eve | I.   On Marking | | |
| Sidgwick | II.   On Stimulus | } 1 Vol. | 2/- |
| Abbott | III.   On the teaching of Latin Verse Composition | | |
| Farrar | General Aims of the Teacher | } 1 Vol. | 1/6 |
| Poole | Form Management | | |
| Locke | Thoughts on Education | Quick | 3/6 |
| Milton | Tractate on Education | Browning | 2/- |
| Sidgwick | On Stimulus | | 1/ |
| Thring | Theory and Practice of Teaching | | 4/6 |

## 7. MATHEMATICS.

| | | | |
|---|---|---|---|
| Ball | Elementary Algebra | | 4/6 |
| Euclid | Books I—VI, XI, XII | Taylor | 5/- |
| ,, | Books I—VI | ,, | 4/- |
| ,, | Books I—IV | ,, | 3/- |
| | Also separately | | |
| ,, | Books I, & II; III, & IV; V, & VI; XI, & XII 1/6 *each* | | |
| ,, | Solutions to Exercises in Taylor's Euclid | W. W. Taylor | 10/6 |
| | And separately | | |
| ,, | Solutions to Bks I—IV | ,, | 6/- |
| ,, | Solutions to Books VI. XI | ,, | 6/- |
| Hobson & Jessop | Elementary Plane Trigonometry | | 4/6 |
| Loney | Elements of Statics and Dynamics | | 7/6 |
| | Part I.   Elements of Statics | | 4/6 |
| | ,,   II.   Elements of Dynamics | | 3/6 |
| ,, | Solutions of Examples, Statics and Dynamics | | 7/6 |
| ,, | Mechanics and Hydrostatics | | 4/6 |
| Smith, C. | Arithmetic for Schools, with or without answers | | 3/6 |
| ,, | Part I. Chapters I—VIII. Elementary, with or without answers | | 2/- |
| ,, | Part II.   Chapters IX—XX, with or without answers | | 2/- |
| Hale, G. | Key to Smith's Arithmetic | | 7/6 |

LONDON: C. J. CLAY AND SONS,
CAMBRIDGE UNIVERSITY PRESS WAREHOUSE,
AVE MARIA LANE.
GLASGOW: 50, WELLINGTON STREET.

# The Cambridge Bible for Schools and Colleges.

GENERAL EDITORS:

J. J. S. PEROWNE, D.D., BISHOP OF WORCESTER,
A. F. KIRKPATRICK, D.D., REGIUS PROFESSOR OF HEBREW.

---

Extra Fcap. 8vo. cloth, with Maps when required.

**Book of Joshua.** Rev. G. F. MACLEAR, D.D. 2s. 6d.
**Book of Judges.** Rev. J. J. LIAS, M.A. 3s. 6d.
**I and II Samuel.** Prof. KIRKPATRICK, D.D. 3s. 6d. each.
**I and II Kings.** Prof. LUMBY, D.D. 5s., separately 3s. 6d. each.
**I and II Chronicles.** Rev. W. E. BARNES, D.D. 4s.
**Books of Ezra & Nehemiah.** Prof. RYLE, D.D. 4s. 6d.
**Book of Job.** Prof. DAVIDSON, D.D. 5s.
**Psalms. Book I.** Prof. KIRKPATRICK, D.D. 3s. 6d.
**Psalms. Books II and III.** Prof. KIRKPATRICK, D.D. 3s. 6d.
**Book of Proverbs.** Archdeacon PEROWNE. 3s.
**Book of Ecclesiastes.** Very Rev. E. H. PLUMPTRE, D.D. 5s.
**Song of Songs.** Rev. ANDREW HARPER, B.D. [In the Press.
**Book of Isaiah. Chaps. I.—XXXIX.** Rev. J. SKINNER, D.D. 4s.
—— **Chaps. XL.—LXVI.** Rev. J. SKINNER, D.D. 4s.
**Book of Jeremiah.** Rev. A. W. STREANE, D.D. 4s. 6d.
**Book of Ezekiel.** Prof. DAVIDSON, D.D. 5s.
**Book of Daniel.** Rev. S. R. DRIVER, D.D. [In the Press.
**Book of Hosea.** Rev. T. K. CHEYNE, M.A., D.D. 3s.
**Books of Joel and Amos.** Rev. S. R. DRIVER, D.D. 3s. 6d.
**Books of Obadiah and Jonah.** Arch. PEROWNE. 2s. 6d.
**Book of Micah.** Rev. T. K. CHEYNE, M.A., D.D. 1s. 6d.
**Nahum, Habakkuk & Zephaniah.** Prof. DAVIDSON, D.D. 3s.
**Books of Haggai, Zechariah & Malachi.** Arch. PEROWNE. 3s. 6d.
**Book of Malachi.** Archdeacon PEROWNE. 1s.
**I Maccabees.** Rev. W. FAIRWEATHER and Rev. J. S. BLACK. 3s. 6d.
**Gospel according to St Matthew.** Rev. A. CARR, M.A. 2s. 6d.
**Gospel according to St Mark.** Rev. G. F. MACLEAR, D.D. 2s. 6d.
**Gospel acc. to St Luke.** Very Rev. F. W. FARRAR, D.D. 4s. 6d.
**Gospel according to St John.** Rev. A. PLUMMER, D.D. 4s. 6d.
**Acts of the Apostles.** Prof. LUMBY, D.D. 4s. 6d.
**Epistle to the Romans.** Rev. H. C. G. MOULE, D.D. 3s. 6d.
**First and Second Corinthians.** Rev. J. J. LIAS, M.A. 2s. each.
**Epistle to the Galatians.** Rev. E. H. PEROWNE, D.D. 1s. 6d.
**Epistle to the Ephesians.** Rev. H. C. G. MOULE, D.D. 2s. 6d.
**Epistle to the Philippians.** Rev. H. C. G. MOULE, D.D. 2s. 6d.
**Colossians and Philemon.** Rev. H. C. G. MOULE, D.D. 2s.
**Epistles to the Thessalonians.** Rev. G. G. FINDLAY, B.A. 2s.
**Epistles to Timothy & Titus.** Rev. A. E. HUMPHREYS, M.A. 3s.
**Epistle to the Hebrews.** Very Rev. F. W. FARRAR, D.D. 3s. 6d.
**Epistle of St James.** Very Rev. E. H. PLUMPTRE, D.D. 1s. 6d.
**St Peter and St Jude.** Very Rev. E. H. PLUMPTRE, D.D. 2s. 6d.
**Epistles of St John.** Rev. A. PLUMMER, D.D. 3s. 6d.
**Book of Revelation.** Rev. W. H. SIMCOX, M.A. 3s.

*Other Volumes Preparing.*

---

LONDON: C. J. CLAY AND SONS,
CAMBRIDGE UNIVERSITY PRESS WAREHOUSE,
AVE MARIA LANE.

# The Smaller
# Cambridge Bible for Schools.

*Now Ready. With Maps. Price 1s. each volume.*

**Book of Joshua.**  Rev. J. S. BLACK, LL.D.
**Book of Judges.**  Rev. J. S. BLACK, LL.D.
**First Book of Samuel.**  Prof. KIRKPATRICK, D.D.
**Second Book of Samuel.**  Prof. KIRKPATRICK, D.D.
**First Book of Kings.**  Prof. LUMBY, D.D.
**Second Book of Kings.**  Prof. LUMBY, D.D.
**Ezra & Nehemiah.**  Prof. RYLE, D.D.
**Gospel according to St Matthew.**  Rev. A. CARR, M.A.
**Gospel according to St Mark.**  Rev. G. F. MACLEAR, D.D.
**Gospel according to St Luke.**  Very Rev. F. W. FARRAR, D.D.
**Gospel according to St John.**  Rev. A. PLUMMER, D.D.
**Acts of the Apostles.**  Prof. LUMBY, D.D.

# The Cambridge Greek Testament
## for Schools and Colleges

GENERAL EDITOR: J. J. S. PEROWNE, D.D.

**Gospel according to St Matthew.**  Rev. A. CARR, M.A.
  With 4 Maps.  4s. 6d.
**Gospel according to St Mark.**  Rev. G. F. MACLEAR, D.D.
  With 3 Maps.  4s. 6d.
**Gospel according to St Luke.**  Very Rev. F. W. FARRAR.
  With 4 Maps.  6s.
**Gospel according to St John.**  Rev. A. PLUMMER, D.D.
  With 4 Maps.  6s.
**Acts of the Apostles.**  Prof. LUMBY, D.D.  4 Maps.  6s.
**First Epistle to the Corinthians.**  Rev. J. J. LIAS, M.A.  3s.
**Second Epistle to the Corinthians.**  Rev. J. J. LIAS, M.A.  3s.
**Epistle to the Hebrews.**  Very Rev. F. W. FARRAR, D.D.  3s. 6d.
**Epistles of St John.**  Rev. A. PLUMMER, D.D.  4s.

GENERAL EDITOR: J. ARMITAGE ROBINSON, D.D.

**Epistle to the Philippians.**  Rev. H. C. G. MOULE, D.D.  2s. 6d.
**Epistle of St James.**  Rev. A. CARR, M.A.  2s. 6d.
**Pastoral Epistles.**  Rev. J. H. BERNARD, D.D.  3s. 6d.
**Book of Revelation.**  Rev. W. H. SIMCOX, M.A.  5s.

**London:** C. J. CLAY AND SONS,
CAMBRIDGE WAREHOUSE, AVE MARIA LANE.
Glasgow: 50, WELLINGTON STREET.
Leipzig: F. A. BROCKHAUS.
New York: THE MACMILLAN COMPANY.

CAMBRIDGE: PRINTED BY J. & C. F. CLAY, AT THE UNIVERSITY PRESS.